SEARCHING FOR 66

SEARCHING FOR 66

Tom Teague

Illustrated by Bob Waldmire

Samizdat House
Springfield, Illinois
1991

Searching for 66

A Samizdat House Book • 1991

Cover art and other illustrations by Bob Waldmire, Box 110, R.R. 2, Rochester, Illinois 62356

Cover concept and design by Bob Waldmire and Becky McVay

Photographs by the author, except as noted

Address inquiries to Samizdat House, 1208 West Edwards, Springfield, Illinois 62704

Library of Congress Cataloging-in-Publication Data
Teague, Tom.
Searching for 66.
I. History, American I. Title
Includes index

Preassigned Library of Congress Catalog Number: 91-090165
ISBN: 0-940859-09-2

Printed in the United States of America

10 9 8 7 6 5 4

ACKNOWLEDGEMENTS

My thanks and sincere appreciation go to Bud Farrar, Ingrid Hansen, Anne Kuchar, Pat Lovas and Marilyn Houston, Becky McVay, Ruth Riley, Bob Waldmire and the family of friends I have met along Route 66.

U. S. Route 66

© RW

FOREWORD

November 7, 1985

Mr. Tom Teague
1208 W. Edwards
Springfield, IL

Dear Mr. Teague:

I am carrying most of your letter on U.S. 66 in our letters column, and breaking a rule by carrying your full address so that interested readers can get in touch with you.

I, myself, started to drive 66 to the University of Wisconsin in 1929, and I cussed and loved it—mostly cussed. Historians of the 26th Century should know that American kitsch and bad taste may have reached its height in 66's old alligator farms and "Indian" trading posts, but it did, indeed, bridge the nation, it gave birth to the motel age, and the winds that blew up its dust also blew up fundamental changes in America.

When you come through Tulsa, please see if I'm in town. I'll take you to lunch.

Very truly yours,

Jenkin Lloyd Jones
Editor and Publisher
The Tulsa Tribune

SEARCHING FOR **66**

ONE

It rose from the shores of Lake Michigan, angled through Chicago's big shoulders, then flowed across the prairie to the Father of Waters and St. Louis. Seven states later in Santa Monica, California, it emptied into the Pacific Ocean: U.S. Route 66. At its birth in 1926, this highway was hailed as a great agent of progress—a concrete ribbon tying the west coast to the rest of America. And for a wondrous half century, it embraced and embodied this nation like few institutions can. TV glorified it. Songwriters romanticized it. Okies drove it out of the Dust Bowl. And scarcely an American alive did not dream at some time of setting wheel to pavement along its way.

But beginning in the mid-1970's, a popular belief spread that 66 was dead—that it existed no more. And it's easy now to see why—the first official image of its dying was so strong. Charlie McLean, who was there when it happened, described the scene.

Michigan Ave. and Jackson in Chicago, 66's eastern terminus.

"It was cold and wet—typical winter weather for Chicago," said Charlie, an operations engineer for the Illinois Department of Transportation. "The American Association of State Highway Officials had determined that Route 66's replacement in Illinois and part of Missouri, because it was primarily a north-south route, should have an odd number. They assigned 55. By 1976, Missouri had finished its share of the road and wanted to officially designate it so they could put up signs and mark it on maps. But AASHO rules prohibited that unless Illinois, as an adjoining state, did the same.

"We finally agreed that when new state maps came out in 1977 they would show I-55 markings instead of Route 66. This meant that the new signs would go up and the old ones come down."

John Chesniak & Gus Schulz, January 13, 1977, Chicago. *Courtesy Chicago Sun-Times*

The last old sign hung from a light standard near the corner of Michigan Avenue and Jackson Boulevard, the route's eastern terminus.

The others had come down without fanfare (though with quite a bit of volunteer help). But on January 13, 1977, when state signhanger John Chesniak climbed a ladder to remove this last one, Charlie McLean, several other engineers and a battery of newsmen were there to watch. Though standard in language and format, the sign's message today was chilling. "END OF ROUTE 66," it said. And when John handed the placard down to his partner, cameras clicked and whirred. That evening, news of John's deed traveled to homes throughout America, where it was received like a death in the family.

Events of the next few years only strengthened the effect. State by state, Route 66's other replacement interstates were completed. Black and white shields disappeared from roadsides and maps; tri-color shields appeared. When the section of I-40 around Williams, Arizona, opened in October 1984, the job was finally finished: Route 66 no longer carried traffic as part of our national highway system. Therefore, it no longer existed. In a final indignity the next year, AASHO officially "deauthorized" the road that was once known as the Main Street of America.

Which all meant little to me until about six years ago. In 1965, I'd come down from Iowa to go to school on 66 at Southern Illinois University-Edwardsville. In 1967, I'd taken a long, rambling vacation on the highway out to Arizona. In 1968, I'd taken 66 to Fort Leonard Wood, Missouri, and basic training. And in 1972, I'd settled in Springfield, Illinois—another 66 town. The highway had been pulling on me for a long time, I see now—it just hadn't announced itself. Then one October afternoon in 1984, at about the same time that I-40 was finishing off 66 in Arizona, I was driving along the route just north of home. It was a four lane stretch, built in the '40s. Flanked on each side by crisp autumn colors of park and woodland, it dipped and curved in rhythm with the land. Ahead, a low-rail bridge excused itself across the Sangamon River. A century and a half earlier, when the highway was merely a trail, I mused that Lincoln had probably ridden it on his judicial circuit.

"This was a beautiful old road," I said, like remembering an old friend. "I should get to know it better." Which has been my fate ever since, for there are no exits from 66—only entrances. In 1985, I spent vacations and many weekends traveling the road in Illinois. I listened, I talked, I read—and only wanted more. So in the spring of '86, I passed up a promotion at work and took a leave of absence instead. The next four months I spent driving from Chicago to Santa Monica, meeting new neighbors and searching for 66. I've never been able to explain fully to myself why I left on that journey—what personal goal I wanted to attain. But I have a lot more time left to think about that and I'm sure someday I'll figure it all out. Meanwhile, I can tell you what I found.

SEARCHING FOR 66

TWO

"Godley? You're driving 66 and you never heard of Godley?"

Rain filled a gray sky as the lunch crowd gathered at the Log Cabin Restaurant in Pontiac, Illinois. Bob Bolen—part-time farmer, part-time realtor, full-time storyteller—was undertaking to inform the well-meaning but naive stranger beside him about the ways of the world and Route 66.

"It was *right* on the road," Bob admonished me, about a quarter turn too loud. "Started out as an entertainment center for coal miners. Got to be a pretty popular place with other people, too—especially with the truckers. With other folks, though, it was like a dirty word."

He paused and curled a hand around his chin in deep concentration.

"Myself, I was 27 before I could find the place."

"You been goin' out to Godley since you were 14, Bobby," said Shirley Stymiest, his friend and fellow realtor.

She had him there. Bob took his cap off a moment, wiped his forehead with a flannel cuff, and launched a lengthy admission.

"I was actually *15*, Shirley. How it happened was one night after takin' a load of stock to Chicago, I had stopped on the way back for a load of coal in Braceville. Got as far as Godley after that, 'bout 20 miles north of here, and the damn truck broke down. Right in front of the main house!

"I was only a kid. And, cripes, nobody was around. It was wintertime and my truck was vapor-locked!"

A suspicious chuckle crept along the counter. Bob adjusted his glasses, trying to ignore it, but smile wrinkles crowded the corners of his weathered face.

"So I thought I'd go in and get a cup of coffee, see?"

Its cue received, the chuckle became an uproar. Bob let it get good and started, then joined in.

"Everytime you went through Godley, that truck broke down," Shirley said.

"Got to cool the engine, I guess," tried another customer.

In Chicago, locals had known Route 66 mostly as Jackson Boulevard or Ogden Avenue—the principal streets it took through town. In the suburbs, a few reminders of the highway started cropping up: 66 Realty, Hi-66 Cafe, 66 Video, and even a singles bar called Kicks on 66. But not until it hit the prairie and became a connector of cities—instead of just a way through them—did memories of the highway truly blossom. By the time I got to Pontiac and the Log Cabin, mere mention of 66 in any public place guaranteed a lively conversation.

The Old Log Cabin Restaurant, Pontiac, Illinois.

"We used to be the halfway point between Springfield and Chicago," said Sarah Hilyer, who runs the Log Cabin with her husband, Jerry. "Everybody would stop here. Then I-55 went through and left us two and a half miles off the route. Now only locals come in, plus whatever travelers who remember us and can find the way."

"Yeah, but we tried to fix that once," Bob said, revving up again. "The new interstate went right by my silo. And it's a big silo, too. So I let Jerry paint a sign on it for the Cabin.

"Well, the damn state people, they got ignorant, you see? They got real nasty with Jerry—made him put up a million dollar bond while they were litigatin' 'im. Jerry finally had to repaint the sign. But he made money off it 'cause it was up almost a year. And you can still see the sign through the paint."

I first met Bob and his Log Cabin crew in 1985. There's a couple of dozen of them—farmers, realtors and other people who can set their own schedules. And that first day, each of them had at least one 66 tale to tell—about Godley, coal miners, farm life and road life. Back home, quite a few of those tales had gone into an article I wrote for an area newspaper.

On my way to Chicago for the official start of my national journey in '86, I stopped by the Log Cabin again. The usual crew was there and welcomed me back. Most folks had read the article. Those who hadn't were complimentary anyway. Bob paid for my lunch and somebody set a piece of pie in front of it.

On my way west a few days later, Paul Gschwendtler hosted a lunch party for me at his farmhouse. The whole gang was there, plus Paul's mom and dad and a few other folks. We had chicken wings and potato salad, pork chops, beans and chocolate—and one ear of corn.

"Paul planted that especially for you after you were here last Thursday," Bob said. "Used a grow light and a tent."

After the food, we retired to a nearby tavern for an afternoon of euchre. I've been back dozens of times since, listening to more stories and working on my euchre game. Once we even went to Godley, but it's a quiet, aging hamlet now—barely an echo of its notorious past.

Paving Route 66 near Dwight, 1927 *(Courtesy Illinois State Police)*

SEARCHING FOR *66*

THREE

Fifteen miles south of Bloomington on Old 66, a natural maple grove interrupts the Illinois prairie. A lone outpost of the eastern forests which drop off at the Indiana border, it stands on a rise, dominating the landscape for as far as the traveler's eye can see—which in this country is a considerable distance.

"There's weather over in the grove," area farmers will say. "Looks like we got about twenty minutes."

In virgin prairie country, timber land was always poorer soil than the grasslands. But the land around this grove has been farmed for more than 130 years. And for that century and a third, prairie winds have been picking up the farm land's topsoil and dropping part of it back on the grove. The result today is sugar and black maples of record size. Also burr oaks, red elms, white elms, blue ash, black walnut and sycamores.

Isaac Funk, formerly of Germany, homesteaded the grove. His first February there, he went drilling among the maples for their sweet treasure. Every February since, Isaac or one of his kin have gone to the grove again.

Steve and Glaida Funk are the sixth generation of Isaac's family to shepherd the grove. Their home is in a clearing near the sap house. The seventh and eighth Funk generations live in a house just outside the grove. Before long, a ninth edition of the Funk family will be toddling among the maples on a sunny winter morning, gathering sap from some of the same trees that Isaac visited.

Steve and Glaida met in Oklahoma during World War II when he was a fighter pilot and she was a smalltown girl. After the war, Steve came home to Illinois and got a job trimming trees near Chicago. But he fell one day and couldn't work for awhile.

"Couldn't think of a better way to recuperate than with Glaida," Steve explained later, "so I got on 66 and went to see her."

Just as Steve's health was returning, he fell again—this time for Glaida—and they eloped.

"It took my mother-in-law thirty years after that to think I was all right," Steve likes to say. "But I couldn't climb, so I got married."

Shortly after their marriage, Steve's Aunt Hazel asked the newly-weds to take over the grove and surrounding farm. It's now theirs under a trust whose principal term is that the grove—though its wood is worth millions—never be used for anything besides making maple sirup.

Steve Funk, Funks Grove, Illinois.

"It's actually worked out pretty nice for us," Glaida said the first afternoon that I stopped by. "We start making sirup in late winter. By the time the buckets are down, it's time to get out to the fields. It's been like another crop."

A pleasant, easy-talking woman with just a touch of gray in her hair, Glaida stood behind the sales counter on the back porch of their home. When she and Steve first took over, the grove was running only 500 buckets. Most of its product was consumed at Funk family tables. But the new trustees studied their art. They began attending international maple conferences and tried out new scientific methods of collecting and boiling the sap. Soon they were running the equivalent of 5,000 buckets and their sirup—which they spell that way because it has no added sugar—was pouring all over the country via Route 66.

"That was when we were using plastic tubing instead of buckets and it would just flow from the tree to the sap house," Glaida said. "What a job that was! It was easier during the season, but not before when we had to put it together—and not afterwards when we had to flush it out. So we went back to buckets. We're running only 3,000 now, but we get out to the fields on time."

Funks Grove Rail Depot

From a three-bucket maple in the back yard, a bird sounded its rain call. Minutes later, Steve came in from the field. He had been spraying corn, but was afraid the leaves were getting too wet. "Route 66, huh?" he said when Glaida introduced us. "Come on in the kitchen."

We sat down around a formica dinette. Steve poured us all coffee from his battered Thermos and we talked in the dim afternoon light.

"Our lives have gone by 66," Glaida said. "We live on it. We work on it. We courted on it. When they built the first road, that's when Steve was born. When our first son was born, they put in the new lane. And when our middle son was born, they made it four lanes."

Steve's face has the ruddy, weathered look of all farmers. Scars of varying length give it character. He spoke in a measured prairie drawl, interrupting his wife and being interrupted by her in a rhythmic pattern.

"Yeah," he said, "we've gotten into a lot of things along the road. One time a soldier came up to the door. He'd been in a wreck and had a broken leg. I ended up driving him and his wife and child up to Chicago. Another time, I loaned my car to a young lady who had to get to a class in

Bloomington. And Glaida can't count all the people we've pulled out of ditches or fed or gassed up."

Glaida broke in. "But people don't stop here so much anymore because we're not on I-55."

"So often, people who need help are just prey," Steve continued. "They've come in here and we've helped them so they wouldn't be prey to somebody else. It's just seemed like the thing to do.

"Now you're not even supposed to stop on the interstate and help anybody anymore. The state police tell you to keep on driving—they'll help the people."

Glaida put on some bean soup for dinner while Steve gave me a tour of their high tech sap house. The energy crunch ten years earlier had threatened the Funks' business. But they fought back by installing a heat exchanger over the boiling pan in the sap house. This funnels heat out to preheat sap in a holding tank. As a by-product, it collects distilled water. Then from Canada Steve and Glaida imported a reverse osmosis machine. This Goldbergian maze of tubes and valves somehow draws water off the cold sap, leaving less of it to boil. Now, thanks to the energy crunch, the Funks were spending less on fuel than they had been before.

Later I helped clear the supper dishes while Steve brought out a copy of the Funk family history. He'd helped research and publish it three years before for a family reunion. His daughter Susan, who's published ten romance novels and children's books, helped write it. A beautifully printed volume, the history is bound in green leather with its title stamped in gold on the cover: *A Tree Grows in Funks Grove*.

Leafing through the book's nether regions with me, Steve found a 50-year-old Andy Gump comic strip. In it, Andy and his friends were spending a Sunday afternoon driving to Funks Grove when they got lost. One by one, friendly area folks stopped by Andy's car to tell him how to find his destination—and each one suggested a different path.

"Things haven't changed much," Steve said in his even tone. "You still can't find Funks Grove. The new highway took us a mile off the route and the feds said we didn't have enough traffic for an exit sign. Sales really hurt. It takes longer every year to sell our production."

Steve pointed out his picture window toward the road that used to be. "They said the whole world went by on 66," he observed. "Well, they don't go by anymore. They're going down that interstate."

SEARCHING FOR *66*

FOUR

New restaurants along interstates tend to have safe, inviting names—like Hardee's, Wendy's, Denny's or McDonald's. Which makes sense. Who wants to invest their personal fortune today into an operation and then turn people away with a questionable name like, say, Pig Hip?

But such things didn't concern Ernie Edwards in 1936 when he opened his restaurant in Broadwell, Illinois. Like he's done most of his life, he just called it like he saw it.

"Harbor Inn," he said. "That was its first name. We got a deal on some wallpaper that had ships on it. Then we went down to the five and dime to buy some glasses. And they had some ships on them. So we called the place Harbor Inn.

"That didn't last long, though. There was an old man out here on the prairie. It may have been the only time he was ever in here, but he came in one day and I had a fresh-baked ham settin' on the back stove. The old man wanted a sandwich, so he pointed at the ham and said, 'Give me a slice o' that pig hip!'

"That intrigued me. I went to my attorney. We got patents on the sandwich and I copyrighted its name. From then on, we were the Pig Hip."

More than half a century later, Ernie is still carving slices off a pig hip and topping them with his patented, pepper-flavored sauce. And outside on Old 66, a neon sign and a quartet of dancing pigs invite travelers in.

Ernie, as he always has, wears a white cook's suit and a paper chef's toque. When he wants, he can tilt the toque forward on his forehead, look a person right in the eye and—without saying a word—tell him he's going to lie.

"Of course we only use the left pig hip," he told me.

"Why's that?" I wondered.

"Because when a hog has an itch, he has a tendency to raise that right leg to do his scratchin'. That makes the meat tough on that side, so we don't use it."

Making sure I could see, Ernie exchanged winks with the waitress.

"And that's a true story," he said. How could I doubt?

Once he had the Pig Hip well established, Ernie said he opened two more restaurants.

""My chain," he called them. "But I'm back to one now. I found out if you got more than one restaurant going, the ones you didn't run yourself would fall apart. Just like a person.

"I had this one in Lincoln, just up the road from here. Tizil's we

The Pig Hip Restaurant, Broadwell, Illinois.

called it. On Veterans Day one year, the people running it told me they were going to go watch the parade. I told them I was going to work and I was the only veteran. So they left and I just turned the key on the building, closed it, and came back here."

It was a light day at the venerable cafe. Virgil Crumpler, who rightfully bragged about 64 years of marriage, was the only customer besides myself. But in its day, the dancing pig has welcomed its fair share of guests, including many famous ones. David Hartman, whose photo hangs over the cash register, has been there. He married a local girl. But perhaps the Pig Hip's most famous guest has been Colonel Harlan Sanders.

"Yeah, the old colonel, he and I were bosom buddies," Ernie let on. "He came in here one day and tried to sell me a franchise. I tried to sell him one. He said, 'Take out a chicken, I'll bring in my mix and show you how to cook a chicken.' So he did. Meanwhile, I fixed him a ham sandwich."

Even Mike Royko, curmudgeon columnist for numerous Chicago newspapers, has visited the Pig Hip. He stopped in one day while researching an article on area resident Emil Verban, who used to play for the Chicago Cubs. Ernie, as a longtime friend of Emil, was interviewed.

"Royko called me an old coot in a rocking chair," Ernie said, trying his best to sound offended. "And I don't even have a rocking chair! So when he got married awhile back, I sent him a congratulations card from 'The Old Coot.'

"Emil didn't take too hearty to the column, though. Royko asked me if he'd been a good ballplayer and I said, 'No.' Maybe it was my use of the word 'mediocre' that bothered Emil. At any rate, we still see each other in church, but at handshaking time now he makes sure to avoid me."

Ernie told me the day we met that he wanted to hang up his carving knife and sell the Pig Hip. But that was five years ago and there just haven't been any offers. Broadwell has an exit off I-55, but few people besides locals use it—long distance travelers all stop at franchise restaurants in nearby Springfield. Ernie's making it on locals and memories, but the new owner would have something additional to contend with: a mortgage. So when I stopped by the Pig Hip one afternoon in 1988, I wasn't surprised to see Ernie still there. As often happens when a realtor hasn't been able to sell a place, Ernie had recently listed himself with another.

"He's a Jewish guy from Springfield," Ernie said. "He says he never heard of the Pig Hip before he listed it, but everybody he mentions it to has. He hasn't got me any offers yet, but he calls every week or so and we have a nice talk."

Meanwhile, business goes on. This day, Ernie was investigating a brochure from a sign company.

"You've seen those new blue signs on the interstate with smaller signs on them for gas stations and restaurants?"

"Yes."

"Well, the state highway people tell me I'm too small to get on a set of those, but I'm still going to figure out a way to do it anyway. They cost $1200 a year, but the way you have to look at it is that's only one customer a day."

Ernie would eventually find a way around state regulations and the signs would go up. But his musings today were interrupted when a regular walked in.

"How about you, sir?" Ernie asked. "The usual?"

"Sure," the man said. "Slice one off—but only if you tell me what you put in that sauce."

"You know I can't do that. But I can tell you about the time I took out a patent on a square ice cream scoop."

"A *square* ice cream scoop?"

"Sure. It happened like this...."

Note to 3rd Printing, 1992. Business got so good along 66 that Ernie and his wife were working 12-14 hour days during 1991. Finally, after Labor Day they retired. "I'm 75," he said. "My wife is 70. We thought it was time to start preparing for old age."

SEARCHING FOR 66

FIVE

Show me a man who's never put pedal to the metal and I'll show you a man with no legs. Ever since Jean Lenoir wheeled that first horseless carriage down a dusty country lane a hundred-odd years ago, Americans have been trying to figure ways to make the trip go faster. In its preamble, our constitution's framers professed to be creating a *"more perfect* union." A merely *perfect* union wouldn't do—it had to be *more* perfect. So it has been with our elapsed times. From little deuce coupes to Z-28's. From crank starters to computer-controlled turbochargers. From zero to 60 in less time today than it took yesterday—we've always wanted more. Or less.

As one of its longest paved highways, Route 66 soon became the nation's longest automobile proving grounds. Top end speed was tested on the road's remote straightaways, acceleration at its thousands of stoplights, and the endurance of car and driver alike on caffeine-powered cross country treks.

And if that wasn't enough—if just a little more speed or a little more danger was needed to complete a driver's thrill—66 offered a hundred little detours to places like the Springfield Speedway.

The fertile prairie soil of Sangamon County, Illinois, has spawned two of this country's fastest dirt racetracks. Both lie along Route 66 in Springfield. One—a mile oval—is at the state fairgrounds. The other—three-eighths of a mile of continuous clay bank—was Joe Shaheen's Springfield Speedway on Dirksen Drive.

The United States Auto Club (USAC), auto racing's dominant body, sanctions events at the fairgrounds. Outlaws raced at the Speedway. Dust and grease from both tracks long clogged the veins of Joe Shaheen (as in "the rain"). He saw his first race ever at the fairgrounds. The son of Syrian immigrants, he could have gotten in for free. But he preferred the view from the top of a nearby silo. As soon as he could reach the pedals, he started racing. Then in 1947, he built the Speedway, vowing to run it until God or the Devil raced him down the last straightaway.

In a life that paralleled the saga of Route 66 and the automobile, Joe always liked to ride up front or on top. As flamboyant as any funny car, he challenged all odds. Shrewd and tough as an old Model T, he usually won out.

Of course, the man always worked to have the odds with him, whether other people knew it or not.

"Back in the '20s, I was a daredevil driver," he told me. "I did what's called the Drive of Death. First, I'd put silver dollars over my eyes. Then I'd cover them with a heavy black blindfold and pull a black hood over my head. Then for $25, I'd drive my car around a track at 60 miles an hour.

"People would say, 'Man, it's impossible for him to see. He must be cheating.' But I'd take the hood and blindfold off, take the silver dollars and throw 'em into the crowd and say, 'See?'"

Joe Shaheen, Springfield, Illinois.

We were sitting in the memorabilia-strewn living room of Joe's trailer on the Speedway's grounds. Joe rummaged around a closet for the hood, showed it to me, then made me try it on. It was heavy and black, like a leaded executioner's mask without eyeholes. I could barely hear through it, let alone see.

"I just told people I drove close to the wall and judged my distance by the sound of the exhaust," Joe explained later. His brows lifted, letting a quick smile sneak from his pale blue eyes. "Everybody was scared I'd die. They'd stand and worry—but not too close to the fence.

"They called me Daredevil Joe. But I was safe. The only way I could get hurt was if the drive shaft fell off and stuck in the ground and somersaulted me!"

The old showman paused to take a pinch of Big Man Tobacco. After eight decades of hard mileage, his voice often struggled to get its words out. But that could not be mistaken for weakness of thought or memory.

"That car had a pipe on it this big around," he said, cupping his hands, then spreading them to the very limit of credibility. "That and racing is why I can't hear now. On the backside of the track, I'd take it easy, so as not to wind the engine out. But coming in front of the judges' stand, I'd put the throttle down all the way.

"Later, I'd take the blindfold off and throw those silver dollars in the air. I'd get $25 and it only cost me two."

The trick was, of course, that Joe could see. That much he admitted. But nothing more. It was his showman's secret. To tell it even now would diminish the thrills his spectators had.

Off the track, Joe approached life just like he did the Drive of Death. Only instead of a steering wheel in his hand, he often held a pair of dice. As a youthful shoeshine boy at the Illinois Central railroad station in Springfield, a madam's boyfriend had taught him how to shoot craps.

"Mike Greckles and myself was pitchin' pennies up against the wall one morning between trains when this guy comes by," Joe said. "The station was right in the middle of a red light district called Rabbit Row and I used to go get a pint of cream every week for this guy's girlfriend. One day he sees us pitchin' and pulls out a pair of dice. 'Here, Joe,' he says. 'This is what you oughtta play. You don't have to do all that work bendin' and everything, see? Just roll the dice and throw 'em out and if your number comes up, you win!'"

"There's a way to win this game," young Joe told himself. Between trains, he started practicing for nickels and dimes with Mike, his skill and taste for the bones growing with each roll. By his early twenties, when he wasn't driving, the former shoeshine boy was running the area's largest craps games—one on Route 66 by the fairgrounds and another in nearby Riverton. Normal limit was $30, though under the right conditions, wagers could hit the four-figure mark.

A 1935 newspaper article about a tavern robbery in Riverton discreetly failed to mention a craps game. But it described young Shaheen, the victim, as being known for "flashing large wads of cash." The article, in numbered paragraphs recounting the incident, said that Joe had begged for his life. But according to Joe, he'd merely explained the odds to the man.

"I said, 'Now you just have a robbery rap. But if you kill me, it's a murder rap.'"

Joe lost $1,500 that day. But it bought him the chance to make a lot more. Besides craps and his own driving, he soon figured he could make money off other people's driving—so he became a promoter. One of his early ventures was the area's first powder puff derby.

"I got seven guys who didn't mind women driving their cars," Joe said. In between stories, he'd just taken two minutes to make a $3,500 deal with an engineer to draw up plans for the new stands the city was requiring at the Speedway. "Sixteen women wanted to drive—all of 'em good ones, too. Well, I grossed $7.50 for 15 customers and I gave it all to the girls."

Other events proved more successful and Joe prospered. Then, in 1942 he was drafted. But that didn't slow him down a bit—it just changed his location.

"I was based at Camp Flora in Mississippi," he said. "I was the only one who had a car—the last '42 Chevy off the line. So I ended up driving this master sergeant and his friends to the horse races in New Orleans. They lost a bundle, but I had a system.

"Then one day during a barracks inspection, the sergeant found seven pairs of cool [certified] dice in my locker. He took me in the latrine and asked me, 'Joe, do you think there's a way we can make money with these?'

"Well, I was just an oyster—he could have put me on KP, wash dishes and everything."

Soon craps games were a weekend fixture at the base. At the first one, Joe and his sergeant made a $1,600 profit. And instead of doing KP, Joe was assigned a job driving a truck. The poor oyster ended up with most of the pearls.

"I got out of the army in '43 when I turned 37," said Joe, scratching his still majestic nose. "They said men my age was too old to fight. But that sergeant, he didn't want to let me go. He was makin' money."

Joe figured auto racing would come back after the war and rolled the dice on an old cow pasture on Bypass 66. Driving his own scraper, he carved a steep oval in the prairie loam and buttressed it with clay trucked in on 66 from Missouri. Next he built stands on the north and south sides of the track and a tavern at the west end. In 1947, Springfield Speedway held its first race.

For four decades, every kind of motor vehicle that could run fast enough to keep from falling off the banks raced around the Speedway—midgets, sprints, stock cars, late models, motorcycles. And when a 1957 race ended in a dead heat, Joe settled the issue by having the top finishers do two more deciding laps around the track—in reverse.

"I've never canceled a show for midgets, either," Joe bragged. "Sometimes I'd lose three or four hundred dollars and sit in the stands by myself—the most expensive seat in the house. That's when the midgets was in decline, when the stock cars was taking over. But I promoted midgets every race night and never did give up.

"USAC even doublecrossed me once. They gave a big race to a friend of theirs out of Indiana. Ran 30 miles from here. Didn't have two people in the stands.

"I got them St. Louis people to come take their place. Ran a benefit race for Rex Easton, a USAC driver. After the race, USAC come here and begged me to take them back.

"I said, 'Wait a minute! Don't you do no begging when you gave the track to someone else! I've had races when all the other promoters dropped them. Those guys had sense! I didn't. I said I didn't give a damn whether I made money or not. And that's the respect you guys give me? Now you're here begging! I gave a benefit race for one of your drivers!"

The memory was so vivid it made Joe stammer. Sally, his helpmate and companion for the past thirty years, brought him his medicine. Emphysema and congestive heart failure had slowed Joe down the past few years. His big cigars—once a facial landmark—were gone. But he was still running the show. He took his medicine faithfully, then said, "Bring me some chewin'."

In midafternoon, a young man fresh out of jail came in to talk about a job grading the track. Joe still preferred to do this work himself—he didn't care what the doctors said. But today he decided to help the kid out and explained carefully how to position the grader's blade so just a slice of daylight showed between it and the ground. Then he asked his new employee if he could count on him.

"Yes sir!" came the answer. The two men agreed to meet the next morning at 10.

Rex Easton ran at the Speedway. So have other champions such as Tony Bettenhausen, A.J. Foyt, and Mario Andretti. Stars or not, though, Joe's best show was always his most recent one.

"You should have been here last Sunday," he declared when I first met him in 1985. "You want to see a show—we had a million dollar one!" He held two fingers together. "Mel Kenyon and Bill Doty was this far apart. Doty was just waiting for Kenyon to goof up someplace so he could drive underneath him.

"I wanted to go up on the judges' stand afterward and ask everybody to pay four or five dollars more. But I knew they wouldn't go for it."

Joe's next show, of course, would be better than his last.

"In August, we're having the USAC sprints here for the first time since I opened up," he said. "We've always had the outlaws before. They have wings, USAC don't. So they'll come here during the state fair and we'll see how they run." Joe was optimistic—his flyer for the event called it "the biggest event in the history of racing in Springfield, Illinois." I didn't bet against him.

Sunday evenings, the neon outline of a midget race car used to light up the corner of Bypass 66 and Clear Lake in Springfield. Behind it rose the floodlit, white frame superstructure of the Speedway. Two thousand people would pay their way in—families, longhairs, rednecks, teenyboppers looking for romance, old men looking for memories. A hundred drivers and their crews work in the pits at the center of the race oval. A hundred other people manned the ticket booths, refreshment stands, sentry posts, tow trucks and ambulances. Joe would make two circuits around the track in the spray truck to settle the dust. A squadron of pick-ups would follow him to tamp it down. It was race night, a perfect antidote to the end-of-the-weekend blues. And after I came home from my journey, it was where I could be found every Sunday from June through October.

The races would start in relative silence with the time trials. The track record for the fastest cars—the sprints—is eleven seconds. Next would come the heats—ten-lap events with six or eight competitors each. Then a score of cars would line up for the 25-lap features, a hundred and sixty cylinders would start banging against each other and it was white noise city.

You couldn't hear the person next to you, but fans would shout encouragement to their favorite drivers anyway. Dust and mud would fly out and build up on people's hair, clothes and faces. Yellow flags were common—spin outs averaged about three a race and you could count on at least one spectacular crash each race night. It was a particular point of pride for Joe, though, that there had never been a fatality at the track. And when the green light would come back on and those sprints would go howling around uninterrupted at nearly a hundred miles an hour, fans held tight to their souls, for the cars could take those with them.

In October of 1987, Joe held a fortieth anniversary party at the Speedway. Three hundred former drivers came back from around the country and made one more lap around the track sitting on the back seats of convertibles. Joe went last—frail but majestic—waving to his standing, clapping fans. Fifteen minutes later, I saw him back at work in the tavern, restocking the cooler.

It was the Speedway's last race night. That next spring, life waved its checkered flag and he died. But on its way to the cemetery, Joe's funeral procession detoured by the Speedway and took him on one last lap around the track. And when he passed those pearly tool gates in the sky, I bet Joe pulled that hood of death off, threw a pair of silver dollars into the air and said, "See?"

A year after his death, Joe's sister Marie sold the Speedway to developers. Today a McDonald's, a Taco Bell and a Walgreen's stand blandly on its site. It's just too sad to think about. I'd look to the other side of the road where Joe's favorite restaurant used to be, but there's a Hardee's over there.

SEARCHING FOR **66**

SIX

Traffic volume and road conditions at Joe Shaheen's Route 66 front door often made Joe's midget races seem like tame excursions. In too many spots along its length, the new highway quickly earned the nickname "Bloody 66"—especially near hills, unguarded railroad tracks and sharp curves along section lines. Eventually the road was straightened and then widened to four lanes most of the way. But until that day, traffic engineers tried no end of other safety improvements.

From the Around the Block Tavern in Glenarm, Illinois, in the 1930s, patrons could enjoy a beer and watch the results of one such test. At the top of a nearby hill, officials had installed a large curved mirror. With its aid, drivers could now see what was on the other side of the hill before they reached its top. This would make passing easier and safer, officials figured. What it actually did was take drivers' attention away from the road. After several accidents, the experiment was retired. Soon afterward, traffic engineers figured to ban passing on hills all together.

The Glenarm mirror.   *Courtesy Phyllis White*

SEARCHING FOR *66*

SEVEN

Like Burma Shave signs of old, the thirteen wooden placards stand in a soldierly line alongside Route 66 near Raymond, about 35 miles south of Springfield. Their precursors offered, for 900 empty jars, a trip to Mars. These signs, mingling with the hollyhocks along a fence row, have a far loftier goal—they want to help you get to Heaven. Just repeat after them for thirteen lines and you've said a Hail Mary.

High school kids and young adults from the local Catholic Youth Organization made and planted the signs in 1959. They came as a modern afterthought to the group's main project immediately to the north—the Our Lady of the Highways Shrine.

It was, as all are, a simpler age. Americans were in their seventh year of liking Ike; soon they'd be loving Kennedy. Vietnam was a distant drum; Dallas was undreamt of. The Catholic youth of rural Raymond wanted to show their love of God and country. Living along 66, it came logically to them that they should build a shrine for travelers.

Francis Marten's daughter, Loretta, was an officer in the CYO, so he volunteered his farm as the shrine's site. The kids spent $400 of their own money and imported a Carrara marble statue of Our Lady of Lourdes from Italy. Rechristening her "Our Lady of the Highways," they spent another $600 building an alcove of brick and wood for her. Then they planted some evergreens and laid a stone walk to the alcove from the driveway. As a finishing touch, they used leftover wood to fashion their Burma Shave litany.

A dedication ceremony for the shrine in 1959 drew four hundred people. A pilgrimage in 1963 drew five hundred. For five or six years, the youth maintained their lady faithfully. Then marriage and maturity took their toll and the group dwindled away. Sometime around 1965, Francis took over the maintenance. He remains today, at age 78, the shrine's keeper.

"When I-55 came through, the feds tried to make me take the signs down," he said, his voice soft as cornsilk. "But I had them measured right.

They were four inches inside my line and there wasn't a damned thing the government could do about it."

Years ago, Francis set a utility spool on his side lawn as a place for just sitting. Hollyhocks grow halfway around the spool now and the semi-retired farmer spends a lot of afternoons there watching the traffic, his land, and the shrine. A bulky, cherub-faced man in overalls and farm cap, he welcomed the chance to talk when the litany caught my traveling eye and pulled me in. He was friendly and hospitable. The day was bright and sunny. But a curtain of sadness cast long shadows on his every word and gesture.

Francis Marten, Raymond, Illinois.

"I spend $200 a year to light the statue," Francis said while giving me the tour. "This spring I restained the wood. Last summer I gave the kids from St. Raymond's $50 to fix and paint the signs. I just do whatever has to be done."

Hands stuffed deep in his pockets, Francis looked down and said, "And that's about all I have to do. My son and a friend, they do the farming. And my wife, she died in January. She had a stroke about ten years ago and I spent the next nine and a half years taking care of her—feeding her, dressing her, getting her in and out of bed.

"She couldn't speak our language anymore, so we learned hers. If somebody came by when she was the only one home, she had a signal for us when we got back. Then we'd ask, 'Was it someone we know? Man or woman? Someone from the country? Someone from church?'"

Francis and I sat on the spool amid the emerging hollyhocks. "Many people get sour or cranky after a stroke," he continued. "But not Ruth. She couldn't smile anymore, but she always had one for us anyway. Sometimes she would even laugh. It might have sounded like a grunt to anybody else, but we knew it was a laugh.

"Then between Thanksgiving and New Year's last year, she had three more strokes just like that. We buried her four months ago and I've never been so lost." He shrugged, but could not shed the grief.

Inside at his kitchen table later, Francis let me look through a scrapbook from the shrine's dedication. While I read, he rummaged through a candy box full of other clippings, looking for a favorite one.

"If Ruth were here, she'd know right away where it was," he said. "I'm just lost without her."

SEARCHING FOR **66**

EIGHT

Early in the nineteenth century, a sandbar formed in the Mississippi River across from St. Louis. Favored by the currents, it soon grew to be a mile long and a quarter-mile wide. Dense with willows and cottonwoods, it proved a popular arena for clandestine cock fights, boxing bouts and duels—and quickly earned the nickname "Bloody Island."

As it continued to grow, the new land mass diverted the Mississippi from its western bank and the St. Louis harbor grew dangerously low. This alarmed residents of that city and in 1836 Congress approved funds for diversion dikes to stop Bloody Island's growth. Built promptly, the new dikes caused the area between the sandbar and the Illinois bank to fill in with silt. Soon island and mainland became one.

Chain of Rocks Bridge, Mitchell, Illinois.

A small community developed in the area. Growth was stymied, though, by frequent floods. Then in the 1870's the community's mayor,

Melburn Stephens, led a campaign to have the entire commercial district elevated fourteen to twenty feet. Millions of yards of dirt were hauled in for the purpose and spread around. The result was early East St. Louis—a city on a landfill by a sandbar.

Blessed by location and resources, East St. Louis became the hub of the Metro East area. Its riverfront boomed. Route 66 cut right through the heart of town. The city's railyards were the nation's second largest. It served as commercial center for a series of adjoining company towns: National City (National Stockyards), Alorton (Aluminum Ore Company) and Monsanto (now called Sauget). Its population reached 80,000. In 1965, *Look Magazine* even declared East St. Louis an All-American City.

But America has a way of using things up, casting them aside, then moving on. Take beer cans, for example. Or campaign promises. Or entire cities. The Interstate Highway Act in 1957 was an early sign that East St. Louis and Route 66 were falling victim to this trait. Bypassing the city was one of the new road network's first goals. When that was achieved in 1965, traffic didn't *have* to stop in East St. Louis anymore. So it didn't.

Then Alcoa Aluminum closed down its smelter as Illinois' high sulfur coal became too expensive to use and labor became cheaper in southern states. Packing houses followed, one by one, as their East St. Louis plants became obsolete. National Stockyards, in turn, became but a shadow of itself.

Each day the morning sun reflected off the new Gateway Arch across the river and back on a scene of growing desolation. A racetrack burned down. The daily newspaper ceased publication. Railyards diminished as the interstate system grew. Route 66 was a memory. A $176 million tax base in 1965 fell straight as a plumb bob to $45 million in 1990.

At the same time, East St. Louis was going through an even more dramatic ethnic change—a phenomenon which people associated with it can only call the White Flight.

"It happened so fast it was mindboggling," said Don Szymula. A member of the last white generation to grow up in East St. Louis, Don, 46, now lives in Collinsville and works in Granite City. "We looked up and in five years the city was gone! With no industrial base, the city's property taxes became the highest in Illinois. Pretty soon, white families were moving to the suburbs for lower taxes and better services. It started pretty slow, but before you knew it, it was like a herd of lemmings."

Before World War II, only ten percent of East St. Louis' population was black. The rest was primarily immigrant stock from eastern Europe. But the war and post war economies drew a steady flow of black migrants from the south and by 1950 the city was one third black. Twenty years later, as the white flight hit its stride, the city was 70 percent black. Today the only whites among its 40,000 residents share a diehard streak. At 98 percent, East St. Louis is the blackest city in America. Even its mayor, Carl Officer, has referred to his hometown only half-jokingly as

"Soweto West."

Soon after becoming the nation's blackest city, East St. Louis received another unsought title: the U.S. Department of Housing and Urban Development declared it the nation's Most Distressed City. HUD keeps convincing tally of seven economic and social indicators to prove this label. But no one familiar with East St. Louis needs a government table to see the truth. Sixty percent of the city's people are on some form of welfare. Another 14 percent are unemployed. A third of the city is vacant lots. The teenage pregnancy rate, nothing to be proud of at the state level, is 360 percent higher in East St. Louis. And when youth escape the early parenthood trap and make it through college, they often don't come back.

"My pat answer to kids who might be considering leaving town is that I want them to stay here," said Percy McKinney, a new alderman. "I want them to live here and help make East St. Louis better. But if they have to leave town to get work, they can use my truck."

Marion Officer was the mayor's father and operator of the mortuary which still handles 85 percent of East St. Louis' funerals. One afternoon he drove with me down Old 66 on the city's east side. In an accent often mistaken for West Indian, he said, "I grew up in this neighborhood. I went to this grade school that you see to my left. And my church is right here on the corner where I grew up.

"See that abandoned shack there? When I was a little boy, there were houses all along that block. Also taverns, whorehouses and dives. It was a terrible, terrible area. But the people were fine people."

While waiting at a crossing for a train to rumble by, Officer shook a Kool deftly out of an everpresent pack and lit it.

"I have an attachment to this area," he said, then paused for effect. "And I have seen it *demolished*. I've wondered—we've all wondered—why? How?"

The elder Officer put part of the blame on "misguided government policies." But he put most of it on his own people.

"When the white exodus started, many black leaders let them go gladly," he said crisply. "They wanted power. They knew how to get it. But when they got power, they didn't know what to do with it. So we got what you see now. It's a disgrace to our city."

Captain Levester Heavens of the East St. Louis Fire Department stood by an aging pumper in the fire house at 17th and Central. On the fingers of a hand which once had 4400 volts of electricity pass through it for twelve minutes during a successful rescue attempt, he counted the firemen who'd been sued recently by hospitals when the city, nominally self-insured, failed to pay their medical bills.

"We feel we have an obligation to the city to do the best we can with what we've got," Captain Heavens said. "But the guys are getting kind of reluctant, you know. And you can't blame them. The state's raised the death benefit to $100,000, but that doesn't help a guy run out on these railroad tracks by Monsanto, try to cool a car off, maybe prevent an explosion—not when he doesn't have any hospitalization. It takes away from his firefighting instincts."

The average age of East St. Louis firemen is nearing 50. A new one hasn't been hired for nearly a dozen years and there isn't even an eligibility list. Heavens asked the city once to buy a pair of binoculars so he could more safely check the contents of a tanker car if one does derail. He was refused. He asked for a $19 part for the firehouse stove so his men could cook themselves hot meals. Again he was refused.

Levester Heavens, East St. Louis, Illinois.

Heavens sighed. "I keep telling people we can't be Keystone firemen," he said. But only two of fifteen lights in his truck bay still worked. One of two heaters needed to keep the fire hose warm and flexible was broken. One truck's cab leaked when it rained. The other truck was downtown being field stripped. Its door at the firehouse couldn't be raised anyhow. The fireman's union once offered to buy diesel fuel for the department, only to be called "fools" by Mayor Officer. And because of faulty wiring in its sleeping quarters, Heavens fears his own firehouse will be aflame some rainy night when he and his men return from a fire.

East St. Louis police are no better off—a women's prayer group held a fund drive in 1990 to buy them two working cars. Law and order in the city are maintained primarily through a 16-man contingent from the Illinois State Police and a HUD-financed drug patrol in the housing authority.

The housing authority itself was taken over by HUD in 1986 because of criminal mismanagement. State Community College faces a similar fate—and for similar reasons. Its population base is too small to support it anyway. And in 1989 the school district, which depends on local taxes for only nine percent of its budget, was paying two superintendents, but had boarded-up windows at East St. Louis High School.

The city's government could address these institutional failures, except it is facing imminent collapse itself—and has been for some time. The plum bobbed tax base would be disaster enough for any city. But the state Department of Transportation has withheld East St. Louis' $81,500 monthly share of motor fuel tax receipts since October 1988 because the city had been using them to pay general operations expenses. And in September 1990, citing mismanagement and poor accountability, HUD ordered East St. Louis to give up control of its $2.1 million a year community development block grant—or lose it altogether.

Municipal garbage collection is infrequent at best in East St. Louis. Children play near ponds created by leaks in the sewage system. City employees go weeks at a time without paychecks. More than 300 dead people were registered to vote in the 1990 elections. And in the fall of 1990, Circuit Court Judge Roger Scrivner ordered that the deed to City Hall be surrendered as partial payment to a man who'd been beaten in the city's jail in 1984. Later, he criticized the city for not factoring rent for the hall into its 1991 budget.

Mayor Carl Officer brought a ray of light in 1985 when he announced plans to redevelop the East St. Louis riverfront. Some $474 million in bonds were sold to build apartments, a cargo port and a recycling center. But that money was soon tied up in a court dispute between Officer and the Connecticut firm hired to develop the project's plans. Three years went by. When building on the project didn't begin, the bonds' authority expired. The project is dead. Two federal agencies are investigating.

Marion and I drove by the site of an old Knights of Columbus Hall where Don Szymula had worked as a teen. Once it had six bowling lanes, two swimming pools, a gymnasium, a ball room, and a dozen smaller meeting rooms. When the whites exited town, the Knights of Columbus donated the building to the community. For a few months, a drug abuse program operated on the site. Then the angry racial days of the late '60s came and a radical group took over the building. Within a year, the hall was totally trashed. Five years later, it was torn down. Now it's just another overgrown vacant lot in a city which has thousands. The only activity there today was three men standing around the open hood of an old Buick.

"I would have made a great naval commander," said Carl Officer, 37. His police driver had just switched on the siren of the mayoral Mercury. He was traveling to the county seat in Belleville with city attorney Eric Vickers to persuade another judge to let the city bolster its coffers by selling cars and other evidence from past criminal cases. "But a couple of weeks before I was to go to Annapolis, my dad got very sick. He called me and my sister and brother home and asked us to go into the family business. So I had to go to Southern Illinois University in Carbondale and enroll in the mortuary program. Pretty soon my father's feeling better and

I'm stuck in embalming school. I just never pursued the military after that."

Carl returned home after college, took a job with the Illinois Secretary of State, and helped out in the family business. In 1976, he ran unsuccessfully for county coroner. Then on a bar bet in 1979, he ran for mayor of East St. Louis and won. The young man collected his wager, then embarked on a career of sixteen and eighteen hour days. His first term was filled with optimism, even though substantial layoffs and other cutbacks were made. The second term was a wash. Then came the third term and its harsh realizations.

On the way back from Belleville, Officer was evasive about the outcome of his meeting. He responded to questions about the budget issues with facile predictions, but no solutions or his usual elan. At a hamburger drive-up in Belleville, he joked with Vickers about who'd paid for an order of french fries. At a gas station back in the city, he stopped to talk with a young woman making a phone call. Returning to his office, there was a joke about raising the city hall rent of an uncooperative newspaper. Somehow East St. Louis was making it through another day.

If he were writing his resume now, I asked Carl, what would he say under the heading "Mayor"?

"That's easy: Mayor of East St. Louis: 1979- ...." he said and spread his hands in a question.

"Life's a strange problem, Teague," Marion had told me. We were sitting at a rail crossing in his Plymouth Horizon, waiting for another freight to rumble by. "I guess that's what makes us all so different. I was listening to a sermon the night before last at the funeral home. The pastor said that none of us should expect any compensation here on this earth, that all of it would have to be in the hereafter. And I said after the service, 'Reverend, why did you say that I should not expect any happiness here? I can't buy that! I don't believe the Master intended for me to live here his estimated three score and ten and not find *some* kind of happiness! You mean I have to *wait?* There ought to be something here that I can find!'

"But his theory was, no, you're not going to get any happiness here. Here you're bound for trials, tribulations. It's a period of getting yourself washed and cleansed for the hereafter.

"I have fulfilled all obligations I should fulfill. I have done everything I thought I should do. That's the key to everything that this country stands for. But then I wait until this age and find out there's a possibility that something's missing! I don't know what, but I often think, 'Well, why don't I just wake up today and get on your 66 and just say good by-y-y-y-y to the whole damned thing?

"That's why I envy what you're doing, Teague. I've enjoyed a couple of trips, but I couldn't be comfortable, conscience-wise or anyway else, to just pick up and walk away like you have. It would be so unfair. So unfair. Something's missing, though, and I'm going to find it. I'm sure of that. I look forward to it happening. I just don't know when or where.

"Those are the things you don't know, Teague. You have to make up your mind. But it's difficult because you really don't know what you're looking for."

The last freight car shook the mortician's Horizon. "Let's go to lunch," Marion said and took the next right turn for the suburbs. Two months later, his funeral home would burn down. Three years later, he would finally give up and die, never having found what he was looking for.

SEARCHING FOR 66

NINE

The Father of Highways met the Father of Waters at the Chain of Rocks Toll Bridge near Mitchell, Illinois. In the encounter, the Mississippi convincingly laid claim to the title "Old Man." Chain of Rocks, which carried Bypass 66 over the river, started out like any other bridge—in a straight line toward the opposite bank. But in midstream, near a Greek Revival pumping station, it took a sudden 45-degree turn north. This accommodated a quirk in the river's currents and let barge traffic flow safely between the bridge's pilings. But for road traffic up above, it often meant the most monumental traffic back-ups between Chicago and Los Angeles. The pavement was only 18 feet wide—Route 66's standard first width—and the shoulders were iron girders. When tractor trailers approached the turn simultaneously from opposite directions, they could not pass by each other safely. One would have to stop, wait for the other to back up (if traffic allowed it), then drive on.

After it finally got across the Mississippi, Bypass 66 skirted the northern reaches of St. Louis, then turned left near the airport and headed due south along the city's western flank. Five miles downstream from the Chain of Rocks, City 66 crossed the Mississippi on the MacArthur Bridge. A spur went north while the main route angled through downtown and the city's south side. By the time the two 66's finally joined again two miles south of Kirkwood, Missouri, they had between them intersected every major thoroughfare in metropolitan St. Louis. If you could find 66, the rest of the city was yours.

And in that city you'd find a rich tradition of commonplace cuisine. The hot dog was born in St. Louis. So were ice tea and the ice cream cone. Seven-Up and Switzer's licorice started there, as did Anheuser-Busch. Carrying on that tradition today in two modest stands on the city's south side is Ted Drewes Frozen Custard.

The original building, constructed in 1941, had been recently modernized and enlarged when I first visited there in 1986. The new stand was four times as large, but it maintained the gabled roof, dormer windows and white siding of its predecessor. There were also no gaudy signs, no drive-up windows with squawk boxes around the corner, no inside seating and no curb service. The only way to get something at Ted Drewes was to walk up to one of the 15 service windows, wait your turn, then ask a human being for it. Which is what I did.

"One medium cone, please," I said to the teenage girl behind the counter. "And would your boss like to talk about Route 66?"

I gave the girl my card, then worked on the cone while she went to find out. Before the custard even began to lose shape, she was back, motioning me to come in the side door.

Ted Drewes, St. Louis

Going inside was like a Cub Scout field trip. The store was a dense array of counters, freezers, prep tables, mixing stands, and custard machines—all stainless steel or gleaming white. Mixers whined, compressors hummed, custard poured softly into cones and cups, orders were called back and forth, and cash registers rang. The place smelled good, too.

Ted Jr., who's run the business in the decades since his father died, stood at the far end of the store, away from the open windows. He'd spread out some bills on a vacant counter and had been working on them until I came in. His voice was medium-pitched and friendly and he spoke in a soft midwestern twang—clipping it only slightly when talking of business affairs.

"Route 66?" he said, as if he'd just heard news about an old friend. "The original reason my parents were so nuts about this lot was because it was on 66! I was only 12 at the time, but I can remember how excited my dad was when he found this place. 'It's on 66!' he said. And my mom said, 'Route 66! Ooh!' She was thrilled to death!"

Before 66, Ted said, the first Drewes "stand" had been a 1919

Cadillac truck with the back cut away and a custard machine mounted on it.

"Our story started in the carnivals," he explained. "My father's older cousin had invented the Caterpillar and he was with the All-American Carnival in New York. One day in 1929 he came through St. Louis and said to my dad, 'Why don't you come and join the carnival, kid? There's no frozen custard stand here. You can build one.'"

Ted's face wore his father's reaction. "My dad said, 'What?' He didn't even know what frozen custard was. He was selling insurance then. My mother was struggling along with three children. But Dad was the kind of person who was always willing to jump at the drop of a hat—I guess that's how the pioneers were or else they would never have come over here—and he was gone. They got an old trade magazine out and found a used custard machine for sale somewhere up in Illinois. And he was off."

Ted's father spent the next six summers touring with carnivals, transporting the heavy custard machine between stops by rail. Then every fall he'd come home, pick up the family, and they'd spend the winter selling frozen custard on beaches of Florida.

Ted Jr. loved the ocean, but his mother didn't like the traveling. So when they went to Florida one winter and the Depression had left the beaches deserted, she persuaded his dad to build a permanent stand in St. Louis. The first was on Natural Bridge Road. This one on Chippewa was the second by six successful years. But with its volume and location, it quickly became the headquarters.

"We all sensed 66 was something special," Ted remembered. "And it wasn't just here, either—it was all over the country. And as soon as you realize you're part of a greater thing like 66, the mere fact that you know you're only part of something larger helps you somehow rise above it.

"Sunday night when everybody came home from the country, boy, this place was swamped! But what we thought then was busy is about a tenth of what we have now. We had four people running the store in the early days. Last Saturday night we had 35."

Few people who line up today at a Drewes stand walk away disappointed. But when Ted talks about the first custard his father made, he almost takes pride in how bad it was.

"According to Dad, the original recipe was terrible!" Ted said with gusto. "It was unbelievable—just terrible!

"Now Dad was not really a gourmet type of person—he didn't go around to the finest restaurants—but he did know what tasted good. So he started fooling around with the recipe. Pretty soon he decided it wouldn't cost him that much more to put real milk in instead of powdered milk, for goodness' sakes! Later he started putting a little cream in. Then he started adding eggs because he knew homemade ice cream tasted better with eggs. After not too much fooling around, he came up with a pretty good recipe—the same basic one we use today."

Behind Ted on the spotless white wall could be seen a menu. Abuca Mocha, Hawaiian Delight and Dutchman's Special seemed a bit beyond basic to me.

"Oh, those!" And the custard king launched into another enthusiastic explanation. "I like to spend a lot of time thinking about people and places. And then I try to get the flavor of the place into my ice cream. The dishes on that menu are all taken from places my wife and I have been to on our winter trips. We were even thinking about a Route 66 Sundae a couple of weeks ago, but couldn't come up with it."

"One concrete fudge!" came an order in the background. Ten staff, most of them high school or college age, were handling the afternoon flow.

"That's Tom," said the boss with a nod in the caller's direction. "Every one of my young people have different capabilities. His is being friendly. He can stand at a window and wait on every customer for long, extended periods of time and still keep his personality high. Others you have to be careful not to stick 'em at a window too long because they're liable to screw up your business. But Tom likes it. So I say let him do it because that's where he thinks best."

Ted took time out to approve an ad agency's new design for his line of souvenirs—a line almost as popular in St. Louis as Anheuser-Busch's.

"We've had some pretty good people work here when they were young," said the line's namesake. "Preachers, physical therapists, film makers, college presidents. The key is I like to hire a kid who has some interests. If they don't have interests, all they do is watch TV, I wouldn't touch them with a pole. 'What kind of work do you do at home?' I ask them. 'Do you ever wash dishes?' If they can't say yes, they're out.

"And they gotta know how to think, too. I'll point out to the road here and say, 'That's Route 66.' And I'll point to my left. 'That way is southwest,' I'll say. And then I'll point to my right. 'Which way is that?' If they can't tell me, they're not going to run one of my cash registers."

Ted hooked a hand on an overhead rack for support and surveyed his custard family.

"The hardest thing, though, is learning how to work," he said. "A lot of kids, they don't even know they don't know how. But that gal in pink there, she's known how to work for a long time. She's joking around now, but that's about as long as you'll ever see her loaf. That's why she's making $9.75 an hour."

He turned and nodded toward the fresh-faced girl who'd waited on me. "I grew up on this job and I really know what they're going through and how hard it is. So I can appreciate how much better they are than I was. This gal here somehow or another didn't have the smarts to go to college. Came from a large family, was backward in a way at first. She's been a pain, but right now I'm happy with her. And the whole thing with her is throughout her lowest, lowest time, she always had a good nature."

Ted had talked long enough without doing some work himself. A small rush developed at the windows and he went to help. Everyone made their own orders, but there was no confusion, no bumping into each other, and no long waits at any station. It was an operation as smooth as their custard—and as good to look at.

When my host returned about ten minutes later, he brought me a dish of concrete—his answer to the blizzards, earthquakes and other natural disasters currently being touted by his major chain competitors. Though its name was no tastier, the custard's flavor was. Later, Ted pressed a Dutchman's Delight on me—custard topped with chocolate, butterscotch and pecans.

The Coral Court Motel, an endangered art deco classic near St. Louis

"See that Baskin and Robbins store across the street?" he asked. "Three-thirty in the afternoon and it's virtually deserted. Many businesses, the owners have so many irons that they aren't really looking after anything. They have the old 'All you need is good managers' philosophy. Which is fine. But if you want something to really do well, it can take your life.

"It's the same way with these kids. They know that I really care about this business—you noticed I wasn't back in the office doing these bills—and I think sensing that helps them really work a lot harder."

At four o'clock, Ted's mother came in for her daily stint.

"This is the person who taught *me* how to work," he said in introduction. Putting his arm around the 85-year-old woman, he smiled down and asked, "Wouldn't it be cute to have a Route 66 day and play the music all day long, Mom? We could call it the Ted Drewes Route 66 Day!"

"I like that!" Mom said, beaming. "You come up with the best ideas! Why, we could even have a Route 66 Sundae!"

SEARCHING FOR *66*

TEN

Leaving St. Louis, Route 66 ambles southwest toward the Ozarks. A land of limestone bluff, hardwood forest and river floodplain, it is, in this native Missourian's opinion, the most beautiful scenery along the route. And until the 1920's, it was lightly settled. But when good cars and good roads came to the area, developers followed. One of the earliest was the St. Louis *Star-Times*. In 1925, anticipating 66, the newspaper bought 650 acres along the Meramec River near Pacific, Missouri. It subdivided the land into 20' by 100' lots and named the resulting community Times Beach. Then, in a reverse merchandising twist, it gave away six-month subscriptions to everyone who paid $67.50 for a lot (minimum purchase: two lots).

Macadamically speaking, Times Beach belonged entirely to Route 66. The new superhighway was the only road into town and the only road out. No other U.S. routes passed through. Nor did any state or county highways. Not even a dirt lane meandered on to the next town or farmhouse. But 66 was enough as factory workers and other folks of modest income from St. Louis began buying lots and building summer cottages. The highway's first resort town was born.

Built by the owners themselves, early cottages were makeshift originals. Because of frequent flooding, most stood on stilts. During the '30s, many owners moved into their cottages fulltime to ride out the Depression. Gas rationing during World War II brought even more of them to "The Beach" permanently, as did the post-war housing shortage.

Fish fries and hoedowns became a weekly tradition in the increasingly tightknit community. The prosperous '50s made it to town only a year or so late, bringing with them an upward trend in development. Makeshift buildings were torn down and replaced by conventional housing. Other homes were built onto. An association was formed to buy the remaining lots from the now defunct *Star-Times* and build a park. And because the floods seemed to have slacked off, new houses were built at street level instead of on stilts. Its change from summer resort to permanent home was completed in 1957 when Times Beach incorporated as a fourth class city.

A low tax base kept municipal services to a minimum in the new city. The town had 16.3 miles of streets, for example, but none besides 66 were paved. They were just graded dirt and during Missouri's hot, humid summers, the dust from traffic on them was so heavy laundry would get dirty before it had a chance to dry. Dust covered the people's houses and lawns and lined their lungs—a nagging, annoying problem, but Beachers accepted it as a reverse cost of living where they wanted.

Then in 1972, Russell Bliss, a waste oil hauler from nearby Rosati, Missouri, appeared before the Times Beach board of aldermen with a solution to the town's dust problem. For only six cents a gallon, he offered to spray his waste oil on the town's streets twice a month.

The board accepted Bliss's offer and he went about his spraying. His bill for that season came to $2,400 but the aldermen were happy to pay—that year, for the first time, Times Beach residents had enjoyed a "clean" summer.

Next year, Bliss came back and made an even better offer. This year he would again spray Times Beach streets for $2,400. Only he would come every week during the summer and spray as much as was needed. The board accepted again. In just two years, Bliss sprayed at least 100,000 gallons of his waste oil on the streets of Times Beach—more than 6,000 gallons per mile. And when the streets could absorb no more, on at least one occasion Bliss dumped excess oil in the undeveloped park.

"I remember my daughter Jerilyn just sitting by the side of the road and patting her feet in this stuff," former Times Beach resident Marilyn Leistner told me. "She was giggling and laughing. And the kids would ride their bicycles through the stuff and come home with big black stripes up and down their backs."

Two years of Bliss was enough for Times Beach and the aldermen decided to get by the next few years on his residue. The hauler did occasional spot spraying in town as late as 1981, but never again had a contract for the whole city.

During Bliss's second summer, Marilyn's husband started having severe psychological problems. He appeared drugged when he drank even a little. Blisters broke out all over his body—a malady later diagnosed as porphyria cutanea tarda. An already strained marriage grew worse and the couple soon divorced. Her ex left town, but Marilyn stayed on the Beach, marrying newcomer Bill Leistner a couple of years later. A dental assistant, the soft-spoken Missouri native showed a flair for community affairs—a flair which was sorely tested in 1982 when her hometown went overnight from riverside obscurity to global notoriety.

On November 10, 1982, reporter Ken Walk sat at his desk at the Tri-County *Journal*, a suburban St. Louis newspaper, going through a stack of government news releases. It was a tedious process, but occasionally he'd glean a paragraph or two of local interest. Today, though, in a cautiously phrased release from the Environmental Protection Agency, he found a single line which would keep him writing for a year and a half: the EPA had just placed Times Beach high on a list of Missouri sites potentially contaminated by dioxin.

Dioxin, a principal ingredient in Agent Orange, might be in the town's soil. Dioxin, determined by a government committee to be the compound most likely to cause cancer, might be working its way into the city's water supply. Dioxin, the most common cause of porphyria cutanea tarda, was threatening the very future of Times Beach.

Walk called Times Beach City Hall for a reaction.

"We had no idea what he was talking about," said Marilyn, who'd just been elected to the board of aldermen.

But Russell Bliss did. The cagey hauler had had a sweet deal with that waste oil. It was a by-product from a chemical company near Springfield, Missouri, and the company for years had been paying him to haul it away. Company officials knew the oil contained hazardous wastes, but claim yet today they thought Bliss was taking it to an authorized dump in Louisiana.

Hardly. Bliss had never left his native state. Times Beach, instead, had become his prime target. A decade after it was made, his offer to the board of aldermen—considered so generous at the time—would prove to be a gooey death warrant.

I looked Marilyn up in her office, the banquet room of a now-abandoned restaurant on the edge of town. Her calm voice and manner less than four years after Walk's phone call almost belied the woman's words. "Chaos broke loose," she said. "No one here knew much about dioxin. But that just made our fear all the greater. A lot of people remembered how the roads had turned purple after being sprayed. They remembered there'd always been an awful odor after Bliss had been in town, how birds and newborn animals had died.

"Then the EPA told us it would be nine months before they could do any testing. We couldn't wait, of course. But at a thousand dollars a test, the city couldn't afford to pay, either. So we raised the money through donations and had a private lab take samples from all over town. They wouldn't be able to tell us what the level was, but they would be able to tell us if dioxin was there."

As soon as EPA learned of Times Beach's plans for an independent analysis, it sent in a cadre of men in white protective suits to conduct a far more elaborate series of tests. Beachers felt temporarily reassured by this gesture.

"Then they told us it would take six months to get results back," Marilyn said. "Our lab said two weeks, so we told them to go ahead."

While residents awaited the tests' outcome, late autumn cloudbursts pushed the Meramec River 25 feet above flood stage. On December 5, 1982, before EPA and the private lab had even completed their first round of sampling, Times Beach fell victim again—this time to the worst flood in its history.

Private insurance companies had long before refused to insure Times Beach homes because they were on a flood plain. The Beach had joined the government's National Flood Insurance Program in the '70s, but had withdrawn from it in 1980 because of the program's requirement that all new housing be erected on stilts. Residents had no insurance, but they'd been through other floods before and had either cleaned up or rebuilt. This flood was a bad one, but shouldn't keep them from doing the same once more.

The muddy waters receded after several days and Beachers started returning home. The rebuilding process was already well underway when the city received what its people now call their "Christmas card." EPA test results, not expected until next summer, were already in—Times Beach was clearly a dioxin casualty. One part per billion in the soil was considered tolerable; samples from the Beach averaged *2,000* parts.

Marilyn's voice remained calm and even. "'If you've gone back, move out,' the government told us. 'If you haven't gone back, don't. Bring in your clothes and anything else which may be contaminated and have it dumped. Don't plan on ever going back.'"

The news brought helicopters crammed with journalists from all over the country and world to cover the story. A government agency set up a guard trailer on the edge of town and wouldn't let anybody in except the people who lived there. Highway crews even came out and removed Times Beach's name from interstate signs, leaving only a ghostly outline where the letters had been.

"By this point, we weren't sure of anything anymore," Marilyn said. "We weren't sure of moving. We weren't sure of our health. We weren't sure of our mortgages and our businesses. We just wanted some certainty restored to our lives."

Even though Times Beach had withdrawn from its flood insurance program, the Federal Emergency Management Administration, decided it should help anyway. To discourage folks from getting on 66 and moving back to the Beach, it offered to pay for their temporary lodging elsewhere until things settled down. Marilyn and her family spent five months in a $50-a-day room at the Holiday Inn near Six Flags. Some families relocated to a nearby trailer park, Quail Run, only to be moved again a month later when dioxin was discovered there. Others ignored the warnings and offers of help and moved back home anyway.

Months went by in this government-induced limbo. Businesses in Times Beach started closing down because there weren't enough locals to support them and nobody else could come in. The Small Business Administration at first offered loans, but subsequently rejected all requests on the grounds that the applicants weren't actually running a business at the time. Homeowners-turned- pariahs, Beachers wondered if their every illness—past and present—was somehow linked to dioxin. Their children were shunned at their new schools and cleaners refused to take their business. A Times Beach man was spotted in an area fast food restaurant and the place quickly emptied. A zealous street preacher from St. Louis even came to Times Beach and proposed it be converted into a center for the *homeless*. He brought two busloads of street people with him, driving one hysterical Beach woman to say, "I feel like they're picking my bones!"

"But there was only one way we were going to get help," Marilyn said, "and that was through the government. You had to ask the government for help and then you had to trust them. So we fought and fought and fought only to be studied and studied and studied. They knew dioxin was bad, but they didn't know how bad. They knew we couldn't go on living in motels, but they didn't know where we should live—only where we shouldn't. And it sure didn't help when we found out some officials had known about the dioxin since 1972."

Ridding Times Beach of dioxin would mean burning it out of the soil in special smelters. This would take years if it could be done at all. And then there would be only the ashes of a town, not its soil. That would make the temporary quality of their lives permanent, so Marilyn and most other Beachers started lobbying for what they thought was the only sensible solution—have the government buy the whole town and let the residents take their money and rebuild elsewhere. When the EPA agreed to use Superfund dollars to do just that, most people thought that would end the town's troubles. In fact, they only intensified.

"Most residents favored the buy-out, but the few who wanted to rebuild were adamant," Marilyn said. "The board of aldermen felt like taffy. Each side made threats. City officials who'd already moved were warned to stay out of town or they would be shot on sight. Those still in town got calls that their homes would be burned. And all of us at one time or another received anonymous, threatening, nasty letters.

"What had happened to our peaceful, friendly little town?"

Two mayors of Times Beach resigned in quick succession because of the threats and pressure and Marilyn was elevated to the post on an interim basis—probably the first dental assistant in American history to attain such office. The formal election on June 4, 1983, became an informal referendum on whether the town would cooperate with the buy-out or not. Threats and vituperation continued throughout the campaign, but Marilyn still came out the winner, 312 to 25. The buy-out would proceed.

"A lot of us supported the buy-out only because it was voluntary," Marilyn said. "So that June when the government hired a firm to handle everything, we thought, 'Oh boy! It's almost over!'

"But we soon found out what voluntary meant. It meant you could either accept the firm's offer or reject it. But if you rejected it, the government would condemn the property, take possession, and evict you. Then they'd still pay you what they wanted."

The first offers were so low that many residents spray-painted them on their houses and invited TV cameras in to witness this latest affront. Eventually, most protesters got better offers. But because the government paid fair market value instead of replacement cost, most Beachers ended up losers on the deal. Complicating this were tortuously slow title searches by a company which had offered a cut rate if it could do them all.

Times Beach, Missouri.

Despite all this, the buy-out continued inexorably; by the time I passed through there in 1986, only one defiant couple still lived on the Beach—and even they had built a new home down 66 near Pacific.

In their final act before disincorporating the city, Times Beach aldermen had appointed Marilyn to monitor the buy-out and be the town's liaison to all the agencies involved. Her primary task these days was to help the reluctant couple move out and then close down the town. It was a job she expected would take another three or four years to complete.

Chief official for a city that didn't even exist, Marilyn was dividing her days between her dental assistant job and her Times Beach office overlooking the Meramec. In a corner she'd stacked all that was officially left of the town—a dozen boxes of files. The guard trailer was next door. A pastoral river mural, the sign from the city's police department, had been bolted to it. Outside it stood the town's only remaining commercial establishment—a Pepsi machine. An unassuming, comfortably-dressed woman in her middle years, Marilyn used to stutter when she spoke to the press. Now she was comfortable with everything from answering the casual questions of a traveling stranger to delivering the keynote speech at the Nation Hazardous Materials Conference (HAZMAT), which she was slated to do later in the year.

"We were all hysterical and abusive at first, though," Marilyn said. "We hated everybody. We know there was something wrong here. The government wouldn't spend $33 million buying and moving us out if they didn't think something was wrong. So we fought with each other, we wrote two or three hundred letters a week, and we threatened to kill the officials who were trying to help us."

"Now I'm no scholar and I'm no expert on chemicals. But since I was in the forefront from day one, I felt it was necessary that I take a leading role. It was the only way I could get rid of the hatred I felt for Russell Bliss and the government.

"At first my husband supported me. Then he didn't. Now he does again. But I realized not too many months after the announcement that you can't be consumed by something like this when one of my daughters tried to commit suicide. Our life had just been a whirlwind. We'd moved to Pacific and she was away from everything that was familiar to her. She'd developed a seizure disorder in 1977 which doctors said would go away when she turned 21. Now she thought it might have been caused by dioxin. It got to the point where she wondered if even the pillow she was sleeping on was contaminated. From TV and newspapers, she developed the impression that her life was no good, so one night she took an overdose of phenobarbs and dilantin."

Sitting at her gray government desk, Marilyn squinted into the late morning sun. Behind her, foliage in a thousand shades of green sloped down to the river. Though it might be coated now with an invisible film of dioxin, Beachers had picked a beautiful place to live.

"After this tragedy, I realized that my bitterness was ruining my family, especially this daughter," Marilyn went on. "I realized I was planting in her the things I was feeling and it was destroying her. It was also scaring the pudding out of my other daughters, my son, and my husband. And looking around the community, I soon learned that the community reacted to my emotions. If I cried, they cried. If I laughed, they laughed. So then I decided I had to be strong for my family and the rest of the community. I kept on fighting—I had to—but I made myself be stronger.

"It hasn't been easy, but it was what I had to do. There still isn't a day goes by that I don't see a guard come in and I wonder, 'Is he tracking this stuff in? Have I taken this stuff home with me? Is it in my house? Is it in my driveway? Have I contaminated the neighborhood?'

"But when you've suffered a tragedy, as the years go by it dims. Most residents have built their new homes and gone on. Even Ken Walk is gone—his paper told him take a transfer or stop writing about Times Beach. He knew he couldn't stay here and not write about Times Beach, so he left.

"But I'm still right in the thick of everything. It's like I haven't yet made the transition. Being a trustee will end someday, but the health problems for my family—are they going to end? Are we going to be okay? Are my grandchildren going to be okay, when and if?"

Marilyn's face suddenly brightened. "Want to take a ride into town?" she asked. I thought she meant nearby Pacific—someplace where we could have lunch. But she meant the Beach. So we went up to the guard trailer where I signed a liability waiver and was issued a protective suit and disposable yellow boots. While a guard drove us along 66, Marilyn sat in the back seat with me and kept up a running commentary about the town she'd called home for 27 years.

Pointing to one of the town's few stone homes, she said, "This house, the top half was once used by gangsters. This next street, Dogwood, is the hottest one in town. We try to avoid it whenever possible. And the woman in this house had a nervous breakdown right after the announcement of dioxin. I don't know where she is now. Last time I talked with her husband she was still in a mental hospital."

Every yard was overgrown. Weeds crept across several of the streets. Most of the houses, modest to begin with, were ramshackle now, having never been repaired since the last flood. Clothes still hung on one line and a wild turkey sauntered across a seldom-used side lane. Marilyn said there were even coyotes in town now.

"Yeah," said the guard, "but they help keep the rodents down."

"Turn right just past Al Campin's house, Mark," Marilyn told the man. Pointing through a rolled up window, she said, "That's where the Essens lived and there's where Chuck Yarborough had his modular park. And this house here was really unique—its whole right wing was a game room. It had an inlaid shuffleboard court and a chess game in front of the fireplace. But everything's covered with mud now."

Back at the office, we patronized the town's commercial district and sat on the trailer steps. Out in the road, a photographer from the Minneapolis Star posed a picture of the town's last two residents, George and Lorraine Klein. Gaunt, defiant and tired, the couple stood in front of a makeshift barricade. Behind the barricade stood a security guard, arms crossed, feet spread, alert. Though it wasn't taken on the right day, the picture would later appear in the book *A Day in the Life of America.*

"One thing I've learned from all this is that people *can* be involved in government," Marilyn said. "Before, we elected these people and thought they were supposed to do everything. But I now realize that just the ordinary citizen can have an impact on what happens just by calling their legislator or writing a letter. We fought for the buy-out and we got it—and that's a good feeling."

Ben Essen, another former Beacher, had a different opinion when I visited him a couple of days later in his new home.

"What I learned was not to have anything to do with the government," he said. And he had more reason than most to say that—his family was one of those that moved to the Quail Run Trailer Park.

"I had a heart attack a week after we moved there," he said. "I was sittin' in the house one mornin' recoverin' and I didn't know nothin'—*nothin'*—about this dioxin business at Quail Run. I was watchin' an old movie on TV when here come these goddurned helicopters and everything else a landin' in here!

"They was in my yard, in the street, everywhere durn place! The news media come walkin' up there and banged on the door. 'Are you the people who lived in Times Beach?' 'Yeah,' I said, 'I lived in Times Beach.' 'So what do you think about this dioxin bein' in Quail Run?' I said, 'Hell, there ain't no dioxin up here.' They said, 'There sure is.'

"And here they come—my whole durned livin' room was wall to wall cameras and people and everythin'."

Late in 1985, the Essens and six other oft-moved families from the Beach bought 15 acres of wooded land up on Jim Weber Road near Pacific and subdivided it. Ben's wife, Rose, wanted to name the development Blissful Acres, but the majority settled on Forest Plus—after the street they had all lived on in the Beach. Home for the Essens now was a double-wide mobile home complete with garage, tool shed and rabbit hutch. Their 66 dioxin odyssey was finally over—even if the memories weren't.

"We hadn't been here a month when the guy across the way approached us about having the dirt road here sprayed," Rose said. "We just started laughing. He thought we were crazy."

"Yeah," said Ben, "and when we found this land, I asked the man at EPA if anybody had ever been up here anytime to do anything. Because if they ever send somebody up here in one of those little white suits, we'll bury the guy. You won't even find his bones."

Later, Ben walked me up the unsprayed road to meet some of his Forest Plus neighbors. Three of the families were out on the slopes of their land that day cutting down dead timber for the winter ahead. We found Chuck Yarborough taking a break by a wood wagon in the middle of the road. Wearing dark blue overalls and chewing some smokeless, he leaned against the wagon and talked about the whole fiasco in the same direct way that all other former Beachers did.

"Are we bitter?" he said amid the roar of chain saws. He gave my obvious question polite thought.

"Yeah," he said, "we're bitter. Wish it hadn't 'a happened...but what can you do? I tell you flat out—I wasn't for the buy-out. And it wasn't the low prices, either. I *liked* what I had. I liked where I was. I liked my neighbors, I liked my friends, and I liked being on 66. As far as fear of dioxin goes, I lived there for 11 years. Any damage done is already done. Time will tell."

His cool blue eyes stared down at the road. Chuck thought a moment more and repeated softly, "Time will tell." Then he straightened up and hollered some directions to his son.

Turning back, he said, "No, I wasn't for the buy-out. I'd already rebuilt my house. But now that it's happened, okay. Fine. Let's get on to something else. You're traveling 66—you can't stay in one place. Neither could we."

SEARCHING FOR 66

ELEVEN

Seventy-five miles further down the road, around Rosati and St. James, the land so reminded early settlers of their native Italy that they named it "Little Italy of the Ozarks." Concords, catawbas, cacos and a half dozen other native grapes already flourished on the area's sunny, gently rolling slopes. Soon, so did several imports. By the 1890's, Missouri was America's second largest wine producing state. And when disease decimated the French wine grape industry earlier this century, it was revived with hardy hybrids from these Ozark highlands.

Then came Prohibition and the Missouri grape industry was itself decimated. For a half dozen years, Little Italy's vintners barely survived by selling their crops to Welch's on longterm payment schedules. Revival eventually came, but it took no foreign paths this time—it came down 66. Thanks to the new road's hard pavement, St. Louisans could now drive down to St. James, have a picnic, buy enough grapes to keep their jelly jars full for a year, and get back in town soon enough to stop by Ted Drewes. A hundred brightly painted roadside stands sprang up to meet these travelers' needs and a Route 66 tradition was born: the annual Little Italy grape pilgrimage.

Phyllis Meagher, a native St. Louisan, remembers her own family's pilgrimages well. She and her brothers and sisters would argue over which stand to stop at, and then in their excitement make it impossible for their father to negotiate a good price. They'd each grab clusters, lean their heads back and gulp in grapes by the mouthful. Tiring of that, they'd turn to squeezing the bottom of a grape just right so the skinned fruit would pop right into their mouths. Her brother Mike even became adept at spitting the seeds at other family members, then blaming Phyllis for it.

Phyllis stayed in St. Louis for college, then took 66 to Chicago and taught two years at a school for deaf children. Later during the afterglow of Camelot, she spent two years in the Peace Corps. Afterwards, she got seriously interested in computers a little earlier than most people and parlayed her way to a successful consulting career.

"It's easy to make a lot of money in the corporate world,"
Phyllis said the day that I met her. "Really easy. But it got a little crazy
sometimes. And at some point I asked myself, 'Why am I doing this?
Why am I batting my head against this wall?'

"Then one day I was visiting my mother in St. Louis and we
decided to drive down to St. James and buy some grapes. It was tradition.
But that day I counted all the grape stands—there were at least forty—and
I said, 'Gee, they sell seventy-five, a hundred tons out of these
stands...there has to be a profit in it. So I rented a little stand up the road
and said, 'I got to do this.'

Phyllis Meagher, St. James, Missouri.

"That first year, the test year, I did everything. I picked the grapes,
packed them, lugged them up to the stand and sold them. In one day I
made $117. Then I went home and there was a check from an investment
for almost the same amount. And I thought, 'Look at how clean this
money is!' Then I looked at the grape money and thought how real it
was."

A decision made itself: Phyllis quit her job, bought the 12-acre
plot that she had picked grapes from the year before, and renamed it Meramec Vineyards. Acting deliberately again, she hired a semi-retired grape
farmer to work the vineyard while she served a year's apprenticeship.
When we met, she was starting her fifth season.

Early on, Phyllis had declined an offer from Welch's to buy her
crops; she wanted to count her money this century instead of next. And a
stand was fun, but couldn't support her year-around. So she started looking around for new markets. The first big one, she discovered, was where
it had always been—ninety miles up Route 66 in St. Louis.

"If people would drive clear down here to buy grapes, I knew they
would buy them in St. Louis," Phyllis said. "So I called two grocery

chains there and they agreed to try a ton and a half. Friends came down from St. Louis and we did everything, even drove the truck back to town ourselves and unloaded it. The grapes sold out in two days and we ended up shipping ten tons that year to those two chains. Now we're shipping to chains in Chicago, Kansas City, Arkansas, Texas, Kansas. Winn-Dixie even took a load last year, which meant our grapes got clear down to Florida."

Cutting the middle man made Phyllis some money. So, too, did cutting her vines. Instead of discarding her prunings, she started weaving the longer ones into wreaths. The shorter ones she packed in burlap bags for use by barbecuers. Both products were selling well at upscale shops in Missouri and Illinois. This year, Phyllis planned to introduce a line of juices—Meramec Concord and Meramec Catawba—and sell it through the same stores which bought her grapes. Also this year, while more established growers were pulling up their vines, she was planting a half acre. They'd later produce wine grapes for sale to area vintners.

"Every year when harvest is over, I re-evaluate to see if I want to go on," she said. "Doing the new things has been fun. I haven't made a profit yet, but I still do consulting work in the off season to keep going. And supervising the workers has been no problem—I had 15 staff in Chicago. But last year, the harvest was really hard. The weather was bad. I had a friend staying with me who was considering suicide. There was trouble with the grapes, trouble with everything—just a whole lot of emotional overload."

Animation crept into Phyllis's voice. She straightened hair which didn't need straightening. "Then a reporter came by and asked me how things had gone the past couple of years. It had been a terrible day and I didn't want to do the happy grape grower story. But I did anyway.

"Then as I talked, I realized how much I'd got done, how much groundwork I'd laid. At that point, I realized how much I really enjoyed what I was doing, how much I got off on it. There's the impact of having started something—the energy, the psychic income.

"There was culture shock when I came here. Some winter mornings I just wanted to go downstairs and turn the heat dial up. But I have a wood stove, so I had to start a fire. Now there's culture shock when I go back to a city in the off season. So when I re-evaluated last year, even with all the hard times, I decided to come back."

She looked at me inquiringly, analytically, to see if I'd computed. I nodded, but it was unnecessary—her eyes already knew.

SEARCHING *FOR* **66**

TWELVE

West of Rolla, Route 66 enters the Mark Twain National Forest. In this land of streams and cedars, it visits towns like Sleeper, Buckhorn and Hazelgreen. West of the forest, it goes on to Lebanon—at 10,000 people, the largest town in a 60-mile radius.

At first, the highway's path through Lebanon looks much like any other commercial strip along the route. Then, in just a three-mile stretch, it passes Ron Ikerd Used Cars, E.B. Auto Sales, George Marcel Used Cars, Alvin Jackson Used Cars, Kelsey's Auto Sales, L & N Auto Sales, Don Farner Motor Sales, and Mark Farner Motor Sales Limited—and also Orby's Body Shop, Riley Automotive, Lebanon Auto Supply, Rogers Wrecking and Salvage, Precision Engine Shop, Superior Auto Glaze and Car Wash.

"We have 114 dealers in all, mostly wholesale, plus all the related businesses," Charley Luthy told me. "They call us the Used Car Capitol of the World."

Charley owns Sho-Me Auto Supply and he's a past president of the city's Used Car Dealers Association. A waitress at the Country Corner Cafe had referred me to him. In tones both Ozarkian and slick, he explained how this modest Missouri city came to have one used car dealer for every eighty-three persons in town—and made it sound like the most natural of progressions.

"We have a lot of hustlers here, Tom, a lot of go-getters," Charley said. "Back in the old days they were horse traders. Then 66 came and there weren't any more horses, so they switched to cars.

"Well, Gene Smith had thirteen kids. All but just a few grew up and went into the car business—buyin', cleanin', fixin', haulin', sellin'. His wasn't the only big family in town, and a lot of the others went into the business, too. Some of them are in the third or fourth generation by now.

"With 66 and now the interstates, we've always had good location. It was easy to get the cars, bring them back home, fix them, get them back on the road to an auction. Help's cheaper here. Rent's cheaper. So when we got to the auction, we could sell our cars 45 percent cheaper than the big city dealers."

"And our boys are sharp," he went on. "Don Farner can just look at a car and tell you within five or ten dollars how much it'll cost to fix it up. When you can come that close, you can make money in any business."

The capitol title was self-proclaimed, but probably deserved. Lebanites still claim it today, only not as loudly as before. That's because Richard King, former director of the Missouri Department of Revenue, once had another title for Lebanon. He called it the <u>Rollback</u> Capitol of the World.

A year and a half before my visit, King had looked at Lebanon's amazing statistic—all those used car dealers—and decided there was no way that many people could be making that much money honestly. So he'd called in four other state agencies, the district attorney, the county sheriff and the FBI. Together, helicoptered into Lebanon one cloudy autumn morning in 1984 and launched a sneak attack investigation of the used car metropolis.

Charley sat behind his desk, leaning back, his cool blue eyes in control. "Three or four days before the investigation, King called in the media," he said. "He told them what he was going to do, what he was going to find, even how many dealers he'd close—at least 30. He even claimed we had some kind of hydraulic machine down here that pulled dashes off cars so we could roll the odometers back. So when King came down here that Monday morning, here come all these TV and media people in their vans and helicopters. And they were going to get their story."

"Don Farner had a kicker on his lot, a totalled car he'd rebuilt. Since it was a rebuilt, its number had been pulled off the original spot and put on the door. That's the law. But some state guy saw the sticker missing and said, 'Here's a stolen car! Our first stolen car!' They called a wrecker with the TV cameras rolling and they were going to impound the car. Before we could get it straightened out, they'd got their pictures and left."

As spokesman for the dealers, Charley spent all his time talking with the press, state officials, his senators and the Governor—defending, debating, counterattacking, pleading. A few officials lent a sympathetic ear, but the tide of King's investigation was too strong. Lebanon was on its own.

"Now I'm just an old country boy that was born here, Tom," Charley said. "So was my dad. And my dad's dad and his dad. You become pretty familiar with a region when your roots run that deep in it. Now I ain't sayin' the dealers is all all-American, but you have to have a certain amount of respect for these individuals out there workin' six days a week tryin' to make a livin'—just like people did all along 66. And it was **dead** wrong when King and his people tried to take these guys' livelihood from them."

Charley leaned forward and pointed a finger. "They were callin' us a rat's nest—illegal this, illegal that. But you know how many charges they leveled out of all this? How many criminal charges?"

"One?" I ventured.

"Zero! That's how many—zero!"

The defense rested.

Before I left, Charley called up Don Farner for me.

"I need a loan, Don," he said, then held the phone away from his ear so I could hear the abuse.

"Actually, I got this guy here wants to put you on TV."

More abuse came over the line, but Don still invited me by. He and his son Mark share a garage, office and lot on the west end of 66 in Lebanon. He claimed business was terrible. But between phone calls, test drives and conferences with his son, Don found only fifteen minutes out of two hours to talk with me.

"You know what the worst thing they got me on was?" he asked after one phone call.

"I have no idea."

"Misalignment of parked cars!"

"I never heard of that."

"I never either. Mark never either. But one of his cars was parked on my side of the lot and they told us that was wrong. I also didn't have a business license, but that's because they hadn't sent it out on time!

"I like the used car business. There's nobody hooked up to you. There's nobody tellin' you what you got to do. But that investigation perturbed me. You work on your reputation for forty years. Then the authorities and the media, they come in here and you couldn't fight 'em. You just couldn't fight 'em."

Fortunately, Don didn't have to fight very long. The investigation was slated to run a week. But at 2:30 p.m. on only the second day, Richard King gathered the media around him.

"The investigation is taking a break," he declared. Then he got in his helicopter and flew back to the state capital. A month later, Missouri elected a new governor. That man, in turn, selected a new director of the Department of Revenue. King took one last flight—home—and his investigation went with him.

Business back in Lebanon hurt for awhile. But most of the dealers' clients were repeats. They knew better than Richard King or the media reports and kept coming back from as far away as Dallas. Life and business in the city were pretty much back to normal by 1986. All that was different was a bad taste for government and a wariness of strangers that shouldn't have to be.

In 1947, at age 42, Bud Riley decided to escape the "rat race of city life" in Rock Falls, Illinois and buy a small business on Route 66 in the Ozarks. Looking for another place, he stopped at a small gas station and cabin near Lebanon to ask for directions—and ended up buying that place instead.

"Our sleeping quarters were in the attic," he said. "It was <u>hot</u> in the summer and <u>cold</u> in the winter. The toilet was outside. We had no phone. It was nine miles to the nearest grocery store. I couldn't sleep—I was so excited and happy."

Ruth, however, wasn't. She had a good job in Rock Falls and decided to stay there for a while with their son John, who was then 10. One September morning in 1947, she and Bud bid each other a tearful farewell as she left for work—Bud had a trailer full of second hand equipment hitched to the family's '37 Oldsmobile and he would be leaving for Missouri later that morning. But when Ruth got home from work that evening, Bud was still there—the trailer hitch had broken just as he was pulling away!

"On the way to Lebanon finally, the hitch broke again," Bud said. "The trailer turned over and my junk spilled all over the highway. My mother was with me. She said, 'Buddie, let's go back. This is Friday the 13th and we are not supposed to go.' But I said, 'Oh no.' I was able to find a fellow with a truck. I loaded it and he drove my junk to my dream gas station.

"Mother and I got settled. She was no help. She had a wooden leg. I did everything. I washed our clothes by hand. We lived on bologna."

When school let out the next year, the Rileys' son John flew down to Missouri to spend the summer with his father. When he decided to stay there for school the next fall, Ruth came down for a visit. The first day alone was almost too much for her.

"I was sitting in the 'store'—some canned goods on a shelf," she said. "I was in a booth that I thought would fall apart, looking out on Route 66 when I see my husband standing at the highway waving his arms to our son John. John was at the wheel of the Olds. He could barely

Riley's Snack Bar, east of Lebanon, Missouri.   *Courtesy Ruth Riley*

see over the wheel and he had Grandma Riley with him. Bud was giving him the signal that the highway was clear. He crossed it and took Grandma for a ride on a bumpy road on the other side. Later Bud built a 'road' in back of the station and John would drive on it almost everyday."

Ruth returned to Illinois soon after that. But in six months she was back in the Ozarks for good. She and Bud and John fixed up a house on the hill behind the station. Using cigarettes as a loss leader and fireworks as a profit maker, they expanded their business. John started taking flying lessons. A graduate of the U.S. Naval Academy, he now flies planes for NASA.

Ruth and Bud sold Riley's Snack Bar in 1965 just as I-44 was pushing them to the wayside. Not long afterwards, the business burned to the ground. Eventually, they settled in Wallops Island, Virginia. Bud died in March 1990 of a heart attack, but Ruth lives on in Wallops Island with John, "thanking the Lord for my good health." John has been back to Missouri to view the station's ruins, but that's a trip that Ruth herself doesn't want to make.

SEARCHING FOR 66

THIRTEEN

If there's ever a hall of fame for logos, a museum for corporate icons, a gallery for symbols which identify their companies better even than their companies' names, then a camel from Springfield, MIssouri, will be a charter member.

In 1868, U.S. Army Lieutenant Paul Beall and his party rode by camel from eastern New Mexico to the California-Arizona border. Their purpose was two-fold: to survey a road and to prove the camel's value as a means of transportation in the American Southwest.

The Beall party achieved its first goal—the road they surveyed would eventually become Route 66. But the camels didn't catch on and not another was seen along the way until Snortin' Norton hit the road in 1926.

A lickety-split, slobbering ship of the desert, Snortin' Norton galloped America's highways for 60 years on the tractor-trailers of Campbell 66 Express. A thousand trucks carried him over 9,300 miles of route in 22 states. And Norton's image was on each of them at least five times. Legs stretched to the limit, tail flying high, a red "66" on his side and his too-long tongue flapping in the wind, Norton actually made travelers happy to see a truck.

Frank Campbell began his 65-year career in transportation as a cinder hauler. Using a horse drawn wagon, he made 35 cents a load filling in ruts made in Springfield's dirt streets by this new machine, the automobile. When 66 came through town, Frank figured it was now possible to drive the 225 miles to St. Louis in a single day. That made trucks suddenly competitive with railroads in the hauling of freight. So the cinder hauler stabled his horse, traded in his wagon, and formed Campbell's Express. The new company had one truck, the one he'd just bought, and one driver—Frank.

Butter and eggs, loads of fresh meat, and kegs of horseshoes were among Frank's early cargoes. As a hub for the Frisco line, Springfield was a loyal railroad town. This forced the first of Frank's many innovations in the trucking business—late night deliveries to merchants who didn't want to risk angering Frisco employees. Later innovations included containerized shipping and less-than-full load cargoes.

At a favorite Springfield cafe of Frank Campbell's, a punning waitress gave him the nickname "Hump." Frank liked that and made a camel the symbol of his thriving new company. At first the new logo featured a bare camel standing solemnly amid palm trees and pyramids. When a cigarette company objected that this resembled its own logo too closely, Frank removed the scenery. He added the red "66" to the camel's hump in the early '30s when he bought out another company, 66 Rapid Express.

A 1957 Campbell rig

By 1935, Frank was doing so well that he had to quit driving and go to work full time in the office. "It was all the red tape and paperwork and requirements of the ICC, the PSC, the OCC, the ACC, FICA, IRS and so forth," he later said. "It got so a truck couldn't move until the weight of the paperwork equalled the weight of the load."

As the company grew, one painter and then two were hired full time to put the Campbell logo on its trucks. In a forty-year career, chief painter Bill Boyd estimated he created 12,000 camels. His fastest time was twelve minutes for one on the cab door of a truck. His largest one was a 32-foot beast which stretched across the front of the headquarters building. Small wonder, then, that it was Bill who gave the logo its name. Stepping back from a new one one day, company legend has it that he said, "Well, that looks like a Norton. I guess that's Snortin' Norton." A motto, "Humpin' to please," came later when Frank's favorite waitress asked him if he were doing just that.

Over the years, Snortin' Norton became not only the Campbell logo, but a member of its family, a barometer of how the company felt about itself. In the beginning, he was a lifelike, but stationary creature. But in the early '40s, when acquisition of Sunflower Transfer and Storage spread Norton's tracks over Arkansas, Oklahoma and Kansas, his eyes opened and his exaggerated lips drew back in a toothy smile. In the '50s, with expansion to four southern states, his ears bent back, steam poured from his nostrils, and Norton took off in full gallop. In the '60s, he soared into full cartoon maturity as Campbell's 66 established its primary, Chicago-to-Dallas route.

Frank always liked to tell his people, "You can't stand still. Grow—or slip back!" And for fifty-eight years, his company grew. Then came government deregulation of the trucking industry in 1984. Frank had always lived by the rules, but now the rules had changed and they favored somebody else. Squeezed between unionized giants and non-union independents, Campbell 66 Express stood still. Then it slipped back. Frank had a stroke in 1985 and his family sold the already-troubled company to a group of longtime employees. The new owners tried cutting back operations to the basic Chicago-Dallas route, but the day and Snortin' Norton were not to be saved. On April 9, 1986, Route 66's most famous namesake filed for bankruptcy.

"We still hope to reorganize as a smaller, possibly non-union carrier," said Campbell Vice-President Bruce Crim when I passed through Springfield. But that wasn't to be, either.

Most Campbell drivers were old enough to take their Teamster pensions. The younger ones found jobs with independent companies. A sign at the headquarters door advertised "1500 good people and a couple of grouches." But when I dropped by barely a month after the bankruptcy filing, Bruce and his office staff were the only ones left. It was a quiet, somber scene, lightened only by the omnipresent image of Snortin' Norton. He was painted in a border on the walls. Official portraits of him decorated executive offices. Images of him emblazoned letterhead, note pads, operations manuals and anything else that take ink. A wooden carving of him, Bill Boyd's masterpiece, hung in the entry hall. There was even a restroom marked "Humps," but I forgot to ask which sex it was for.

Bruce had time to give me a tour through the logo's history.

"You'll notice that at one time we'd paint him with steam comin' out his nose," he said by one portrait. "Then as we got more sophisticated, you can see here he's kinda slobberin' a little bit. There was always a different expression on his face, too. Each one of 'em had its own different personality."

Bruce, who's the proud owner of a Route 66 sign ("I cobbed it one night when they were takin' 'em down"), is a second generation Campbell employee. His father drove a truck and Bruce joined him as a relief driver while he was still in high school. After college, he rose through the drivers' ranks to the office. Now, thirty-five years later, he was presiding over the end.

"It was hard filing for bankruptcy," he said. "It sure was. If I had a nickel for every mile I ever drove on 66, I'd be a rich man. In the early days you couldn't make a run from here to St. Louis without pretty well figurin' you were gonna have to overhaul the gearbox."

Bruce stood admiring the carving. "For fifty-eight of our sixty years, we were a profitable company," he said proudly. "But those last two years killed us."

It was almost a year after our visit before Bruce could finish up the paperwork and the last rites could be administered. Campbell 66 Express has slipped back into history now. Other companies have bought most of its trucks. Just as the government has paved over Route 66 in many places, they've painted Snortin' Norton over with their stylized, abstract logos—a strange sort of burial for a family member.

A year after my 66 journey, I was driving in downtown Springfield one day when a plain red cab crossed my path pulling a Snortin' Norton trailer. I made an illegal left turn and followed the truck until it stopped at a warehouse on the west side of town. I pulled in behind and caught the driver before he went inside.

"Did Campbell's 66 make a comeback?" I asked.

"No," he said, "but I pulled these trailers 25 years for them. I bought this one when they sold out and I was going to be goddamned if I repainted it. But take a good look at him. He's the last one left."

SEARCHING FOR 66

FOURTEEN

Late last century, Jesse James plundered his way throughout the west and midwest. But when he wanted to take refuge somewhere, he called Missouri home. Abundant ground water had worked on enormous limestone deposits in Missouri, honeycombing the state with caves. With 5,000 known caves and a hundred more still being discovered every year, Jesse seldom had to stay in the same cavern twice.

Before air conditioning, Missouri's caves were its community centers. Indians carved weapons and buried chiefs in caves. Entrepreneurs mined onyx from them. Outlaws, runaway slaves and bootleggers hid in them. Religious revivals, KKK rallies and romantic trysts took place in them. And in their cool depths, mushrooms were grown and ice was stored. Caves still serve most of these uses in Missouri. But with 22 show caves drawing two million visitors a year, tourism has become the state's leading speleological business.

Four of the show caves—Meramec Caverns, Onandaga Cave, Fantastic Caverns and Crystal Cave—are on Route 66. I resolved to go to each of them in order. But the tour guides' memorized spiels at the first three caves tired me and I wouldn't even have gone to Crystal had I not found an ad for it in a 1941 Route 66 tour guide.

"Most wonderful cave in America," the ad said in confident hyperbole. "Nature's underground wonderland in miracles of jeweled beauty. Competent guides, electric lighted, a beautiful underground mystery of the ages. Mann Sisters, Proprietresses."

Though wary of more subterranean schlock, I gave the ad's lure a chance and followed the guide's blue lines to the Crystal. Once I got there, Loyd Richardson, the cave's current owner, took all of 30 seconds to set my mind at ease.

"I don't have a regular story," he said, writing a receipt for my admission fee on a piece of scratch paper. "A standard spiel gets boring after awhile. When I'm down in the cave, I'm as likely to be talking about Dolly Parton as anything else."

There are no scheduled tours at the Crystal. We just waited a few minutes to see if anyone else was coming down the road. When no one showed, Loyd locked up the souvenir shop and we walked down a grassy slope to the cave itself.

"My wife Edith and I bought this place in 1980," he said. "It was a retirement project, but it was a lot like comin' home, too. Edith was raised around here and when I was courtin' her, we used to come out here to see the Mann sisters all the time. They was like grandmas to us.

Loyd Richardson, Crystal Cave, Missouri.

"My daddy-in-law even helped build these stone steps when they opened the cave back in 1893. They paid him 50 cents an hour. He was engaged to the oldest girl at one time and they even built a honeymoon cottage that's still standin' over here. But then he got in a fuss with the old man and he and the sister didn't get married. As a matter of fact, none of the sisters ever got married. When they died, they willed the cave to my wife's sister, who'd taken care of them. Then she got arthritis and sold it to us."

In barely as many yards and seconds, Loyd had sketched 83 years of Crystal's history and had not once mentioned Jesse James. So far, so good, I thought.

My guide unlocked the cave's gate, a wrought iron relic from a turn-of-the-century jail, and slowly swung it open. Gesturing me inside with his flashlight, he said, "And this is the only cave we know of that Jesse James was never in."

Though a battle with pneumonia earlier in the year had intimated his mortality ("I never been that sick before"), Loyd was still a sturdy 68. His forearms looked young and strong from work in the cave. Streaks of black hung on in his silver hair. He spoke in a low, soft voice, his native Arkansas twang flattened by forty years at the Cessna plant in Kansas.

"The Mann sisters came over from Brighton, England, when the oldest 'un, Ada, was five years old," he said in the cave's entrance gallery. "Their mother was real sick—best we can figure is she had TB—and she never came down here until after they got the steps built. And she was standin' right here, pretty feeble, and she said, 'Oh my, it looks like crystal.' So they called it Crystal Cave."

A tiny lizard, colored a translucent earthy orange, darted out from its hiding place. Loyd nudged it back with the toe of his boot.

"Now that's the actual story," he said. "It's not somethin' I made up. My daddy-in-law told me."

As we walked up and down his daddy-in-law's handiwork, Loyd showed me the cave's formations and their typically fanciful names: Washington's Monument, Abraham Lincoln, the Upside Down Well, the Lost City. "You can see about anything you want to in a cave," Loyd said. "We had a baseball player come in here one day and look at this formation and say, 'Why there's a bat and glove.

"And here's a stalagtite that has another one wrapped around it. Now why would Nature do a thing like that?

"And here's a section that's a total dead end. I let kids run up there and make up their own stories. They don't want to listen to me anyway."

Business isn't too brisk at Crystal Cave—about a dozen guests a day compared to five hundred or more at nearby Fantastic Caverns. But that's okay with the Richardsons. Loyd uses the time between guests to dig clay out of "new" sections of the cave. He'd planned on opening one of those sections this spring, but missed the state's inspection deadline because of his pneumonia. Tourists aren't allowed if a section hasn't been inspected, but we snuck up there anyway.

"I love workin' down here," Loyd said. "I have this crooked little stalactite timed—it drips every seven seconds—and I set a jug under it for drinkin' water. Me and my dog come down here and I just work. You forget about everything down here. Time don't mean anything and you forget about it. Like if I need to go to dinner, my wife has to come out and turn the lights off on me. She'll flash the lights and I'll know I need to go out for somethin'.'"

We talked that morning until Edith flashed the lights for lunch. Afterwards, I drove the guide's blue line back to Route 66, a less cynical person than the one who'd driven in.

SEARCHING FOR 66

FIFTEEN

In the early 1980's, Missouri tourism officials decided to change the state motto. The old one, "Sho-Me State," projected skepticism. Something more inviting was needed these competitive days. They settled on "Wake up to Missouri." Though on a bland par with Illinois' "You put me in a happy state" and Indiana's "Wander Indiana," the new motto did imply you'd at least want to stay overnight in its state.

At the same time, officials dropped mention of the state's official mascot, the mule, all together. After all, what kind of tourist draw is a sterile animal?

Down in the Ozarks, though, homefolks still prefer the old slogan. "Wake up to Missouri" means nothing to them—they do that everyday. "Sho-Me" at least tells the way they look at things. As for the mule, they have some not-so-subtle pride in it, too.

"Why, in Missouri we have mules that can even jump fences," a man had told me in Rosati.

"Jumpin' mules, huh?" I'd asked.

"You damn betcha! We got mules here that can clear a four- or five-wire fence without so much as a running start. The best ones can even clear six feet."

I didn't pursue the point. The man was just giving me an Ozark howdy, I figured, a good-natured jab that said "Wake up to Missouri, slick." But as 66 took me to the rest of the state, the subject of jumping mules kept coming up in chance conversations. I remained skeptical. But when a very proper lady at the general store in Halltown said, "Yes. Yes, I believe there are such animals", I decided to see for myself.

At the newspaper morgue in Joplin, I sifted through the file on mules. Articles said George Washington, a founding father of our country, was also the founding father of American muledom. He knew an expanding America needed a dependable work animal and he knew mules were stronger, more durable and cheaper to feed than horses. He also knew that Spain had the finest jackasses in the world. Though the Spaniards jealously protected this national resource, the General prevailed upon Spain's King Charles III to send over a pair of jacks in 1785 so a new line could be started on the American continent.

One jack died on the way over, but the survivor, Royal Gift, went on to become the Father Abraham of this country's mules. Once he even went on a breeding tour of southern states. His progeny went on to help build a nation—plowing, hauling, mining, logging, clearing the wooded wilderness, breaking the prairie sod. Most parts of the original Route 66, in fact, were built with mule-drawn equipment. Today, however, most mules are used only for recreation—trail rides, shows and coon hunting. They can be contrary creatures with minds of their own. But that doesn't bother Missourians much—it reminds them of themselves.

Dave Baugh, Carthage, Missouri.

The clips told me all this, but said not a word about jumping mules. There was only a single, slim lead—one article told of a man in nearby Carthage, Dave Baugh, who edited and published a magazine called *Mules and More*. Carthage was just up 66 from Joplin, so I gave the man a call.

"Jumpin' mules?" said Dave. He had the purest Ozark twang I had yet heard and didn't hesitate to use it. "Shur, we have 'em! Why don'tcha come up tomorra afternoon 'n see fer yerself?"

We met about 4 p.m. the next day at a Carthage pancake house run by C.D. Baugh, a cousin of Dave. My host smoked cigarettes, drank coffee and talked about his circulation, but his resemblance to other editors ended there.

"I only got through the eighth grade and I may be lying about two subjects," said the wiry hill man. We were waiting in the cafe for a heavy spring rain to let up. "But I'll tell you, Tom, I know mules. And I'll tell you, they ain't stubborn—some of 'em are just smarter than their owners!

If you take off runnin' down that road and get to hurtin', you're gonna quit! Well, a mule will, too. He knows what his limit is and he quits. An' if you're out ridin' and want him to jump over a dangerous cliff, he might just say 'To hell with you!' and tell you to go on over by yerself.

"Mules are a lot more durable than horses, too. An' a lot smarter. A horse is really a dumb animal. He'll get into his feed barrel and eat enough 'til it kills him. Let a mule get in there, she'll eat what she wants 'til she gets full and quits. Same with a horse and water. You run a horse hot and he'll drink 'til he kills himself. But a mule might walk up to the trough, maybe dip her head in, then come back in an hour when she's cooled off."

Dave won his first mule in a poker game in 1974. He's had about two dozen since. That was time and animals enough to have more than just a few stories and opinions.

"Mules ain't stubborn, Tom, no" he offered. "But if they figure out they're smarter than you, you've had it. They won't do a damn thing for you. That's why Ann Landers says when somebody calls you a jackass, you take it as a compliment.

"In the end, it looks like a man's got mules, he oughtta have a sense of humor. If he don't, he ain't got no business messin' with 'em."

Dave called for more coffee. He poured a shot of cream in it, let his spoon rattle around the cup two or three times, and tested his work. Satisfied, he set into another muleskinner tale.

"I know 'n old boy hitched his mule up to th' wagon one day and that mule wouldn't move for nothin'," he testified. "The old boy, he cussed 'n hollard and jumped up 'n down. But that mule, he just wouldn't budge. Finally, the old boy built a fire right under the mule's belly. The mule moved then, but only enough to pull the wagon over the fire!

"And then one night this old boy in a bar says, 'Hey, you don't know where I can buy me a good mule to plow my garden with, do ya?' I said, 'I got one right out home. It's a white mule. Everybody know you got a white mule, your garden'll turn out better.' He said, 'That right?' I said, 'Yeah.' 'Well, how much do you want for it?' I said, '$50.' He said, '$50? That's pretty cheap!' I said she didn't look so good. He said he'd be out tomorra to get her. He comes out, she runs into the side of the barn, and he says, 'Hell, this mule's blind!' I said, 'Well, I told you she didn't look so good.'

"But he loaded her up anyway. Then I run into him about 30 days later and asked him how she was doin'. He said, 'Hell, I sold her!' I asked him how the hell he did that. He said, 'I raffled her off! Got a thousand dollars for her at a buck a chance.' I said he must have pissed a lot of people off and he said, 'Just one—and I gave him his money back!"

More rain. More coffee. More cigarettes. More stories. Traffic outside on Old 66 sloshed by as Dave spun on. His newsletter, he said, had come to him the same way his first mule had—by chance.

"I got a hold of a coon hound magazine one day and was lookin' through it," he said. "It was just a lot of show 'n tell, a lot of see 'n tell, a lot of guys lyin' about their dogs. Kinda down to earth. So I decided to do the same with mules.

"I ain't gonna show you what those first few issues was like. But I've been doin' it six years and I got a little better. Circulation's about two thousand now. I'm goin' to 49 states. Even make a profit now 'n then. And the more subscribers I get, the easier it gets—a guy'll go out huntin' or to a show, write an article, take some pictures, send it to me, and I'll print it."

Good enough, maybe, but Editor Baugh has grander plans. "The way I see it, Tom, my dad and his brothers, they was all contractors," he said. "They all worked for theirselves. Any kind of construction you wanted, one of the Baugh boys'd do it.

"But nobody had a pot to piss in! Most everybody around town would say, 'Yeah, them Baugh boys, they're hard workers, hard workers.' Now I done a jillion hundred things in my life. You have to when you're raisin' four kids. But damn! When I get to be fifty years old, I don't want to be known as just a damned hard worker. I'd like to be able to *retahr* by the time I'm fifty! I turned 41 just last Saturday and I'm still shootin' for it. I'm hopin' this magazine'll help me make it."

Dave pulled a couple of issues of his journal out of a hip pocket and let me look through them. Inside, there was a healthy amount of ads, plus pictures of show mules, mules on trail rides, mules at "Show de-ohs," mules pulling wagons, even mules playing polo. Stories had headlines like "Fast Ass," "Crazy Ass," "You Bet Your Sweet Ass," "Texas Muleskinner," "Okie Muleskinner," and "Muleskinners Engaged." There were calendars of coming events, poems about mules, and such homey bits of advice as "If you got a drunk in the family, feed him scrambled owl eggs."

Only one thing was missing.

"Where are the jumping mules?" I asked.

"Jumpin' mules?" Dave looked surprised. "You mean there ain't none in those issues?" He grabbed the magazines from across the table and quickly leafed through them.

"Well, I'll be damned, Tom!" he said, still surprised. "But honest to God, I swear we have 'em. We use 'em when we go coon huntin'. It's a lot more fun than *walkin'* after the hounds. But we got so many fences in this country, it was either teach the damn mules to jump fences or carry 'em over. So we teach 'em to jump and some of 'em learn pretty good. A good mule can clear a four- or five-wire fence easy and the best ones'll top six feet.

"And honest to God, Tom, I swear we have 'em. Soon as this rain's over, we're gonna go see some."

Finally we drove Dave's battered pick-up out of town on 66, turned right on a black top road, left on a gravel lane. rattled past a house at the top of a small hill—"That's my cousin Ben's place"—and down a slope to a corral. "And this is where he keeps his mules."

Dave cut the gas and pulled in by the corral, parking his truck where it stopped. We got out and walked over to the fence where a stocky, blonde-haired man with a moustache and cowboy hat was brushing down a large black mule.

"This is my cousin Ben Baugh," Dave said. "And that's his wife Carol over by the shed with the other mules. She's the one with the short ears. And this here's my friend Tom. He's a good old boy, but he's never seen a jumpin' mule. Can you help 'im out?"

"Sure can," said Ben. "I was just getting ready to give Jingles here a little exercise." He laid a blanket on the top strand of the four-wire fence and led Jingles over to it.

"Now didn't I tell you mules was smart, Tom?" Dave asked. "First of all, you'll notice she ain't carryin' Ben over that fence with her—he'll have to get over on his own. An' second, he has to lay that blanket there 'cause she ain't gonna take a chance on no barbs."

Ben stood right next to the fence and by Jingles' side. He said a quiet word to her, then pulled gently on her rein. The jenny backed away two steps and sat expressionlessly on her haunches. She nosed the blanket to make sure it was secure, rocked back twice, then launched herself over the fence in a sideways flop. Ben climbed over after her and had her jump again. Then again and again. Each time Jingles cleared the height easily.

Dave tugged on his cap in salute. "Well, that's how we do it, Tom," he said. "Did we show you or not?"

"You sure did! I feel like a Missourian again."

"Good! Now we can go to dinner!"

SEARCHING FOR 66

SIXTEEN

In carving their smooth and true channels across this country, leviathan interstates bypassed thousands of towns. But in Kansas, they bypassed an entire state. US 66 hewed due west from Joplin, Missouri, crossing into southeastern Kansas a mile later. The old road first passed through Galena, continued west a few more miles to Riverton, the Cherokee County seat, then arced south for Baxter Springs and the Oklahoma border. A bare twelve miles after entering Kansas, Route 66 left it. But its successor, I-44, doesn't even pay that token. The new road takes a hypotenuse southwest from Joplin straight into Oklahoma. Southeastern Kansas is off its map all together—yet another detour for a region whose history has been molded by them.

In 1863, for example, Confederate guerrilla William Quantrill dressed in a federal uniform and detoured a company of Union troops to nearby Fort Blair to be massacred.

After the war, Baxter Springs became a booming stop on cattle drives. An annual festival still celebrates the town's early claim as "The First Cow Town in the West." But the cattle trade ended abruptly a century ago when Kansas ranchers forced tic-infested herds from Texas to take a detour around their state.

For 30 years after this, southeastern Kansas subsisted on farming—remote, peaceful and clean. But the world's richest deposits of lead, zinc and cadmium lay as close as fifty feet to the surface in this area and boom times came again in the 1920's when mining companies moved in. By the time Route 66 passed through in 1926, the 500-square-mile district, most of it in Kansas but some in Oklahoma and Missouri, was producing more than half the world's supply of industrial metals.

More than 1,400 mine shafts were sunk during the new boom. Mine heads and excavation rigs swarmed along the roadside. Acid smelters were built. And where once the area's dominant landscape feature had been prairie grass, it now became chat piles. Hundreds of 20-story mountains of mine tailings, awe-inspiring heaps of sharp limestone fragments laced with unretrieved metal, lined 66 on both sides. Manmade, lifeless mounds, they presented more a moonscape than a landscape.

Mickey Mantle grew up in this area. At Baxter Springs Kiwanis Park as a youngster, he hit many a home run and foul ball over the fence and on to passing cars on 66. As an older teenager, he worked summers in area mines. After high school, he became a New York Yankee. Mickey's father never got to see his son in the Yankees' pinstripes, though. "Mutt" Mantle died of lung cancer before that chance came—another victim of what many people call one of our nation's most devastating environmental disasters.

Elmo Burrows, Baxter Springs, Kansas.

Area natives bristle understandably at the term "disaster." This is, after all their home and mining was their livelihood. But evidence of disaster has been accumulating too long to be denied. Locals have known for some time, for instance, that their rate of lung disease was fifty percent higher than the national average. The same holds nearly true for cancer, heart disease, strokes and kidney disorders. The people have known, too, that Tar Creek, which Route 66 crossed near Commerce, Oklahoma, has flowed heavy and orange with lead, zinc and cadmium for as long as anyone can remember. And they've known when the acid smelter in Galena was operating that homeowners downwind of it were often driven away by billowing clouds of fumes and dust.

All this was known. But the scope of the area's environmental and health problems was not truly realized until the mines which caused them started closing down. This started in the 1960's as the metal yield of the ore dipped below eight percent. Had it been an island away from nature, southeastern Kansas might have retired once again to peaceful obscurity. But when the mines turned their pumps off, water flowed back into the shafts and flooded them. Debris-laden, the water then flowed back out—horizontally to places like Tar Creek or vertically down open mine shafts to the Roubidoux Aquifer, prime source of the area's drinking water.

Up on the surface, thin shelves of land above the mines started caving in. Fields, roads and whole sections of towns were swallowed. And the new fire station in Galena sank five feet before it could even be completed.

Still higher up on the surface, the loose chat piles became dangerous playgrounds. Area children fashioned sleds from cardboard boxes and went sliding down them. On weekends, off-road vehicle enthusiasts came from all around to roar over the larger piles. And on smaller piles around open mine shafts, adolescent boys played a game called "Ring Around"—running in narrowing circles around the shaft to see who could get the closest without falling in.

Even people who didn't go near the chat piles felt their lethal effect. The metal content of chat particles made them sharp enough to be used for sandblasting oil wells in Saudi Arabia and many piles were hauled off for that use. Others went to pave roads or line railroad beds. But hundreds of piles remained. And when spring and winter winds whipped across the prairie, they would pick up sharp metallic particles from the chat and deposit it elsewhere—to no good effect.

Many home owners in the tri-state district, unable to afford indoor plumbing, had substituted by drilling holes through their floors and down to a mine tunnel. Mine shafts and subsided areas became trash dumps. Though the acid smelter in Galena has been gone more than 15 years, the land around it is called "Hell's Half Acre" because nothing will grow there still. And Galena once decided against chlorinating its water supply several years ago because mining companies couldn't use chlorinated water in processing their ore.

When Superfund, the Environmental Protection Agency's clean-up program, was created in the last year of President Carter's administration, it declared Tar Creek to be the number one hazardous waste site in America. A mining company spokesman disputed the title. "The Tar Creek problem is a naturally occurring condition of minerals held in the ground," he said. "No one's drinking the water from Tar Creek," said a Kansas health official, "so there's probably no health problem there."

Superfund money was set aside to start a clean-up program. But with three states and more than 50 public agencies involved, the clean-up soon needed a clean-up itself. Soon Kansas and Oklahoma couldn't even agree on which way the water flowed underground. Mining companies fought the clean-up because they would have to pay for it. And local citizens asked the EPA to look for environmental causes of their illnesses, but the EPA said it could do that only if it already knew the illnesses were environmentally caused. By 1986, seven years after Superfund was created and Tar Creek was targeted, only four mine shafts had been plugged and only a few diverters for polluted streams had been built.

In late 1985, the Wichita *Eagle-Beacon* assigned a team of eight reporters to study the tri-state area and all its issues. They spent five months at the job and in late April, 1986, published a four-part, 20-page series. Its logo was a skull and crossbones buried in the ground. Only the top of the head and the tips of the bones—represented by chat piles—showed above ground. Called "A Legacy of Neglect," the series told in exhaustive but evenhanded detail of the tri-state tragedy.

My search for 66 brought me to the tri-state area only ten days after "Legacy of Neglect" had debuted. The people, not surprisingly, were bewildered, angry, and reluctant to talk to strangers who carried tape recorders and asked questions. Baxter Springs mayor Elmo Burrows summed up their feelings: "It's real hard for a person who's been fed all his life on mines to turn on them and say they did nothing but harm."

A former miner and contractor, Elmo, at 69, was in his second term as mayor of his hometown. I waited in his office, noting a Route 66 sign on the wall, while he talked with a phone caller about the city's new trash pick-up system. "This unit we bought looks like a machine from outer space," he said. "It's made ours one of the best trash pick-up systems in the state. One man can do the whole town in just four days and spend the fifth working on the truck."

Elmo spoke to his caller in assuring, mayoral tones. But when he turned to me, the verbal fists were up. Neatly dressed in doubleknit shirt and pants, he looked younger than his age, but sounded much older.

"I don't really have much to say," he told me. "Those newspaper stories pretty much told it all." So I started talking instead—about Route 66.

"Jumping mules, huh?" Elmo interrupted. "We used to use mules in the mines all the time."

"Is that so?"

"Yeah. We had to lower them down in special harnesses. Even had underground stables for them."

Soon we were down at the local historical museum, where Elmo has assembled a mining exhibit—drill bits, hats, goggles, picks, a miniature smelter, ore samples, explosives artifacts, stretchers, hundreds of crew photographs—plus an outdoor display of drilling rigs, rock crushers and other heavy equipment. Elmo showed me all around, providing expert, fond commentary. At one point, he even dipped into a bucket of ore samples and insisted I take some home with me.

"I started in the mines in 1935 after I graduated from high school," he said. "If there was a bulldozer there you wanted to run, you got on the bulldozer, you ran it. If there was a cutting torch there or a welding machine there, you ran it. That's why when they started building gas tunnels all over the United States, they came to the tri-state area for help."

We'd just climbed the steps from the downstairs exhibits. My guide stopped for awhile and I could hear his labored, wheezy breathing.

Emphysema?

"I saw the writing on the wall a long time ago and got out of the mines in 1953," he said. "But I still think there's twenty to thirty years of mining left here. It's low grade ore, but someday they'll figure out a way to get it out."

"But we don't have to depend on just the mines in Baxter Springs," His Honor continued. "We're diversified here. We have Ozark Salad. We have a terminal for Yellow Transfer, a branch of Ingersoll Rand, and a fellow's done a real nice job of reclaiming some farm land west of town. I don't say this boastfully, just proudly—in 1984 we were the city leader of the ten southeastern counties in creating jobs."

We went outside to inspect a keystone rig. One of the museum's most prized exhibits, the ancient excavating machine literally pounded holes deep into the earth. When working, its blows could be heard and felt for miles.

"And of course we were always proud to be on the Main Street of America," Elmo said after the inspection. "It made us really feel we were part of this country. But we lost even that last winter when they took the old signs down.

"Then the newspaper came along with its articles."

Elmo waved at the passing garbage truck. A streamlined, side-loading vehicle, it truly did look like a moon craft.

"It's a thing you never expected to happen," he said. "They made us sound like a disaster area, like there was something wrong with people for wanting to live here... I just don't know what to say to them."

I didn't, either. So I asked, "Would it make any difference *what* you said?"

Elmo considered the question silently for several moments. "No," he finally said, nodding. "No, I guess not. We'd be here anyway. We'd be home."

SEARCHING FOR 66

SEVENTEEN

Had she lived anywhere else in the Midwest, Carol Riley would probably have painted barn scenes. But she lived in Baxter Springs. So she painted smelters, mine heads, ground shacks, and frameworks. A few of those paintings hung in the museum. Before Elmo arrived, I'd spent some time looking at them. Their colors were rich and sentimental and the subjects always seemed to be caught when the sun's angle was strongest—at sunrise, sunset, or high noon. I liked them and said so to Elmo later on.

"Why don't you go see Carol then?" he asked. With an introductory phone call from him, I did.

Carol Riley and her husband John live in a brick ranch home on Baxter Springs' east side. It's on a circle drive in a subdivision. Not a smelter or a chat pile was in sight and I thought I could be anywhere in America as I rang the Rileys' doorbell. John answered and welcomed me inside. He was an older, white-haired gentleman with strong blue eyes—courteous, but a little apprehensive.

"Carol's had Alzheimer's Disease for the past year," he explained. "I know she's glad to have you see her pictures, but sometimes they take her back."

I sat in the living room and talked with Mrs. Riley while John brought in painting after painting from other places in the house. He leaned them against the wall, the couch, the chairs and the lamp posts until the room was full. Then he brought in some more. Individual scenes were not pretty in my conventional sense, but their beauty accumulated.

"I've been painting these about twenty-five to thirty years," Carol said. "Now I'm in museums all over the country. In the '60's, the Smithsonian even had an exhibit of my work."

She spoke graciously and with intelligence. Then in the middle of our conversation she turned to her husband and, as if I weren't even there, said, "I'm not going to sell him one, John."

"He just asked to look at your paintings, sweetheart. He's not here to buy them at all."

Carol drew back a bit. Her head shook uncertainly. John and I sat quietly in the afternoon sunshine and waited.

"It's not that I don't want to let you see them," she said presently, "but I don't want to let them go."

I understood. John brought more paintings in.

"I waited until my kids were old enough to fend for themselves before I got serious about my art," Carol said. "Then I just painted what I saw. I thought they were pretty."

Again as if I weren't even there, Carol turned to her husband and spoke urgently, "We have to go, John."

"No, we don't," he reassured.

"But we have plans."

"We don't have any other plans, honey."

SEARCHING FOR 66

EIGHTEEN

The Cherokee Hunt Club stands in the peaceful shadows of an oak and hickory glen a dirt road mile off Route 66. For seven days and six nights a week, it is a tranquil, pastoral scene, almost deserted. But every Sunday evening, it becomes a crowded and bloody battleground. Every Sabbath at sundown, the cocks fight.

A pawn shop owner in Joplin had told me about the fights. So one rainy Thursday afternoon, I pulled up the club's "Members Only" driveway to see if I could wangle an invitation to next Sunday's matches.

A two-room shotgun of a house squatted at the head of the drive. Leaving camera and tape recorder in the car, I walked up and knocked on its screen door. Nobody home. I checked the low wooden shed to the house's left. Nobody there, either, except about twenty bantams in cages.

I thought about staying a moment to admire the future fighters. But if there was anybody around here, I felt I should find them before they found me. So   I dodged the rain and ran over to what had to be the arena—a high building of corrugated metal which might have held a couple of combines anywhere else.

"Hello!" I hollered in my best twang. "Anybody home?"

I heard a dog's answering bark and then what could have been a human voice. Maybe it had said "Come in." So I did.

Hollering "Hello!" periodically so my progress could be monitored, I explored the arena. In back of the stands, a series of small, closed-off rooms lined the walls. Waiting rooms, I figured. Owners didn't want their cocks to see too much action before it was their turn to fight. Also in back of the stands there were several small pens with red dirt floors. Prep pens, I thought, or maybe they were used for side fights.

The stands themselves were raw wooden planks held up by native oak logs. Rising in a hexagonal pattern almost to the roof, they held in their center the main fight pen—a six-foot dirt square bordered by a low fence of white iron and chicken wire.

I felt I was either on a movie set or in another century. Stopping my own hollering, I stood in the dim light and listened to the roar of fist-shaking, cigar-smoking, money-waving crowds. Violence filled the ring, the air, the people's eyes. Roosters cawed horribly in the lust of battle. Feathers and dust clouded our vision. A drop of something fell on my shoulder. Blood?

"What do you want?"

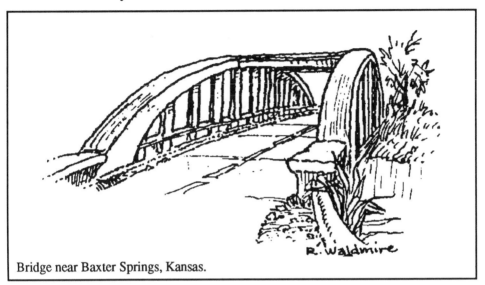

Bridge near Baxter Springs, Kansas.

It was that same quiet voice I'd heard before. I looked over to the refreshment stand. There, by a Pepsi sign, stood its owner—the club's ringmaster.

He was a small, stout older man in green overalls. With close-cropped gray hair and a shuffle, he didn't look like an impresario of violence at all—he looked more like Uncle Henry. His dog, a long, low mongrel with her teats dragging, didn't look too vicious, either.

"What do you want?" the man repeated.

He didn't sound in the mood for blue sky, so I quickly explained my trip and my interest. Just as quickly, I found I didn't know beans about getting into a cockfight.

"I can't believe somebody sent you here," said Mr. Greenjeans. We were sitting in the first row by the main pen. "We don't do that [cockfighting]."

He looked away in disgust at whoever had sent me.

"It's just a sport anyway." he whispered.

I asked the impresario why bantams were used so much in this "sport." "Because they have the best power to weight ratio," he said. "And their stamina."

Lightly encouraged, I told the man a story or two from my trip to further soften him.

"I don't believe you," he said. "You're either from the government or the Humane Society."

I assured him I was searching for 66 and just wanted to learn about chickens. He assured me I was lying.

"I've been raisin' chickens fifty years," he said, looking away still, "and I ain't tellin' you nothin'... It's just a sport."

Keeping a respectful distance, I showed my bantam host some pictures from my trip. They didn't sway him. I talked about jumping mules. He was unmoved. I even took him outside and showed him my car's license plate: KIX ON 66. He remained belligerently unconvinced.

"I saw that when you came in," he said, "and I still don't believe you. You're from the government or the Humane Society and we don't want you here."

I didn't see other people around, so I figured the "we" could very well mean the man and his 12-gauge. Trusting that to instinct, I bid a respectful farewell and climbed back into my car for the trip to Oklahoma.

SEARCHING FOR 66

NINETEEN

Sixty-Six dipped south into Oklahoma and the toenails of the Ozarks. I was traveling now through a land which lay on the cusp of several regions: the Midwest, the Southwest, the Prairie, the Plains. Natives call it Green Country and hasten to correct people who assume it was part of the Dust Bowl. "Don't believe everything you read," they say. "Steinbeck's geography was all wrong."

Diner near Quapaw, Oklahoma.

I cruised smoothly toward Miami (pronounced "Miamuh" in these parts). Rivers flowed full from spring rains. Wildflowers bloomed in huge patches on roadsides and medians. Except for the fields of winter wheat, everything else *was* green. On H Street in Miami, I stopped to visit Ladeen Johnston. Before I'd left on my journey, I'd written public letters to the newspapers along 66. asking for people's help, advice and comments. Ladeen was one of two hundred folks who'd responded. On this warm afternoon, she invited me in for a glass of cherry Kool-Aid.

"Everything in my life is connected to that highway," she said. "I just hated to see it go. For me, it's gonna mean sitting out there and not seeing anything. It's going to turn from meeting people and making friends to boring people.

"Saturday night all the farmers would come to town. We joked that they used to hold up the bank. But life has got so fast now people don't have time to make friends anymore. And these turnpikes and freeways help make it that way.

"To me, the real life is gone and it'll never come back. That's what 66 meant to everybody around here—it was a way of life. Now it's gone."

And Ladeen was only 44.

With 396 miles of 66 in Oklahoma—more than any other state—it wasn't too hard to find folks who shared Ladeen's plaint. Down the road a piece, where Route 66 crosses Little Cabin Creek, the vernal gridwork of a pecan orchard interrupts the irregularity of the other roadside scenery. The trees, some standing as high as forty feet, have greeted three generations of transcontinental travelers. But the orchard's current owner, Don Gray, worried that people can't find it anymore.

"They took the Route 66 signs down last year," he said, "and I was so busy workin' hard I didn't even notice. Then one day they were gone! And I think it's disgustin'—a damned dirty shame.

"I'm hopin' we can still get traffic to stop, but the change confused people. For fifty years, we advertised we were east of town on 66. Last year, though, we had to change to 'East on 60,' another route that used this same stretch of road for about forty years. Just a few weeks ago, a lady come in and asked my wife, 'Where's 60?' And she'd lived in this area all her life! People can't get it out of their heads that this isn't High-

Don Gray, Vinita, Oklahoma

way 66 anymore."

Later on in Vinita, the road's popularity made me a celebrity. Reading my letter in the Vinita *Daily Journal*, members of the Eastern Trails Historical Society had elected me an honorary lifetime member of their group. After some discussion, they'd also agreed to waive the usual $3 fee for a membership certificate—if I'd pick it up in person at their May 18 meeting.

Vice-President Don Roberts and his wife Cora escorted me to the meeting hall after an Oklahoma breakfast of scrambled eggs and brains (which don't taste bad if you take a piece of bacon with each bite, then slug down a dose of Oklahoma moonshine). Twenty-five people were there, a good crowd. Secretary O.B. Campbell started things with a formal reading of last month's minutes. Treasurer Warren Fetter reported they had the same amount of money now that they'd had for the past three months. President Annabelle Southern led a discussion about an excursion to Fort Smith, Arkansas, the next month.

Then it was my turn. I stood and talked until just before folks got tired of me. I told them about myself. I told them about Francis Marten, about Ted Drewes, Times Beach and Snortin' Norton. I told them about the incredible freedom I felt every morning when I woke up. My trip wasn't such a big deal, I said. It was merely the time of my life.

Then I shut up and let them do the talking.

SEARCHING FOR 66

TWENTY

Between Miami and Afton, Oklahoma, there's a stretch of ancient pavement that local folks call the Sidewalk Highway. When 66's route through Oklahoma was designated in 1926, counties had roadbuilding responsibilities in the state. But not always the money. Which is what happened when it came time to pave the ten miles between Miami and Afton. Highway commissioners in neighboring Craig and Ottawa Counties added up their cash. Even with a limited amount of federal aid, they had only half of what was needed.

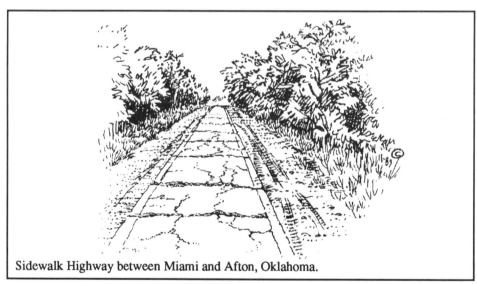

Sidewalk Highway between Miami and Afton, Oklahoma.

The officials considered their options. They could pave a two-lane west from Miami and east from Afton until their money ran out. But that would leave five miles of dirt road in between. This, in turn, would disqualify them for federal funding and leave even more of the road unpaved.

Highway engineer George Klein proposed the ingenious solution to the dilemma. The feds required only that the road be paved, he said. They didn't say how wide it had to be. Instead of paving 18 feet for half the distance, Klein suggested, why not pave nine feet all the way?

Like many portions of 66, the new road was brick. Borrowing an innovation from Missouri, it also had concrete lips on either side. There was no passing lane, of course, and when cars approached from opposite directions, they had to run their right tires over the curb to get by. Besides Sidewalk Highway, the stretch also gained notoriety as the Scotch Highway and the Bicycle Road.

Klein's creativity in Miami-Afton later helped him gain appointment as the state's highway commissioner. One of his first projects was to replace the Sidewalk Highway with a new, two-lane alignment. The old road survives, but is used now only by the farmers whose fields have always crowded in on its sides.

With the help of Miamian Paul Watt, another letter-writing friend, I found the Sidewalk Highway one morning. It was dry and deserted. Asking Paul to watch for traffic, I got out of his car and lay down on the pavement. Stretching out on my belly, I touched one curb with my toes and the other with my fingertips. Thousands of people have made the journey to Lake Itasca in Minnesota so they could plant one leg on one side of the Mississippi and one on the other. But I had just become the first person I knew of to straddle Route 66.

SEARCHING FOR *66*

TWENTY-ONE

Though he didn't live long enough to travel it more than a few times, no man is more widely linked with Route 66 than Will Rogers. He was born near 66 in Oolagah, Oklahoma. He had a ranch near Santa Monica, where 66 met the Pacific. He was mayor of Beverly Hills on 66 and won worldwide fame as a movie star in Hollywood—another 66 town. He lies buried in Claremore, Oklahoma, on a hill overlooking 66. The road was renamed in his honor when he died and his son Will Jr. was honorary president of the U.S. Highway 66 Association for several years.

So I decided to check this man out. I'm not a ceremonially religious man and neither was Will—we were both raised Methodists—so neither of us was going to call him a saint. But that seemed to be what other people were doing. All I knew about the man, though, was what I'd read in the papers and books. They said he'd been an observational genius, a humorist, a philosopher, a philanthropist, an avid sportsman, a devoted family man, and a friend of all America.

Which had me wondering about the man as I walked into his memorial in Claremore. Being from the Aquarian Age, I'd only known icons who wore their foibles on their sleeves. Kennedy had dallied. Lennon had been cruel. And athletes used drugs. Didn't Will Rogers have any character flaws, however minor? It would make him more believable—also contemporary. Or was he indeed the peculiarly American blend of Renaissance Man and Everyman that his legacy said he was?

A statue of Will greets visitors at the memorial's door. Its shoulders are sloped, its hands are stuffed into its pockets, and its left foot is cocked forward. Visitors stop automatically to gaze at it. They want to shake Will's hand, but that's up too high so they rub his shoe before passing on. Further inside, exhibits include Will's saddle collection, posters from his movies and the clothes he was wearing half a century ago when his plane crashed off Point Barrow, Alaska. There is also a theater and, for the serious scholar, access to an extensive collection of the man's letters, columns and other writings.

Dr. Reba Neighbors Collins is the memorial's curator. She'd answered an earlier letter of mine with an invitation to come by and talk. After giving Will's toe a rub, I went to her office.

Reba greeted me dressed in slacks and a shirt that hung out. Disdaining her office and its distancing desk, she sat us down at a folding table in the bay area of the memorial's headquarters. We didn't get up again for three hours.

Will Rogers' Statue at his memorial in Claremore, Oklahoma.

The good doctor needed no warming to the subject, so I got right to it: "I've known of no man or woman in my lifetime who was as universally loved and respected as Will Rogers."

Reba adjusted her glasses, folded her hands lightly, and settled in. "It may have been a one-time phenomenon," she said. "It's hard to explain and it's hard to understand—and I've spent twenty years studyin' it.

"The charisma was there, charisma of a magnitude that is almost unexplainable. And that was a word that would have been foreign to Will. He couldn't've spelled it. But he had it. At least as much as Elvis. Probably more.

"I was too young to know who he was, but I remember when he died. I thought it was a relative and I kept wondering when we'd go to the funeral. I just knew it had to be somebody close because my mother and daddy wouldn't have cried if it hadn't been."

In Joplin a week earlier, I'd talked with Will's cousin Bruce Quisenberry, who'd been the humorist's gofer on many lecture tours. I'd wondered aloud to him what the country's reaction had been on hearing of Will's death. Remembering my own passed icons, I'd compared it to John Kennedy's.

"I hardly think it was a similar reaction," Bruce had answered. "There was shock and sorrow both times, of course. But with Kennedy, we lost a glamorous figure, a Camelot man. The public reaction when Will Rogers died was 'We lost an old friend.'

"I had the privilege of watching Mr. Rogers perform hundreds of times. It was amazing! He could hold an audience for two or three hours easily. Just one man commenting, one man expressing himself. The audience just felt like they knew him. And he made all people feel that way. He made you feel like he'd known you for years!"

Reba is a native and lifelong Oklahoman. But her interest in Will Rogers had been only average until she reached her forties. "We were at the World's Fair in New York in 1965," she said in a soft, assured accent, "and they were playin' recordings of Will Rogers' voice from his radio programs. I sat there and saw how everybody was entranced and how they listened and how they laughed and how pertinent his stuff was to today...and I was impressed! Here I was a journalism student from Oklahoma and I felt really ignorant. I just didn't realize these people at the World's Fair were going to be that impressed.

"So we stopped by the memorial on our way home to Oklahoma City. I thought there would be just a few statues. But I spent all afternoon reading everything on the walls."

That afternoon for Reba became a Ph.D. dissertation, then a seat on the memorial's board of directors, then her present position when the original curator, Will's niece Paula Love, died in the early '70's. In 1983, Reba even took a teenage acting troupe on a tour to California. Following the same Route 66 that the Dust Bowlers had, they presented a play on Oklahoma's history as narrated by a young Will Rogers.

"I fell in love with Will Rogers," Reba said, unabashed. "He said what I wanted to say. He lived the kind of life I wish I could. Will Durant, the philosopher, asked Will once to write about his philosophy. He kind of foundered around, but what he finally came up with was a little bit profound: 'Always live your life so that whenever you lose, you're ahead.'"

I recalled a bumper sticker I'd seen in a country grocery along the way: "Will Rogers Never Met Khomeini." Was it really true, as Will said many times, that he never met a man he didn't like?

"Yes, it was," Bruce had said. "I called him The Great Man."

"Now that's one Will Jr. and I have argued about many times," Reba answered. "Will Sr. had a non-judgmental quality that was almost innate. Will Jr. is simply not that way himself and he finds it hard to accept that his dad was. He doesn't believe it. But I do. You can get angry at your brother and sister and yell at them, but that doesn't mean you don't like them. Will did the same thing with Mussolini and Stalin."

Speaking later from the tack room of his Camarillo, California ranch, western movie star Joel McCrea came down somewhere between Bruce and Will Jr. McCrea had met Will Sr. in 1930 when he was cast as the juvenile lead in one of the older star's movies. Though there was a 27-year age difference between them, the two men had been close friends the last five years of Will's life—with McCrea even being accorded the singular honor of taking Will's daughter, Mary, on her first date when she turned 16. As unabashed as Reba, he said several times during our conversation that Rogers had meant more to him than any other man except his father.

"I didn't really know him well at first," the retired actor said in firm, well-modulated tones. "Then one day—we were shooting on location—I needed a ride back to the hotel and he gave me a lift. We were driving down an old backcountry road and Will saw some men cutting hay. He said, 'Lets stop and see how these fellers are doin'.' So we pulled over his LaSalle and went wading through the uncut part of the hay. The men recognized Will right away, but that's not why he went. He just liked people and wanted to talk to them—wanted to learn all about them.

"But as for liking everybody he met, I'd have to disagree. Will just wasn't mean spirited about it. I remember another day when we were on location and had to go to the privy to take a leak. It was a three-holer. While we were in there, a fan came in and asked Will for an autograph. The fan didn't have anything to write on, so he actually tore off a piece of toilet paper and handed it to Will!"

McCrea enjoyed a short, hard chuckle at the memory. "Will didn't say anything. He just stood there and stared at the man with those icy blue eyes he had. Pretty soon, the man turned and left. Even then, Will didn't say anything. Just zipped his pants up and went back to the set. But you can't tell me he liked the fellow."

When our conversation concluded well past the lunch hour, Reba gave me phone numbers for McCrea, Will Jr. and Jim Rogers, Will's other son. Using those numbers, I'd continue searching for links between Will and 66. On my way out, though, I had one last query for the good doctor herself.

"There are a lot of ties between Will Rogers and Route 66," I said and listed them for her. "Do you think they have any meaning?"

"You'll have to ask other people to get all the historical facts," Reba said. And then she smiled. "But I'll tell you this—I can't think of a better person they could've named the highway after. He was always on the move, always looking for adventure. Always had to see what was over the next hill. So did most everyone else who drove that road.

"And when Will wrote about all these things, he made us see how much in common we really have with other people and other countries. That was his genius—he brought us together, helped us understand and appreciate each other. If you're looking for answers, you could say that 66 did the same thing."

SEARCHING FOR 66

TWENTY-TWO

"Sometime ago, a group of Oklahomans happened to foregather in Washington City. After a fanning bee on the personalities of their great state, its wonderful resources and development, it was decided that each Oklahoman present should donate the sum of $5 which would go into a pony purse, this to go to the one who would tell the most improbable and unreasonable story about some Oklahoman.

"The eldest man in the party, by reason of his age, was given the right of way. And it so happened he was a real Sooner who had somehow or other gotten into Oklahoma ahead of the '89ers. This is the way he began:

"'Once upon a time in Oklahoma, there was a small gathering of people in a schoolhouse. Among those present happened to be a man named Cy Avery. The speaker slated for the occasion failed to arrive and it was necessary for someone to entertain the crowd. Cy was called upon, importuned and earnestly urged to make a speech, but for quite awhile positively declined. He was finally prevailed upon and consented to address the meeting.

"'Mr. Avery spoke for two and a half hours, discussing matters in general, and during the entire time did not say a word about good roads.'

"This is as far as the narrator got with his story. He was interrupted with the exclamation, 'Hell, take the pot!' and the rest of the party adjourned to a thirst emporium to drown their sorrows, for this was in the days before Mr. Volstead messed up the Constitution with his dry amendments."

American Saturday Night
A Tulsa news magazine
April 22, 1922

Cy Avery was 14 when he and his family moved to Oklahoma in 1885. They came from Pennsylvania in a horse-drawn wagon. The three-month trek, besides making young Cy a man, made him a passionate life-long advocate for good roads. Which is good for Route 66, because as surely as Will Rogers would later become the highway's Favorite Son, Cy Avery would be its Founding Father.

Cy Avery, Father of Route 66.   *Courtesy Ruth Avery.*

American Saturday Night's mid-career assessment of Cy was a bare exaggeration of the man's passion. After graduating from William Jewell College in nearby Missouri, he had sold insurance and real estate in Oklahoma, living first in Vinita, then Oklahoma City, then Tulsa.

But even then Cy spent more time talking with his customers about good roads than about policies or land parcels. He joined the U.S. Good Roads Association, the Bank Head Highway Association, the Albert Pike Highway Association, Associated Highways of America and many other groups which included "Road" or "Highway" in their names. In 1913, he was elected Highway Commissioner of Tulsa County. Among his innovations in that post was development of the state's first road grading system, a technique called the split-log drag. In 1915, he led a successful drive to build a highway from Colorado (through Oklahoma) to Arkansas with convict labor. In 1924, he was named highway commissioner for all of Oklahoma.

"With highways, a fusion of the different modes of life, of city and country, is underway and that is possibly the best thing that can happen to us," Cy once told the Tulsa Chamber of Commerce meeting. "It's building gradually a new conception, a new consciousness, a new problem. Our great cities are legal abstractions. Their form dates back to the days of oxcarts and walled cities. Their modern realities, which are water, sewer, drainage, highways, railroads, utilities and—above all—human beings, transcend artificial political boundaries. In the stead of cities, a metropolitan or great urban region is emerging. 'Back to the farm!' may be an idle cry, but decentralization is not. We must prepare and be ready for the changes that means."

Cy was a small, thin man, and folks don't remember him ever moving fast. But they don't remember him ever standing still, either. The changes he foresaw at the Chamber of Commerce meeting required an increased federal role in the roadbuilding process—and he and his associations set to work lobbying for it.

"Motor vehicle traffic does not stop at county lines," Cy reasoned. "Neither does it stop at state lines. America's roads must soon forsake their provincial, farm-to-market orientation and assume a truly national character."

Cy's vision was logical, even prophetic. But the federal government was slow to share it. Officials as prominent as President Coolidge opposed federal aid to highways. The Bureau of Roads, which would become today's Department of Transportation behemoth in the interstate age, was only a sub-agency of the U.S. Department of Agriculture until well into the Twentieth Century. And as late as 1918, only three thousand miles of "postal" roads had been built with U.S. government funds.

But when doughboys came home from Over There and started pounding their swords into Model T's, good road advocates gained a powerful ally—the masses. Until then, automobiling had been largely a rich man's hobby. But now popular pressure was building—and people like Cy were molding it. In 1925, his years of patient lobbying and courtship were finally rewarded with the arrival of a letter from the U.S. Secretary of Agriculture.

The letter announced the Secretary had created a board to "design and number a system of routes of interstate and national significance." The system, once approved by the Secretary, would be paved with the help of $30,000 a mile in federal aid. In his eminent position as Commissioner of Highways for the State of Oklahoma, would Mr. Avery so honor the Secretary as to serve as consultant to this most important board?

Cy not only agreed readily to the densely-worded invitation—he talked his way into a spot on the board's allocation subcommittee—the five-member group which did most of the actual decision-making.

When Thomas Jefferson paid France three cents an acre for the Louisiana Territory, he envisioned an eventual national gridwork of roads to bind this country together. Nearly a century and a quarter later, Cy and his fellow committee members applied our third president's grid principle as they designed their system. East-west routes were given even numbers, growing consecutively higher from north to south. North-south routes got odd numbers, with the low ones starting back east. Existing roadbeds would be used in the beginning, but only until pavement came.

The new system's western linchpin—and its national show-piece—was to be a single route connecting Chicago and Los Angeles. In early discussions, other committee members suggested this road run southwest from Chicago to Springfield, Missouri, then due west through Kansas and Colorado to California. Cy Avery, who'd by then perfected the technique of making other people think his idea was theirs, agreed that this would certainly show off Colorado's mountains nicely. But wouldn't a more southerly route through the flat lands of Oklahoma, the Texas pan-handle, New Mexico and Arizona be far cheaper to build? And with its much lower elevations, wouldn't this southerly path also have the distinct advantage of being an all-weather road?

Other committee members agreed and Cy's route was chosen. Now what should they call it? The grid pattern allowed three choices: 62, 64, or 66. When Kansas interests succeeded in getting a secondary route, that took away the first option. No reason is recorded for the choice between the other two, but when the full board submitted its map on Armistice Day in 1926, the Chicago-Los Angeles road was called U.S. Route 66. The Secretary of Agriculture approved the map only two days later and a legend began.

In 1926, Steinbeck's future "Mother Road" was a jerry-built con-glomeration of existing dirt, gravel, cinder and even plank roads. As events conspired, it wouldn't even be fully paved until 1938. But in 1927 Cy Avery was already predicting it would become the nation's most heav-ily-traveled road to the west, our Manifest Destiny cast in concrete.

To nurture his new prophecy, Cy co-founded the Highway 66 Association. Towns along the way contributed $47,000 for promotional purposes. At the new group's first meeting in the fall of '27, it accepted the publicity committee's recommendation and proclaimed their new road to be the Main Street of America. The Highway 40 Association, which had been using that same motto for a year and a half already, objected strenuously. But it did them no good—the boastful title would soon go to Route 66 by public acclamation. Cy Avery would later go on to such civic triumphs as developing a dependable water supply for Tulsa and spear-heading a drive to build the city's first airport. But in Route 66 he had already sired his masterpiece.

Ruth Avery, Cy's daughter-in-law, sat in the sunlit study of her Tulsa home and patiently outlined all this for me. I'd missed Cy by quite a bit—he died in 1963 at age 92—but she has preserved his files and scrap-books as a private memorial. Joe Howell, transportation writer for the Tulsa *Tribune* and Ruth's long ago boyfriend, arranged for us to meet. Though she'd recited her father-in-law's 66 history to dozens of other journalists over the years, Ruth politely sketched it again today.

"I just don't know if I can tell you any more," she said about half an hour into our conversation. "But I'd be glad to leave you alone and let you read these files."

"Can you tell me one thing first?" I asked.

`"Yes?"

"What kind of *person* was Cy Avery?"

Ruth smiled. Twenty years disappeared from her face. She pulled up a hassock and sat beside me by the file cabinet.

"I just adored Cy," she said gladly. "I lost my own father at the age of four. When I got engaged to his son, a lot of my friends said, 'I know why you're marrying Layton—just so you can be with Cy.' And we did get along beautifully together. We were very buddy-buddyish. We used to go to an experimental farm he had near here and just walk along and visit.

"I was even the only person who ever got Cy Avery to dance. He said you might as well be sitting down talking because that's what you're doing while you're dancing—so why not concentrate on it?"

"And he was a talker," his daughter-in-law said, showing a bit of the same gift (I wouldn't leave for good until well after lunch the next day). "You could never sit down for a meal with him but what he was interrupted on the telephone. He would talk with anybody about anything whenever they wanted to talk.

"We got stuck once in the middle of nowhere in Arkansas. Cy got out of the car and immediately saw somebody he knew—a man who used to work for his father."

"Sounds like a fellow up in Claremore that I've just been study-ing," I said.

"Cy did love people," Ruth said. "He made you feel good. It was only a forty-five minute walk to the farm, but it would take Cy and me two hours. He knew all the kids along the way by name, how old they were, who was sick. And if he saw Old John, the black sharecropper, working in his field, why he had to go talk to him, too.

"And just like Will, Cy was always busy. All the time we would be walking and visiting out at the farm, he'd be looking at the stock and watching posts along the road to see if any wires were out. And he'd fill my hands with sweet clover or timothy or rye seed and have me throw it out as we went along. That's the way he was—he told me never go out to do something without something else to do while you're doing it."

With all his careers and projects and connections, I figured Cy Avery must have died a wealthy man.

"Cy made his money," Ruth confirmed, "but he lost a lot of it, too. He just gave all his time and interest to civic work and let his business go to pot. My husband was just exactly the opposite and that caused some problems between them. But it didn't change Cy."

If money hadn't motivated Cy in all his dealings, then I figured pride or political ambition must have. Had he, for example, been proud that he'd had the Main Street of America routed through his home state?

"No, no," admonished Ruth gently. "It might look like it, but Cy just wasn't that kind of person. He was glad he was able to do it, but he didn't dwell on it. And he didn't try to make money off it, either. His mind was always more for tomorrow.

"From a political standpoint, he was a dreamer, too. They nominated him for Governor once. But he lost badly—he just didn't campaign!

"But Cy was a wonderful salesman. He'd say 'It sure would be nice if...' and then he'd describe something he wanted. And it usually got done. If he couldn't go over or around something, he'd go under. There was bound to be a solution—all you had to do was figure it out. If it was a manmade thing, a man could figure out the answer."

Would Cy Avery have any advice for a man on a search like mine?

Ruth smiled again. "He did tell a reporter once you should live so you have good health and have ants in your pants," she said. "But as far as his main advice for you, I think you just heard it."

SEARCHING FOR **66**

TWENTY-THREE

General News Item: Two young girls were walking down a country lane in Oklahoma one morning in 1986 when a frog jumped out from behind the bushes and said, "If you kiss me, I'll be your oil man!" The older girl walked over, picked the frog up, and examined him carefully. Without a word, she stuffed the talkative amphibian into a bag she was carrying.

The two girls continued down the lane. After fifteen minutes of silence, the younger girl could stand the mystery no longer.

"Why didn't you kiss him?" she asked.

"What would I want with an oil man?" her elder replied. "I'd rather have a talking frog!"

Police Beat Item: Three prostitutes were arrested in Tulsa's red light district last night. Two of them were still virgins.

Business News Item: An area bank has opened a record number of new accounts by offering free toasters. But they ran out of toasters, couldn't get anymore, and have started giving away oil derricks instead.

Future Obituary Item: The Oklahoma Oil Industry?

As a traveling man with no income, I considered the steep decline in oil prices in early 1986 a windfall. But for Oklahoma and the rest of oil country, it meant Depression. Maybe most girls would have kissed that frog. Maybe the bank just gave discounts on derricks. And maybe the prostitutes weren't virgins. But that was oilfield humor and it took exaggeration as a First Amendment right. As one veteran oilman said, "You have to be half silly and laugh easy to be in this business. Otherwise you get crushed."

Not far beneath its gallows veneer, though, oilfield humor told the plain truth: Business was bad. Awful bad. How do you get an oilman out of a tree?—Cut the rope!

Route 66 cuts through half a dozen Oklahoma oil fields. The largest is Glen Pool, which has offered up a billion barrels of crude. I had seen at least fifty wells on my way to Tulsa. But not one had been pumping. A year ago, the state had counted 239 of the country's 1,821 active drilling rigs. Today, it counted only 109 of 723. Five Oklahoma rigs had closed down just the week before and analysts feared the well count might go as low as sixty before it bottomed out.

Tulsa, Oklahoma.

"We're just hangin' by a fingernail," independent oilman Tommy Thomas told me. "They're paying us just $15 a barrel for oil [It would later drop to $12]. That's like giving 'em a $5 bill with each barrel."

I was visiting Tommy because he had been recommended by his good friend and fellow oilman Pat Murphy (Pat had been recommended by his son Mike, who had read my letter in the Tulsa *Tribune*). He sat across from me at his Texas-size desk, wearing a sports shirt and a very nice haircut. He spread a field map out on his desk and, like so many other people along the route, spoke no louder than he had to.

"The north end of the state's biggest field, Glen Pool, touches on 66 northeast of Tulsa," Tommy began. "And if you'll look at the map, you'll see all the fields were indirectly lateraled into 66. I certainly traveled it extensively. But the interstates squeezed out 66 and all its little towns. And now the banks and the major oil companies are about to squeeze the little oilmen out."

Tommy was raised in the cotton fields of eastern Oklahoma. He moved to Tulsa when the Dust Bowl wiped out his father's farm. While his dad clerked in a grocery store, Tommy worked three jobs and put himself through college. His ambition was to be a cartoonist. Walt Disney even offered him a job after college—he could have worked on *Snow*

White. But the pay was too low and Tommy turned to the oil business instead. For the first fifteen years, he worked for the major oil companies.

"I did everything," he said. "I drew geological maps. I operated all kinds of instruments to find the oil and gas. I ran the rigs. I even helped them pour nitroglycerin when I was a boy. But I won't help 'em do that no more. I was young and wild, I guess."

And ambitious.

"I didn't have any dough. I didn't have a damn bit. But this long-time banker friend of mine, we was like brothers. He saw how hard I worked and he loaned me money on insurance policies and old cars to help me get started on my own—my insurance policies were always in hock those early days. Now my banker quotes me on *my* philosophy of how to loan money. I don't remember it. He quotes it, but I forget it every-time."

Eighty percent of Oklahoma's oil wells are "strippers," producing ten barrels or less a day. Tommy started repaying his banker's trust and loan by specializing in them.

"I followed the major companies," he said. "Things they'd goof up on or get tired of, I'd come in, buy their lease, and get it to workin'. It would be economical for me because they had so much overhead. They had district offices and general offices and engineers and geologists and liaisons all over. I did it all myself."

Now Tommy's geologist alone was making $200,000 a year. Until recently, Tommy was doing well himself. His company's motto, "From Idea to Mailbox," explains how.

"We call ourselves TECO," he said, "for Thomas Exploration Company. I'll figure out a place to drill, lease it, drill it, produce it. If it's too big for me, I'll get people with tax money or something like that to go along with me. All they got to do is go to the mailbox, get their check out every month."

"I didn't ever think I'd own a barrel of crude," he said, and spread his hands to envelop his penthouse office. "But the Good Lord led me along. The main thing is work on the Golden Rule and try to meet every-body halfway. All you have is your character or your word. If you don't have that, you're a poor man."

Oil magnate T. Boone Pickens, who's headquartered down 66 in Amarillo, has been known to drill three hundred new wells a year. Tommy does four or five. Though the year's mid-point was fast approaching, he had yet to drill his first well of 1986. Nor did he have plans to.

"There's an Amoco research center here," he said, pointing out somewhere into a high rise forest. "It's forty acres of doctors. All they do there is research on oil and gas. Years ago they discovered a process that pumps oil or gas or water into the formation and changes the elevation of the earth—that made this area pay off another twenty-five or thirty years. But even they can't figure this one out."

I set aside a disturbing image of the earth being pumped up and down and asked Tommy the basic question.

"Are you going to survive?"

"Oh yeah," he said, as if he'd never considered another possibility. "A lot of independents are going under, going broke. I'm not in debt too much—we've always tried to set a little nest egg back. But if you're in debt these days, you're in trouble. With fourteen- and fifteen-dollar oil, if you owe the banks anything at all, it'll break you."

"We're pushin' for a tax on imported crude," he said. Then his voice turned suddenly hard. "But you know Congress. They're so socialistic, communistic and illiterate. Their motto is why be ridiculous when it's so easy to be impossible? With that in mind, we're fightin' an uphill battle."

Would he wish OPEC, then, good luck in getting its members back in line?

Tommy glanced at my tape recorder and considered his answer—but only briefly.

"Yes, I would," he said calmly, yet with a note of independent defiance. "I would!"

SEARCHING FOR *66*

TWENTY-FOUR

It was another one of those absolutely beautiful spring days that they seem to have so many of in Oklahoma. I was cruising 66 about 40 miles out of Oklahoma City, describing the flowers and tress and bushes and whatever else struck me into my tape recorder. On the advice of some folks at a gas station-cafe called Luther's Oil Slick, I was going to see a local landmark—a round barn near Arcadia. The road slid smoothly under my wheels at 45 miles an hour.

Midway between Luther's and Arcadia, a '76 Chevy topped a rise a quarter mile behind me and shot the day's easy rhythm all to hell. The car was first a shimmer in my rearview mirror, then a roar in my ears, and then sheer terror—all in about three seconds. As it neared me at 80 miles per, it swung loosely out to pass. A stream bridge lay barely a half mile ahead. At the rates we were going, I figured the Chevy and I would reach it in a dead heat. And then the unforgiving concrete railings of the bridge would break the tie.

I hastily considered my alternatives. I could speed up, but that would only put the finish line a little further out on the bridge. I could slow down, but what if the Chevy dipped suddenly back into the lane where it belonged? I could pull over on the shoulder, but even that chance disappeared as the road banked up to cross the stream.

Which left the perilous status quo. Small comfort.

At the last fearstricken moment, the Chevy braked and swerved back into its lane. But the quick move pulled the right front wheel off the pavement and then the whole car. With the driver struggling furiously to regain control, the Chevy careened sideways along the brushy embankment.

Now the bridge offered relative safety and I sped up to reach it. Looking back from the other side, I saw the Chevy get a wheel back on the pavement just in time to spin itself broadside into the far guard rail.

The Chevy folded in on itself as the rail pierced it. Great clouds of smoke and vapor erupted from under the hood, and a body came flying through the open passenger window and slid face down across the pavement.

A half dozen other drivers who'd seen the accident stopped to either help or look. I drove up to the first side road and went looking for help. On returning to the bridge, I found as well-ordered an accident scene as a person could ever hope to see. A paramedic had been coming from one direction and a nurse from the other. Both were now tending the victim, putting towels under his head and turning it to one side so blood could not clog his nose and mouth. Somebody else had run to use a CB. A farmer, who'd been out plowing, was squatting over the victim, holding a palm between the man's face and the sun. Two other men stood at the ends of the bridge and directed traffic over its open lane.

Round Barn near Arcadia, Oklahoma.

"Somebody's got their foot on my neck. Get your foot off my neck!"

It was the Chevy's driver, a slight, balding man. From his car registration, we knew his name was Hershel Butler.

"I'm all right," Hershel said. "Let me up."

"Just relax," said the paramedic. "If you go movin' around, you might hurt yourself."

"Let me turn over. I need to turn over."

The nurse was a beautiful young brunette in a pink tank top and running shorts. "Does it hurt, Hershel?" she asked gently.

"Yes, it hurts. It hurts all over."

"Then it will hurt even more if you move. Now promise you won't give me a hard time. I'm only a little girl. I can't fight you."

Ten minutes later, we heard the first siren.

"I still hurt. Oh shit, I'm hurtin'."

"Relax, Hershel," the paramedic said. "You're fightin' it. Your muscles are tensin' up and they're hurtin' you."

"All right, I'll lay still. I'm gonna try to rest and take the sobriety test."

"Okay. Okay."

A sheriff's car finally pulled up. Smoking and steaming from a blown fan belt about a mile and a half back, it looked as bad as Hershel's. A deputy and two friends got out, saw everything was under control, and just observed.

Soon afterwards, two cars of highway patrolmen drove up and took over. Two troopers stopped bridge traffic completely. Another two checked with the paramedic about the victim's condition—he would probably make it. Then they bent over to talk with the studious Hershel himself.

"Do you have a license, Hershel?" asked one.

"No sir, I don't."

End of interview.

At last we heard an ambulance siren from the other side of the rise.

"Do you hear that, Hershel?" asked the nurse. "We'll have you in the ambulance before you even know it. We'll put you in the air conditioning."

The paramedic briefed the ambulance crew on Hershel's injuries and how his vital signs had been for the past half hour. At last they loaded him onto a gurney and transferred him to the ambulance.

"I love you all," said the reason for our little community. "I love you. I love you all."

A middle-aged woman and her daughter ran up to the accident scene. They'd recognized the nurse from down the road and thought she might be hurt.

"Nothing's wrong," she said, holding her dripping red hands casually by her sides. "I'm just doing my thing."

The ambulance took Hershel away, a tow truck took his car, and an emergency truck sprayed debris off the road surface. Its purpose met, our little community disbanded. I now knew first hand why this highway had so often been called Bloody 66. But I also knew why it was called the Main Street of America. This accident probably wouldn't have happened on an interstate—its multiple lanes, wide bridges and broad shoulders are safer and more forgiving—even to drunks like Hershel. But if the accident hadn't happened, our community wouldn't have, either. I would have zipped on by. I got back in my car and resumed my journey, wondering which I preferred—safety or community—and wondering why I couldn't have both.

I drove on through to Oklahoma City, barely stopping at the round barn. Doubling my daily motel budget to $40, I found a nice room with a whirlpool and a TV on casters. I filled the tub with hot water, turned on the whirlpool, pulled the TV within view, and climbed in. I'd had enough searching for the day. It was time to relax.

SEARCHING FOR 66

TWENTY-FIVE

There isn't much in this country that somebody won't collect, catalogue and lovingly display. Every day on 66, my search led me to at least one proof of this. Over four months, I toured museums dedicated to everything from insects to the nuclear bomb, from meteor crashes to neon art. In Oklahoma City alone, I found halls and galleries specializing in cowboys, firemen, photography, Indian art, the 47th Infantry Division, softball and fishing tackle. Somewhere around Amarillo, I started to fear if I walked into just one more museum that the information accumulated within me would reach critical mass and my brain would vaporize. But I kept going anyway.

Someday, I often thought, they should build a museum to Route 66. It would have signs, maps, photographs and hundreds of displays. It would have a theater for watching the old TV show and use car bumpers as guard rails. It might even have a strip of actual pavement brought in from somewhere in numbered pieces.

And for sure the museum would have an entire wing devoted to all the great races, treks and other processions ever staged on the mother road. In 1986 alone, Hands Across America linked its way along 66 from Los Angeles to Amarillo and the Great American Race (antique cars) and the Race Across America (bicycles) both followed 66 for more than half their distance. In 1984, the Olympic Torch was carried along 66 through New Mexico, Arizona, and California. Five years before that, Bob Wieland, who lost his legs in Vietnam, strapped blocks to his hands and pulled his way along the highway on a pallet. And fifty years earlier, Paul Wilson walked the route on stilts. There just has been no end of wondrous, sometimes wacky journeys along 66. But the very first one is the king of them all.

C.C. "Cash and Carry" Pyle would later bill himself as the greatest promoter of his age. But in 1926 he was just a theater owner in Champaign, Illinois. He had no knowledge of professional football, which was then in its infancy. But he recognized opportunity when it knocked—it sounded a lot like a cash register. And he heard it ringing across town in the person of Harold "Red" Grange, the already legendary Fighting Illini running back.

When he saw Grange enter his theater one day, Pyle had an usher call the football star to his office. The very day after the Galloping Ghost played his final college game, he signed a personal services contract with Pyle. The budding impresario in turn immediately signed a contract with George Halas for Grange to go on national tour as the new star of the struggling Chicago Bears. From that, in Pyle's own words, "came professional football as it is known today—clean, hard played, well patronized."

Andy Payne, center, in El Reno 1928 *(Courtesy Merle Woods)*

A dapper, modishly-dressed man, Pyle in 1927 tried to field his own football team. It failed. Then he tried to organize a professional tennis circuit featuring Suzanne Langlen. This also failed. Consequently, his ears were especially attuned when opportunity knocked in the form of a wire from Tulsa's Cy Avery.

Fresh from the creation of 66, Cy tried his standard technique on Pyle. Wouldn't it be nice, he said, if the distinguished Illinois entrepreneur would organize and promote a transcontinental foot race along this new national highway? It could start in Los Angeles, follow 66 to Chicago, then go on to New York by whichever path Pyle chose.

Towns along the way would bid against each other to be named stopping points on the race, Cy said. Tens of thousands of dollars could be made from the sale of programs, souvenirs, and refreshments. Shows and carnivals could be held at night. The Highway 66 Association, with members in every town, would be an active booster.

Pyle knew no more about Route 66 or foot racing than he'd known about professional football. But he heard those cash registers ringing once again. On March 4, 1928, he declared C.C. Pyle's First International Continental Foot Race would depart Los Angeles on a 3200-mile journey across Route 66 and America.

Offering a $25,000 grand prize, Pyle advertised for runners in papers all over the world. He named himself the event's general director; crowd pleaser Grange, still under contract, was appointed assistant general director. True to Cy's prediction, towns along the way hotly contested the right to be named race checkpoints. What had been a mere suggestion was soon being hailed, by Pyle, as "the greatest, most stupendous athletic accomplishment in all history." It remains today the longest competitive-timed race ever run.

Foyil lies between Bushyhead and Claremore in the heart of country which later inspired the musical "Oklahoma." Andy Payne, a local farm youth, had recently graduated from high school when he read one of Pyle's ads.

"The race kind of appealed to me," Andy told a reporter on the fortieth anniversary of the event. "Particularly the $25,000. I was a strong lad and I was more or less at liberty. I mean I didn't have anything else to do."

His mother said, "Don't." His father said, "The boy don't know when to quit." When Grange lit the fuse of the starting bomb at L.A.'s Ascot Speedway, Andy was among the 274 runners who took the first stride.

Doctors said the race's strain would take ten years off the lives of those who finished it. Seventy-seven entrants believed them and dropped out the first day. A dozen gave up the second day and another eighteen the next. Only fifty-nine survivors would cross the finish line in New York.

Willie Kolemainen from Finland and Charles Hurt, a 63-year old marathon runner from England, set a fast pace the first day. Kolemainen led alone after the second. Another Finn, Ollie Wantinend, took the lead on the third day as the "titanic struggle between the greatest long distance runners of the entire world" continued through California's San Gabriel Mountains. Entering high desert country on the fourth day, competitors like Harry Abrams, who had chosen to walk instead of run, began showing up well in total time figures.

Runners covered fifteen to seventy miles a day, which quickly gave the event its nickname: Bunion Derby. Pyle led the way in a $25,000 bus equipped with a kitchen, radio-phonograph, air-conditioning, and wicker chairs upholstered in mohair. Trainers and officials followed in cars. Also in the retinue were a portable radio station and a 3,000-gallon Maxwell House coffee pot.

The runners' passage through each town soon became a parade. Their final checkpoint each night, which usually took place in a stadium, became a spectacle. Grange would speak, a band would play, and the runners would come through. Programs sold for 25 cents ("Pay no more!"). They bragged about such race features as chief cook Butch Burcher, "a former Army dietician," and "separate tents for Negro contestants." Later in the evening, local citizens could patronize a side show which featured a five-legged pig, a fire eater, a tattoo artist, a wrestling bear, and the mummified cadaver of a genuine Oklahoma outlaw.

Andy stayed away from the excitement and spent his evenings writing home. Trying to reassure his mother, he promised he was running for the family farm. Competing against experienced mountain runners, he stayed back in the pack but strong through California. "Once plains country is in sight, though, I expect to pick up materially," he wrote,

And he did. But in New Mexico, tonsillitis slowed Andy down to a walk for three days. Outside Amarillo, freezing rain and snow slowed the entire field to a slog. But on the leg from McLean, Texas, to his native state, the part-Indian lad from Foyil was challenging for the lead.

Before the race, Andy had astonished the Chamber of Commerce in nearby Claremore when he asked it to sponsor him. He wasn't taken seriously. But as he edged closer to Oklahoma and the lead, he became a state hero. The daily greeting on Oklahoma streets changed from "Howdy" to "How'd the boy come out yestiddy?" Classmates recalled how Andy used to lope the four miles to school each day. His track coach remembered how Andy used to warm up for the mile by running the half-mile. And neighbors bragged how they'd seen him herding horses—on foot.

The Tulsa *Tribune* only slightly exaggerated the popular mood as C.C. Pyle's "race of the century" neared Andy's home county of Rogers:

"Soon watchers will mount every high hill and with keen, excited eyes scan the great, gray western trail that winds and undulates up from the bigger cities of the state. As David held the breathless attention of the surly ranks of grizzled warriors in King Saul's army when he went out to confront Goliath, so will those county men watch the son of their native soil as he comes and will vanish in the dust and distance that leads to the city of Manhattan. But along the route through his own home state, this youth will be served. He has already won that affection which endurance, pluck and intelligence alone can win.

"This youth has a background full of contrast. Enured to hardship from his boyhood, cribbed and cabined and confined on a windswept limestone hill farm, shut into a tax-crushed poverty, he broke out of it and wrested an education, graduated with honors in the high school. Amid the temptations that lured to laziness, drunkenness and vice, he kept his body lithe and fit and his mind clear. This superb athlete has by the stamina of his young American manhood and without any mechanical aid arrived up from the deserts."

A contingent of Andy fans followed the race in from the Texas border. Schools throughout Oklahoma were dismissed as the runners approached. Crowds lined 66 solidly from Bristow to Foyil. When Andy entered Claremore, he was greeted with a mortar salute and a rousing rendition of "The Thunderer" from the municipal band. But when he finally reached his hometown, the clear leader for the day and also overall, there was silence for a moment.

"But it was not the silence of indifference," reported the Foyil *Times*. "It was that silence which, once perceived, broke into cheers and Andy took a break from the race and sat down by the old country store and rested for a few moments. And his hands reached out to clasp hands of old pals, old bonneted women, and apple-cheeked country lasses.

"And then the boy ran on and was hid in the great distance of the powerful highway. He ran on and doubtless ran faster and fresher for the cup of affection he had drunk in Foyil.

"They were his ownest folk."

Andy battled back and forth for the lead with Englishman Peter Gavuzzi until well past Chicago. Then an infected tooth forced Gavuzzi out of the race and Andy took a lead he'd never let go. Amid threats from fans of a New Jersey runner, he was escorted across the Garden State by New Jersey's finest, the race's foregone winner. Eighty-six days out of Los Angeles, on May 28, he strode the last several miles through Manhattan, crossing the finish line eight hours ahead of the field. He had just run a marathon and a half a day every day for nearly three months, averaging just a shade over four hours per marathon.

Pyle had promised to pay the prizes the following day. But he'd been plagued by debts, hounded by lawsuits, and had already lost an estimated $60,000. Postponing payment until May 31, he worked out a loan from Tulsa fight promoter Tex Riccard in exchange for promotional rights to future Payne races.

On June 1 at 9 p.m., Andy finally stepped up to a platform in Madison Square Garden and collected first prize. But it wasn't exactly cash. It wasn't even a check. It was two promissory notes for $5,000 apiece—one due on June 4 and the other on September 4. Several months would go by before Andy collected the whole prize.

"Oh yeah, we wondered about getting paid all right," Andy later told a reporter. "Especially during the race. But we were in. And when you're in, you're in. There was no dropping out for those dedicated to winning the Bunion Derby."

Andy ran a race later that year in Tulsa against the Arab El Quafi, winner of the Olympic Marathon. Ineligible for Pyle's second and final cross country extravaganza in 1929, he accompanied it as head patrolman. This entailed dressing like a cowboy in the evenings and doing rope tricks at the side show. But after that race, Andy retired from the celebrity life, remaining unimpressed by his win the rest of his life.

"I owe all my success to cornbread," he'd answer when asked to explain his spectacular feat.

True to his promise, Andy used his winnings to pay off the family farm—and also to buy other land. But it was land soon rendered valueless by the Depression and in 1934, Andy, only 26, found himself running for clerk of the Oklahoma Supreme Court for the same reason he'd taken up Pyle's challenge—he needed the money.

Andy's aura, though he didn't curry it, carried him to an easy victory. He settled in Oklahoma City, earned a law degree at night, and was reelected sixteen times by comfortable margins. On slow days, newsman Joe Howell says he can't remember how many hours he spent playing Pitch in Andy's back room.

Later, oil and gas were discovered on the Payne family farm. Buying more land and managing it well, Andy became a quiet millionaire. He retired in 1968 and died in 1977, only slightly less an Oklahoma and Route 66 hero than Will Rogers had been.

"He did know a lot of people," his widow Vivian told me. "And I think he liked most of them, too. But it was kind of strange the people he was closest to. People who had nothing and people who had a lot of things were his friends. All people were just equal as far as Andy was concerned. He wasn't too impressed with anybody.

"On the other hand, everybody was as good as he was."

When I stopped by to visit her in Oklahoma City, Vivian, a former teacher, received me graciously. But before she'd talk, she sat me down at the dining room table and had me go through three scrapbooks about Andy's life. After two hours, she invited me into the living room for coffee.

"Andy was pretty conscious of his Indian heritage," Vivian said, "and that led to his only disappointment in life. He used to attend those meetings they had and all. Some folks even tried to get him in the Indian Hall of Fame, but he couldn't prove enough Indian blood. His grandmother was Indian, so he did have enough. But his father had lied about how much Indian blood he had because it made it easier to sell his land. So Andy had enough blood in his veins, but not enough on paper and they didn't let him in."

Vivian sipped lightly from her coffee, then shook her head.

"But that was probably the only thing he might have wanted different. It took a lot of guts to stay in the Bunion Derby for that many days. You know you're not gonna feel like running part of that time. But if you can make it through those eighty-six days, you can make it through anything.

"I never heard Andy say that, though. He didn't seem to think it was such a wonderful feat or anything. He just did it. But that's typical of Oklahoma and 66. A lot of people think that way along this road."

SEARCHING FOR *66*

TWENTY-SIX

At Oklahoma City, Route 66 took a right turn and got down to serious business. Nearly half of its 850-mile length so far had been spent going south. It was time now to head due west.

I passed through Bethany, where my letter to the editor had inspired a sixteen-part series on Route 66. West of town, the earth stopped rolling and began to flatten. By the time I reached El Reno twenty miles away, it had turned from orange to tan. I was entering the third great region of my journey: the Plains.

Here, where the '89 Land Rush had ended, the true Dust Bowl had begun. But there's little chance of its return. Windbreaks have blunted the air currents. Smarter farming has held down the soil. And a massive water conservation program has given Oklahoma more surface water per square mile than even Minnesota.

Roadside flowers near Hydro, Oklahoma.

But even these measures weren't needed today. Fields of winter wheat stood ready for the harvest along both sides of the road. Local farmers and traveling combine crews had gathered for the job. But steady spring rains were keeping them from it and the men cursed their luck. The click-click-click drifting from a dozen smalltown domino parlors along the way gave clue to how they were impatiently passing the time.

On a rainy Sunday morning, I dawdled over my third cup of coffee at a Weatherford cafe. While farmers and combiners complained about not working, I was trying to figure out a way to take the day off—my first in seven weeks on the road.   But if I took Sundays off, that would be like taking 17 days off the length of my journey and it was short enough already. So I finished my coffee and got back out on 66. There were still more neighbors to meet.

Lucille Hamons' store near Hydro, Oklahoma.

Down the road near Hydro, by a slight southward bulge in the pavement, stood an all-purpose roadside business—gas station, store and motel. In front of it, on a 25-foot standard, hung a massive wooden sign. Usually signs name a business or tout a product. But this one did neither. It said simply: "Lucille's 66 Historic Highway."

I parked to the side of the building and walked in. A glass display case by the door served as the sales counter. Behind it, slide-top coolers stood against the walls to about halfway back. Racks of combs, aspirin, jerky, potato chips, cigarettes, billfolds and other conveniences of life hung from pegboards above them. Along the other side wall, steel shelves stood heavy with canned meat, cornmeal, flour, sugar, soup, Jello, and other dry groceries. Cans of oil were stowed on the floor underneath. In the back, which wasn't that far away, there were refrigerators, more coolers, a microwave, a built-in air conditioner, and a large color TV on a shelf. A kitchen counter, white wooden cabinets, a sink and an oven lined the back wall. In between stood a pair of dinette table. And in a corner, a dog with too much Pit Bull in her lay watching me.

A woman with a mass of red curls swept atop her head sat at the rearmost table smoking Bel Airs.

"Hi," I said, "You must be Lucille."

"I am," she answered. She spoke in a question and the purest, heaviest Oklahoma accent I had yet heard.

"Your daughter Dene in New Mexico wrote me about you. She said we should get in touch."

"You must be Tom," Lucille said. "Dene wrote to me, too. Come on back 'n have a seat."

"Can I get a soda first?"

"They're in the refrigerator on your left there. Just take your pick."

Her tone was neither bossy nor lazy, but more like that of a fraternity cook. I did what the lady said and sat down.

"I used to have two signs on that big pole—a Conoco and a big neon," she drawled between puffs on a Bel Air. "At that time, I called it Hamons' Courts, but everybody else called it Lucille's.

"Then a wind storm broke the signs loose last year and took 'em down the highway. I was debatin' whether I needed to put up a new sign 'cause everybody already knew where I was when the state came along and took down all the 66 signs. I thought it was so stupid! Route 66 rose from nothin' to the greatest highway we ever had back to nothin'. A lot of people's lookin' for 66 and they can't find it. So I put up the new sign—Lucille's 66 Historic Highway—to let them know the road was still here.

"The interstate bypassed me twenty years ago. I was shut off. But I said I was going to stay here to spite it. Now I'm doin' the same thing with that sign."

A small but steady flow of customers came in as we talked. If they knew their way around and had exact change, Lucille would have them help themselves and leave their money on the counter. When an off duty sheriff's deputy came in, she greeted him with a question: "Why haven't you caught all them people been stealin' things down by Bridgeport?"

"Couldn't catch 'em *all*," the man said. "We had to leave some for seed."

"I've been here 45 years and I've done everything there is to do along 66," Lucille proclaimed early on. "I've run a gas station, a cafe, a grocery store and that motel next door until about four years. And I've seen most everything happen."

As Dene had predicted, Lucille offered more than a few examples.

"One mornin' about seven o'clock my youngest daughter was gettin' ready for school, a lady came in here and she told me her husband was dead down the highway! I got all shook up and I called a doctor. He said, 'Well, what you need is an undertaker.' So I called the undertaker in Weatherford, about eight miles west of here.

"He drove clear to El Reno looking for this man. He had a radio in his car, so when he got over there, he calls and says, 'Lucille, where'd you say that man was? I can't find anybody!'

"In the meantime, this woman was walkin' the floor and cryin'. She had me all shook up. I called all her kids, you know, and told them their father was dead.

"Then about noon, I got a telephone call—it was from the woman's husband in El Reno! He'd just been sleepin' and when he woke up, he'd gone lookin' for her. He'd filed a missin' person report with the police and had found out from one of their kids where she was.

"Now she'd been cryin' around here, but when he called, she gave him a good cussin'!"

Lucille lit a cigarette to give the punch line time to build.

"So when the headline came out, it was 'Dead Man Goes Looking for Missing Wife'! We all had a good laugh about that."

Lucille had another good laugh now. It was not bashful.

"But I've loved it here," she said later. "I always wanted to work. And I always wanted to work in a cafe. I don't know why. I just wanted to get out into the public and work."

After her two daughters were born, Lucille finally got her wish, working three days a week at a cafe in town. A few years later, she and her husband bought her current place. Then he bought a truck and drove off in it, leaving Lucille to run the store.

"My kids helped me when they were here," she said. "Now I'm doin' it all myself—from 10 a.m. to midnight seven days a week. I have a real nice trailer with a sunken living room I added on. But all I go there for is to sleep or do laundry."

A migrant broccoli picker came in and asked to cash his paycheck. Lucille stood at the counter and gave both the check and the man a good going over.

"A hundred 'n thirty-two dollars, huh? You buyin' anything?"

The man shuffled his feet, stuck his hands in his pockets.

"Well, I guess I could use a couple of cases of beer."

Lucille got her cash box out of a back drawer. The man left with $25 worth of beer and groceries, plus his change.

"You have to do a lot of things like that in a business like this," she said afterward. "Whatever it takes. Like in '55 I started a gas war. Gasoline was 19.9 and 21.9. But there was a Western truck driver stopped here and I said to him, 'If you tell all your trucker friends, I'll give 'em a two cent discount.' Just don't tell my gas man.

"Well, I had traffic galore here. I was pumpin' gas right and left. One mornin' I got up and there was eleven trucks out there waitin' to be filled."

The Pit Bull stirred gently by my feet, nudging herself closer. Lucille continued her proud oration.

"But I got 'em all filled. Fixed 'em coffee, too. Th' war lasted six months or a year and I don't think my gas man ever found out."

"I never used to sell beer either until they closed me off the interstate," she said, lighting into a new cigarette and a new story. "I was gettin' ready to send my youngest daughter off to college then and I said 'I got do somethin' to make more money!' Now I make more money on beer than anything else.

"But this isn't a beer joint. It's just that I have a few friends—local friends—that like to come here after work and sit and drink a few beers before they go home. I sit and talk with 'em, but when other people come in, I haveta go."

"The house was always full of kids," Dene told me later in Grants. "They fixed their cars there. They spent the night there. They ate there continually. The door was always open. We thought they were our friends. But they were our mother's. After we were grown up and gone, they kept coming by."

A few minutes before 3. one of Lucille's young friends, Twilah Johnson, came in. She'd been slated to keep the books at the grain elevator that day, but there was no business.

"Are you gonna watch the game this afternoon, Lucille?" she asked.

"I have a guest here talkin' with me about Route 66, Twilah. I don't know if he likes basketball."

"Go ahead and watch," I said. "I don't mind at all."

"Okay, but you're gonna have to let me feed you first."

The lady just had a knack for making you see things her way. Twilah got drinks. I made sure the TV was working and from various coolers and refrigerators Lucille dished up ham, creamed peas and potatoes, rice casserole with broccoli and cheese, a cold salad of broccoli and cauliflower, cucumbers and onions in vinegar, and a way-too-large bowl of bread pudding with custard topping. Then she sat across from me and made sure I ate it all.

"You said you liked okra, didn't you?" she said, extending a jar of the pickled variety.

"Sure did," I said and took one.

"I thought you said you liked it."

I took a second.

After nearly half a century of them, Lucille's 14-hour days finally took their toll; in early 1989, she had a heart attack. But she was back on the job by August. Her daughters wanted her to retire, but knew they were overmatched. They did get a concession, though: someone else stocks the beer now. And because her storage tanks are so old, the Environmental Protection Agency may force her to stop selling gas soon. But she'll still be on 66—her own living museum.

SEARCHING *FOR* 66

TWENTY-SEVEN

> *My friends, just because you live here among them all, do not lose sight of the fact that there are literally thousands of travelers who have never seen an Indian. Indians have tremendous pulling power. And don't forget the value of the cowboy, either....*
>
> *We've got it, folks. All we have to do is go after it right. People must be sold on coming to 66 before they leave home. So let's set aside all sectionalism and strive for the greatest good for the greatest number. Let's do it the American Way!*
>
>

Ralph Jones, New Mexico Motel Owner
Postwar Reorganization Meeting of
the U.S. Highway 66 Association
Oklahoma City
October 23, 1947

The Good War was over. The good times began. Their horizons broadened by the foreign experience, Americans hit the road again with an exultant rush. Just a decade earlier, the Okies' flight over Route 66 had been called the greatest peacetime migration in American history. But that exodus would be equalled every year now as returning GI's and their countrymen descended on California to claim their share of its continuing prosperity. Their path of choice: Route 66. Steinbeck's mother road was now the mother lode.

Frank Lloyd Wright said the continent was tilting and Route 66 was a chute down which everything loose was sliding into southern California. Ralph Jones described it perhaps more prosaically. But the people who listened to him—a thousand innkeepers, cafe owners, gas station operators and other merchants from every state along the highway—were a most receptive audience.   In that audience, to his own surprise, was Jack Cutberth, a middle-aged barber from Clinton, Oklahoma. He'd come out of no self interest—simply as a favor to a friend. But by the time he died 31 years later, he was known up and down the route as "Mr. 66."

"Jack didn't see 66 as a highway—he saw it as a community," said his widow Gladys. "He lived it. He breathed it. It was his life.

"He never got tired, either. As long as it was 66, he was just as happy as a lark. And as much as we ended up traveling it together, I don't think I ever heard him make the remark, 'I'm glad to be home.'"

A note of surprise entered Gladys' lilt.

"We didn't go to that reorganization meeting expecting all that. We sure didn't. It came out of the clear blue sky. I never knew Jack would care for that type of work because he'd always been at home. But he came back from that first meeting as the state secretary. He never said why he felt so special about the highway, but he got interested in doing work with the national set-up and just assumed more and more and more. Five or six years later, they made him the national executive secretary. And that's what he was when he died."

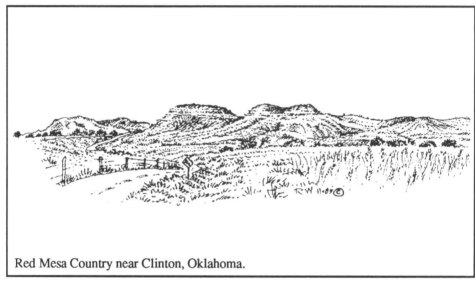

Red Mesa Country near Clinton, Oklahoma.

As executive secretary, Jack's duties included collecting dues, lobbying legislatures and politicians, and arranging the national conventions. That took about ten percent of his time. The rest he spent on the road.

"He got a couple of other fellows to run the shop," Gladys said. "I'd keep a little bag ready and go with him whenever I could. We'd load the car down with brochures—even in the front seat. Sometimes I could scarcely get in the car. Then off we'd go.

"Advertising will do a lot for you if you stay with it. Just keep hammering away at it. That's exactly what Jack and I did every day of the year—place brochures and talk about Route 66.

"And when we had an election and got a new governor, Jack was on his doorstep the very next morning. If he wasn't over in Oklahoma City at least once a week, they'd call and ask what was wrong with him.

"It was expensive to stay on the road. And Jack's work was not a money-making proposition. But he loved it so."

After checking into a motel, Gladys' house had been my first stop in Clinton. When she wasn't home, I'd left a card in her door. At 9:30 that night, she called me.

"Why don't you come over right now?" she asked. I made a lame excuse about not having eaten supper yet and begged off. The poor lady had just had a pacemaker implanted a month before; I didn't want to tire her. As things developed, I was the one who wore out.

Gladys started our visit the next morning by stationing me at a small table in her breezeway. From another part of the house, she started carrying in box after box of Jack's files. It was three hours, though, before I could give them my attention.

"Jack was tall and handsome and an excellent dancer," the aging belle said. "It was at a dance in Butler where we met. And the dancing led to romance and two months later we got married. I was still engaged to another boy at the ti-em."

Gladys left me alone for five minutes of uninterrupted study. Then she returned with coffee, cookies and more memories.

"And when there was a problem, it didn't take Jack two or three days to get started," she said. "He started as soon as he got off the telephone. If something needed to be done, it was done right the-en. Not the next day, next week, or next month. It was done that day.

"Jack was a soft-spoken man and he did things with the greatest of ease and calm. Members would be having problems, tantrums, almost like children. Well, I don't know, Jack would just sit down with them and start talking about *everything* but the highway. But before long, he was talking about the highway. It's just like a mother and a baby. If the mother's agitated, then the baby becomes agitated. But if the mother's calm, the baby will be all right. That works between adults, too."

Gleaning through the Cutberth archives in between chats, I found a promotional blurb on the back cover of 1961's brochure:

"Tod Stiles and Buzz Murdoch—broke, homeless, but resourceful, they pooled their assets and bought a car. Route 66 is the backbone of the American Dream. But with the dream comes its price. Tod and Buzz found the road doesn't end in California—it ends beyond the shoulder at every point along this 2,000-mile dream."

"That's an ad for the TV show," Gladys said. "But that's the way it was. Nowadays you go into one of these new motels and all you see is employees. And Indians are buying so many small motels—we're going to be foreigners in our own land. But our association had some up and at 'em businessmen who saw things the same way Jack did. They got behind the organization and worked at it just as hard as Jack. Whatever he asked them to do, they did it. It was more than an association. It was like they became personal friends. When they quit a year after Jack died, there were still eighteen hundred members."

The members gathered at least once a year at a city along the route for their national convention. According to the minutes of the 1958 convention—held in Needles, California—events started with an early bird luncheon at the Methodist Church. Duplicate bridge games and color movies of a member's world tour were featured in the afternoon. At the evening banquet, held in the high school cafeteria, Will Rogers, Jr., the association's honorary president, was guest speaker. The meeting concluded with a group sing of Bobby Troup's hit song, "Route 66."

"And it wasn't one little group here, one little group there, and another little group down the road," Gladys went on. "They worked at it as a whole. One time, some people wanted to build a toll-road across western Oklahoma to replace 66. A coffee company near here came out in favor of it. Well, when our members found out about that, they stopped buying that coffee all up and down the route. It didn't take that company long to change its mind. No-o."

The 66 Association won that fight. It also resisted Lady Bird Johnson's highway beautification plan with some success. And when the Highway 60 Association put up billboards which deceptively led people to believe they could reach the west coast on that road, the 66 people won a legal battle to have the boards taken down.

"We fought a lot of battles in Washington, too, and we usually won," said Gladys proudly. "Originally, the interstate system was designed to bypass cities along 66 by as much as fifteen miles. We succeeded in drawing it closer. And business loops with their green signs were also our brainchild.

"But we lost our bitterest battle of all when they got around to naming the interstates that replaced 66. We fought tooth and nail to have it named I-66, but we lost. Now look—it's taken five interstates to replace it!

"A lot of our members stayed in business quite awhile after I-40 came because they didn't have the bypasses finished. But then it was time for them to retire and things sort of all jelled at once. Jack died eight years ago yesterday. The association rocked along for about a year after that. They were trying so desperately to make something out of nothing that they stayed with it. I had to remind them that Jack didn't want it that way.

"So the Association is gone. But Route 66, I call it the highway that won't die. I get telephone calls and letters all the time. The government called it just a route. But I'd say it was a shrine. It was a road for the common man. The common man built it, the common man drove it, and the common man ran its businesses."

After nine hours of talking and reading, Gladys and her son took me to dinner. She would have talked even more after that, but I was tired and begged off again.

Next morning, though, Gladys wasn't home. Figuring another meeting just wasn't fated, I left my card in her door and traveled on to the next town. And the next town and the next. I went to a historical museum and a domino parlor. But my steady push westward, a satisfying habit for nearly two months now, left me flat today. Early evening came and I found myself on the road back to Clinton.

"Tom!" said Gladys. "I was gone only a few minutes when you stopped by. I thought I'd lost you!"

George Maharis and Martin Milner of *Route 66.*

SEARCHING FOR 66

TWENTY-EIGHT

By the time Route 66 entered the Texas panhandle, the terrain was flat and semi-barren. Local postcards featured pictures of cattle ranches and rest stops. A truck stop advertised Diesel Happy Hour: 4-5 p.m. and 4-5 a.m. A sign by a high school proclaimed the institution was home to state champs or runners-up in debate, calculator, and shorthand. Roadkill rabbits grew longer ears.

The first town of size in the panhandle was Shamrock. Bill Howe, editor and publisher of the Shamrock *Texan*—"The Biggest Little Newspaper in Texas"—had printed my letter about Route 66. When I stopped by to thank him, he made time to explain the town's unlikely name. It took him most of the morning.

"It all began" he alleged, "around the turn of the century. A posse of kids were on a picnic outside town when they found a sizeable chunk of the original Blarney Stone half buried in the sand! They dug up the oddity and brought it home. But folks didn't realize what it was and it was cast quickly aside. Later, when "Sport" Pendleton built his drugstore, he picked the stone up and used it as a dead man for the hitching rack."

Some years after that, Editor Howe further alleged, an unruly horse kicked a chip off the stone. On that chip, these words were discovered to be engraved: "All men who cross this spot will be received with tolerance and consideration, for they who reside here are as wise as New Englanders, as hospitable as a Kentucky colonel, and have the keen eye, good soul and hearty smile of a true son of the old sod."

"Then in 1910 we got our first postmaster, George Nickel," Bill said. "Up until then, the closest thing we'd ever seen to a shamrock was in the Sears catalogue. But George needed an address so people could send us mail. Being an Irishman, he chose 'Shamrock.'

"There have never been any more Houlihans and O'Connors here than in any other town in Texas. But what's a little thing like a surname have to do with being Irish?"

In truth, Shamrock actually does have a piece of the genuine Blarney Stone. And each year on the weekend closest to March 17, Miss Irish

Rose approaches the stone. A local colleen elected to the honor by her high school classmates, she leans over and plants a quick smooch on the fragment. A band celebrates the feat and the second largest St. Patrick's Day celebration on Route 66 (after Chicago's parade) begins.

Shamrock, Texas.

High school bandmaster Glenn Truax started the annual celebration in 1938 to salve his students' disappointment over not getting to march in the Rose Bowl Parade. It now includes a parade, an antique car show, a banquet, and dancing. People come from miles around, swelling Shamrock to five times its normal size of three thousand. Bill contributes by publishing the St. Patrick's Week edition of the *Texan* on green newsprint. And since Shamrock is in a dry county, the whole celebration is conducted without a legal drop of alcohol.

A highlight of each year's festival is the beard-judging contest on Saturday. For this, all men in town must grow beards—-or face jail terms and a $2 fine every time they show their bare mugs on the street. Bill, who was clean shaven when we met, said most men take this rule good-naturedly. As a matter of fact, some go it one better by actually sporting green beards.

"You mean they dye them?" I asked.

Bill leaned back in his chair and adjusted the pens in the pocket of his seersucker jumpsuit. "I seldom ever tell this story," he lied, "but I actually grow mine that way. Twenty years ago, a fellow by the name of Kuhn McFarland of Ireland saw a story about our celebration in a newspaper over there and wrote to ask if he could serve as our Irish correspondent. I wrote him back that we had no earthly use for an Irish correspondent. But it would be very helpful if he would send us clippings from over there about anything Irish that we could use for feature stories in our St. Patrick's Day edition.

"Kuhn was very gracious and sent us reams and barrels of stuff. This was very helpful because it takes a lot of material to fill a 60-page special edition.

"About a dozen years ago, I got a note from Kuhn a couple of weeks before the celebration, saying, 'I am enclosing a small supply of what we refer to as authentic Irish green chlorophyll tablets. We use them to turn our beards green for special celebrations and festivities and the like. I thought you might like to try them.'

"This was the craziest thing I ever read. But the further I read, the crazier it got. He said that if I took a tablet every morning after breakfast for a week that it would turn my beard green! And the beauty of it, he said, was that it would not affect the color of my hair. His only caution was that if I ever stopped taking them for even a day that my beard would revert back to its original color.

"Well, I opened the little inner envelope with his letter and—sure enough—there were some little old white pills. They looked kind of like aspirin tablets. I thought, 'Well, what have I got to lose?' While no one was looking, I popped one in my mouth and then started taking them every morning.

"About the third day, I caught myself looking in the mirror. But nothing had happened. On the seventh day, I looked in the mirror and said, 'Bless Pat!' That thing was just as green as a gourd!

"I wouldn't have believed it if I hadn't seen it myself. And, like I say, no one else ever believes this story. But it's the absolute truth. I have told it so many times that I have come to believe it myself!"

By then it was time for lunch. Bill's civic club, the Boosters, was meeting down at the Methodist church at noon. Would I like to come?

I followed Bill through a long back room full of printing machinery and old furniture and out to his car. In three minutes we were in the church basement meeting and greeting the other men folks of town—most of whom were also clean shaven.

The ladies' auxiliary had prepared a classic church basement meal—fried chicken, mashed potatoes and gravy, green beans, salad, and apple pie. We passed it around family style in platters and bowls.

After dinner, guests were introduced to the "Boss Booster." I was one of six. Next came a discussion on whether to help promote a wagon train which was passing through town in August in observance of the Texas sesquicentennial. Members agreed that would be a good thing to do, but left details for a later meeting.

At meeting's close, the Dues Booster took the floor for the ritual weekly fining of the members. One fellow was levied a dime for writing a check during the earlier discussion ("I saw you taking care of business."). One was docked a quarter for missing last week's meeting; another paid a quarter for making this one. Bill laughed at a fellow member's misfortune and had to ante up a quarter himself. He protested and got pinched for an extra dime.

SEARCHING FOR 66

TWENTY-NINE

Earlier in our verbal ramblings, I'd wondered to Bill Howe what the story was about all the domino parlors I'd been seeing along the road lately. Every town of size since Baxter Springs had counted at least one domino parlor—and smaller ones had domino tables in their bars. Cruising town before going in to see Bill, I'd even noticed that Shamrock had not one, but two parlors.

Bill generously left one story for somebody else. "Don't know," he said. "You oughtta ask our mayor, Doug Rives. He runs a game every afternoon in that storefront across the street."

"Don't know," said Doug when we met at the Boosters meeting. "Why don't you come by the game this afternoon and see if you can find out?"

Dominos became popular in the Bible Belt portion of 66, Doug later explained, because so many cities had passed laws against card playing. During the Roaring Twenties and the area's various oil booms, dominos was played enthusiastically in virtually every small town hotel along the route. Action was spirited and the stakes often high—well leases and property deeds were known to change hands on the outcome of a single match. Stakes today are generally a little friendlier. And small town hotels don't host games anymore, primarily because there aren't any more small town hotels. But the bones are still clicking in hundreds of parlors and bars.

Doug Rives' parlor defined the species. Its peeling stucco exterior was stark and bare. Its interior equally glamorous—a metal coat rack in a corner, a window fan on a chair, sheets of paneling nailed lengthwise to the lower walls, and outdated calendars and starving artist prints hanging here and there.

From family gatherings as a child, I thought I knew a little bit about dominos. But the farmers and townsmen who gathered at Doug's soon set that thought to rest.

The day's gaming had already begun when I walked in. All four tables were full and had players waiting to get in. There were, as is customary in most domino parlors, no women. I took a seat at the corner of Doug's table across from another spectator, the town's deputy constable, and watched.

Each game began with a shuffle. Raised wooden rims bordered each table's playing surface, keeping the bones from flying off during this swirling, palms-down exercise. Then before the pieces even stopped, each competitor was drawing out the seven nearest ones as his own.

Dominos in Shamrock, Texas.

In front of each man, the formica playing surface was worn white in two arcs where thousands of players before him had arranged their pieces. Under the tabletop at each corner was a shelf for sheltering smokes and drinks from the action. Squares of brown slateboard were screwed into opposite corners of the playing surface. Stubs of scoring chalk hung nearby on strings. On a nail by each corner a wet rag was kept for erasing the score between games.

A few polite seconds went by after each deal while players sorted their pieces. Then they went at each other like Korean boxers. Play began to the dealer's left, usually with a double spot. Some players, such as Doug, artfully flipped their dominos out, landing them like clever jabs. Other players, like Constable Jerry Berten, disdained such subtlety, wound up, and slammed their men down. The pace of play was unforgiving and a man would be accused of dawdling if he didn't have his next punch already on its way before his opponent's landed.

Between turns, each player practiced a nervous habit with his remaining dominos. Some shuffled them around. Others clicked them on the table top. Still others clicked their bones against each other. Whatever its style, each habit's pace picked up as play went on. There were occasional snippets of conversation—primarily criticism of a partner's play—but mostly I heard just the click, clatter, shuffle and slam of dominos, punctuated by stabs of chalk against slate whenever a man scored.

At the end of each game, wallets would open and dollar bills would change hands. Doug seemed to be taking in more dollars than he gave out, but he was still the target of many verbal jabs from the other players—particularly his partner, Jerry. He took it in obsequious good grace, though. Often, he would even laugh. And when he did, other players would laugh with him—knowing it could provoke their mayor to nearly uncontrollable giggling.

Folks started drifting out at about 4:30. By six o'clock, the universal closing time for domino parlors, only one table was left. Play ceased automatically and without debate. Homes and supper were waiting. It was time to go.

That evening, I drove twenty miles back to the Last Stop Bar in Texola, Oklahoma, and watched the domino game there. Compared to Shamrock, this match unfolded at a positively leisurely pace. The players were much younger and a woman even sat in on a couple of games.

After a while, I got invited in. I played slowly but passably and after two hands in a 250-point game, our opponents had only doubled the score on my partner and me. Then in the third hand, I blithely and unwittingly laid down a piece which allowed the next man to score 30 points and end the game. It was nowhere near closing time, but everybody suddenly decided they'd had enough dominos for the day. I retired with only one blemish on my record.

SEARCHING FOR 66

THIRTY

Cruising west again early next morning, I saw a cherry '56 Chevy coming the other way—pulling a trailer. I didn't know whether the driver should be congratulated or arrested. Then it was on past McLean, the next-to-last 66 town to be bypassed by I-40. Near Britten, a water tower took a cockeyed slant like the Tower of Pisa. Windmills and oil rigs stood erect but silent in the expanses of brush and stubble. On the rare stretches of interstate I had to traverse, crossovers from one side to the other were clearly marked and frequently used—and there were gravel lanes connecting rest stops to the frontage roads. In range country, the roads are truly open. And though the range itself isn't open anymore, cattle are still its main business.

Longhorns—tough, rangy descendants of cattle brought over by the Spanish—were ideal early inhabitants of the open range. But when barbed wire fenced off the range and rail supplanted trail as the means to market, the longhorns' eight-foot spreads made them unwieldy, then obsolete. Hereford, Texas, is named after their replacement.

Just as the postwar 66 heyday began, a new aquifer was discovered in the panhandle. This allowed irrigation, which allowed grain crops, which allowed ranchers to bring food to their cattle instead of sending them out to find it themselves. Cattle could be fattened for market in a sixth the time now and at less cost. Cheaper and faster meant better, so range became ranches became feedlots.

On the east end of City 66 in Amarillo stands one of the cattle industry's focal points—the Amarillo Cattle Auction. Two million head a year change hands there, making the Auction one of the largest livestock exchanges in the world. The holding lot itself, a twenty-acre maze of pens and passage ways, is positively Boolean in its complexity.

At the Auction's center stands the bidding arena, an amphitheater of tiered wooden benches kept shiny by generations of blue-jeaned bottoms. There were about 150 people there the day I attended, most of them middle-aged or older men—small scale ranchers looking for feeder stock or packing house reps looking for hamburger. Headgear was de rigeur, with work caps running a close second to straw Stetsons in popularity. Most folks had clean-shaven, ruddy faces and if you didn't wear boots and smoke or chew something, you were in the minority. Everybody knew everybody else and the talking was constant, even during the bidding.

Fred and Virginia Dillard have been Auction regulars for five years—ever since two heart attacks in a year retired Fred from his job with an oil company. Now they run about thirty head on a Mom-and-Pop feedlot on 66 west of Amarillo. Today they were looking for just one head, a white-faced bull to improve their breeding stock.

"The first feedlot that I know was east of town here on 66 in the early '60s," Fred said. His accent, though twangy through long habit, was clear and sharp—unlike the full, heavy sound of Oklahomans. "They fed 'em milo, by golly, and they got fat."

The entry gate swung open and a lot of cattle, urged on by electric prods, bolted into the bidding ring. Fred, who was doing about six things simultaneously, appraised them in a glance and checked the toteboard for the weight. Then Virginia did the bidding while Fred scanned the crowd to see who their competitors were.

"They just sell small lots in the morning—old cows, culls, sick ones, maybe a few nice calves like that one we just bid on," Fred said. "But this one here's got a twisted head. That one has a tumor on his eye. He'll pass inspection, but only if they slaughter him quick. This one with the bare spots on his rear flanks is a rider—got that way from the others trying to mount him. And the bigger the spots get, the more often they'll try. Talk about dumb animals."

A relief auctioneer came on duty. Scanning the crowd, mine may well have been the only unfamiliar face he saw.

"Before we start the biddin' on this next fine lot of Texas beef, I'd like to welcome Bill Wolverton back into our company," the new man twanged. "Bill's been away a few days and we missed him."

Heads turned; there was a general chuckle in the arena. Two rows behind the Dillards and me, an octogenarian gentleman tried hard to appear ignorant of all the attention.

"Bill's been comin' here for fifty years," Fred explained. "So when he missed last week's sale, we were worried. Turns out he was in jail for solicitin' an undercover policewoman down on Amarillo Boulevard."

In 66's packing houses back in East St. Louis, Slavic immigrants and southern blacks took their first steps toward the middle class by taking the menial and undesirable jobs—which meant the killing floor. Today that tradition continues at Amarillo's biggest slaughterhouse, Iowa Beef Products—only Vietnamese and Laotians have replaced Slavs on the floor.

"I think those folks are gonna make it," Fred told me. One reason is that he's helping them out. They get no discount from their employer, so every weekend Fred sells one of his steers to a group of them.

"They slaughter 'em right at my place," he said. "I got racks and hooks and everything for 'em. They'll cut it with the hide still on and stack it up in piles of about the same value. Then they'll draw lots to see who gets what. There's no arguin' or anything.

"Yes sir, I think those folks are gonna make it."

The exit gate swung open. Cowhands stood behind shelters of two-inch pipe and prodded the old lot out. A single steer came squealing in, eyes protruding and tail hiked high.

"That one I know real well," Fred said. "Bought him two weeks ago in a lot with some others. Sold 'im last week, and now he's back again. See how his toes are turned up? He got that way from eating feed that's too rich too fast. They got shots that'll cure 'im, but nobody wants to pay the money."

"You've heard that hamburger commercial about 'Where's the beef?' Well, I'll tell you where it is," he said and pointed at the three-time loser. "It's right there."

SEARCHING *66*
FOR

THIRTY-ONE

"I'm gonna pack my pa and I'm gonna pack my aunt
I'm gonna take 'em down to the Cadillac Ranch"
Bruce Springsteen

Brochures on Amarillo offer specific directions on how to find a monument to something as ethereal as helium. But Bruce Springsteen and all other travelers are left to chance or their own devices to discover Cadillac Ranch. So the element of surprise is often complete as motorists top a rise on Route 66 just west of Amarillo and see ten old Cadillacs—one for each style of the car's tail fins—buried nose deep in the middle of a wheatfield.

There are no billboards, no markers, not even a parking lot—just a graveled wide spot on the shoulder and a narrow dirt path two hundred yards through the field to the Cadillacs. Once there, you'll find no brochures, no guides, no explanatory plaques—just ten Cadillacs planted in a line at the precise angle of the great pyramids and pointing west.

To some, the skyward-stretching fins are like a pagan prayer. For many, they are comic relief to the barren scenery they've just traveled through. To others, the Ranch brings back memories of an era when every young man's dream was to have a big Cadillac and a beautiful blonde.

Stanley Marsh 3 ("Not III") commissioned a San Francisco architecture commune, the Ant Farm, to build the Ranch in 1974. A local boy who made good, Stanley alternates between calling it a joke and the American Stonehenge.

"When I was a kid, I just lusted after having a car," he said, his voice high-pitched and twangy, but always articulate. "I know the first job I ever had, I made enough money to make a down payment on a car. And I don't know that I would have worked if I couldn't have made enough to do that.

"And the nice thing about Cadillacs is they depreciated so quickly that anyone could afford one. Right here in Amarillo when I was a kid if you wanted to be real high class, you drove around in a Cadillac. But your maid had one, too. So you had to buy a new one every three or four years so it wouldn't look like your maid's car parked out in front."

Which has been something Stanley's never found hard to do. A Wharton graduate, he inherited a natural gas fortune, married into a cattle fortune, and built his own from such shrewd investments as Bar Mitzvah coins and a string of Texas TV stations. And for the past thirty years, he's devoted a fair portion of those fortunes to the arts—if you accept objects such as Cadillac Ranch in your definition of the subject.

Cadillac Ranch, Amarillo, Texas.

A lanky, mustachioed man who will someday be called portly, Stanley would much rather do his art than talk about it. He was in Tokyo on my first pass through Amarillo, but made time for me on my way home—as curious about my project as I was about his. After a tour of his land, we sat for three hours in his well-cluttered office and talked.

"I've known the Ant Farm since the hippie days," Stanley said. "They called themselves a commune back then, but they didn't really live together and share the same bowl of soup. They were all educated people, east coasters.

"They grew up as war babies. It was this kind of Saturday Evening Post, Eisenhower-was-the-President life and you wanted glamour. And the glamour was called Hollywood and the movies and the beach and Marilyn Monroe and Las Vegas—and all of it involved getting into a car and going to Lotus Land.

"During the time when all that was the American Dream, the Cadillac was the standard of cars. If you didn't have a Cadillac, there was a reason why. And as the Dream got more sophisticated, cars did, too. More and more, they became places to escape to and go driving through the country in a climate-controlled dream. The aerial goes up and down. You can find a radio station with your foot."

Stanley's secretary called in with a reminder that he had a meeting with international bankers at 4. He gave her a quick set of instructions, opened his day's sixth can of Sprite, leaned back again, and went on.

"When the Ant Farm decided to build a monument to their youth, they came to me because I'm a friend of theirs," he said. "At first they wanted to build a house that looked like a praying mantis. I already had enough house, so I turned that idea down. We settled on Cadillac Ranch because cars were the chief status symbol of that time and Route 66 was where everybody went when they got one. Had I lived on Highway 40 in Kansas, the Ant Farmers might have come up with something entirely different.

"They said that since the beginning of time, all people of consciousness—especially adolescents—wake up sometimes in the middle of the night and they're mad about something or somebody. And they fantasize themselves out of their hut or igloo or tepee or cave. In the past, they've just gone to another hut or igloo or tepee or cave. It's better in this new place because they're away from their homework or they're away from having to say their prayers or they're with their girlfriend or they have a deck of cards.

"So people did this until the invention of the automobile. They still dream, the Ant Farm said, but now they fantasize themselves into a car because cars represent liberty, wealth, sexual freedom, the ability to explore—plus they get you away from schoolwork or home or the mom that wants you to weed the garden."

With the plan set, the Ant Farm—Chip Lord, Doug Michels and Hudson Marquez—came to Amarillo in May 1974 and spent two weeks combing the junkyards and garages of town for the cars. The '49 Caddie was the most expensive and the '57 was hardest to find. Then they borrowed a back hoe from Stanley's other ranch, dug holes, poured concrete in, and lowered the cars into permanent anchorage.

The Caddies stand in chronological order, from 1949 to 1963. Like a wave coming to shore, their fins start gently with the vestigial stubs on the '49. They build to the aeronautic roar of the '59, which had stabilizers and rocket-shaped tail lights. Then they come down and recede once more. At about the same time that shots rang out from the Texas School Book Depository to announce the end of the Fifties, the tail fin era ended, too.

At first, the Ant Farm wanted to plant the Cadillacs haphazardly in the field. But Stanley said no, they should be lined up in a row facing west. He wanted archeologists of the future to know that some highly intelligent life form had put them there for a purpose—even if the purpose could not be figured out.

"And at first I didn't want to put the Ranch out there on Route 66," Stanley said. "All my other art has been hidden—I want people to come on it unexpectedly and let it totally change their lives. And my family had objections to the Ranch because it was junky looking.

"And it *is* junky looking. But it's wonderful! We were prepared to tear it up in a month or two if it didn't work out, if it looked like the side of town where people just have old cars stacked up. But it's stayed. A couple of years ago, we even had a tenth anniversary party for it.

"And you know what the best thing about it is? It's useless! It's perfectly worthless! I can't do a thing with it."

The Cadillacs had originally been painted in their years' most popular colors. But last year a gang of young vandals came to the unguarded Ranch one night, painted all the cars primer red, and sprayed the word M-E-A-T-P-U-P-P-E-T on them. Numerous other graffiti of the most standard variety also blemish each car. Everything but the trunks and the hubcaps has been stripped from them—and those stay because they were welded on. I asked Stanley what he thought of such disfigurement.

He ran a hand through hair which will never be wholly domesticated, shrugged, and said, "I think it shows Americans know how to treat their monuments."

The Cadillac Ranch is just the best known of Stanley's feats. But coming from the man who's the self-proclaimed U.S. Professional Fun Champion, it scarcely stands alone. Stanley once talked a group of friends into dressing in short pants like Boy Scouts and flying to Alaska just to see if "we would be taken for sissies." In the '60's, he won nomination to the White House Enemies List by offering to establish a wing in his proposed Museum of Modern Decadence exclusively for the display of Pat Nixon's wardrobe. In 1977, he dressed in red tails and sneakers and refereed a wrestling match between champion Dory Funk, another son of Amarillo, and a worthy but losing opponent. To a dinner once for visiting Japanese businessmen, he invited only Texans over 6'4".

When John Connally stood trial for bribery, Stanley and friends flew out to Washington to cheer their former governor on. Dressed in cowboy garb, they carried along a case of Lone Star Beer for authenticity. For atmosphere, they dipped their hand-tooled boots into a box of genuine Texas cow manure before entering the courtroom.

And in a semi-apocryphal tale, Stanley once discovered a fur poacher's live traps in a lake on his ranch. Rather than merely have the man be arrested, Stanley bought five dead monkeys from an animal laboratory. He dressed them in miniature scuba gear— complete with snorkels—and placed one monkey in each of the illegal traps. He's never been bothered by poachers again.

The man enjoys skewing environments and thought patterns. He once had wings tattooed on a pet pig. He has a zebra named "Spot," a home named "Toad Hall," and a gas tank at his ranch painted like a Campbell's Soup can. In his office he serves business lunches on a bearskin rug. Or he'll wear a checkered suit made from the same fabric as his desk chair.

Want something on a larger scale? Try meandering out to a remote spot on Stanley's ranch and shooting a game on his Phantom Soft Pool Table—a 90 by 180 foot rectangle of painted grass with stuffed canvas pool balls and a 100-foot cue (startled airline pilots are the table's most frequent viewers). Or go a little further into back country to the Amarillo Ramp—an elevated, 400-foot, spiral of crushed rock which reaches out into Tecovas Lake. A walk up the ramp gives one a constantly changing perspective of the surrounding landscape. Stanley's been known to stroll up to its top, take a leak, then walk back down.

And out near the border of the Marsh landholdings, Stanley had a series of steel panels bolted just below the rim of a mesa. When the atmospheric conditions are right, which is about twice a year, the color of the panels matches the color of the horizon and the mesa's top appears to be floating.

"All my projects fit my theory that the best art is good—yet it has no value," Stanley said. "I can't sell them. I can't move them. They're just there."

Most of Stanley's major shenanigans took place during the '60's and '70's. In the '80's, though, he'd mellowed a bit. Oh, there was the trip he and some friends took to Africa's great ape country to wander among the simians dressed as gorillas. But that was an exception. Perhaps it was because his wife Wendy's transplant surgery in 1985 gave him intimations of his own mortality. Or perhaps it was because four of his five children were teenagers now and he enjoyed spending time with them.

"As a matter of fact, I just sent my 17-year-old son on a car trip to Cape Cod yesterday," Stanley said. "He and a friend are going to visit relatives. Traveling's so much faster and safer and easier now—it's just like a trip I took to El Paso when I was a kid."

Dad gave his thinning hair another swipe. "It's a long trip all right. But I think kids should try things like that. If my children just grew up as carbon copies of my values without having some kind of rebellion and figuring out things on their own, thinking their own thoughts about religion, lifestyle, being a vegetarian—any number of things—I'd be disappointed. I think interesting people, especially during their college years, tend to have flexible ideas and they try out different things.

"I don't mean go off and be a Baghwan or something like that. But it's tradition in the United states to come back from college and offend your elders. When it was considered rebellious, I had long hair. So now my daughter's dating a skinhead. And if I didn't look just a little appalled, she'd be terribly disappointed...and so would the little skinhead.

"But I don't care if he's a skinhead. He plays an awful game of pool, though. He looks real funny at the table, too, leanin' all over there. He's in a band and they're all skinheads. Get them all together and they look like little birds in a nest.

"But they're all nice kids. They're tryin' to look different from us for a number of reasons."

In a Christmas note to me after I got home, the man who so many people call a zany eccentric betrayed even more normalcy.

"I suppose all Americans with families look on Christmas as a time to spend with those families," he wrote. "But when you have five children at home and you live in the Midwest, the answer is 'Yes, but only more so.' What I like is that Wendy and I do things the old-fashioned way and don't do much. We stay home. Good things happen to us. Relatives come. Santa comes in the middle of the night, and our children wake up at 3 or 4 a.m. We force them to pretend to go back to sleep. But, they don't go to sleep. They peek. We never go to see if Santa left footprints on the rug until 5 a.m. One year, Timmy, in despair over the long wait, opened our bedroom window and shouted up at the sky, 'Hurry up, God!' God didn't hurry, but he was there."

On their level, Stanley's links with Route 66 are as strong as his ties to family, business and art. They began when, as an Amarillo ninth grader, he had to write a class report on a local business. On his father's advice, he wrote about Route 66.

"Dad told me it was the third largest employer in Amarillo," Stanley said. "But it didn't have anything to do with tourism like Yellowstone. It just meant people and companies and places that were in Amarillo because it was 300 miles from Albuquerque and about the same from Oklahoma City. And so we had motels, restrunts, and say every 250 miles or so an International Harvester dealer.

"The highway really was a big industry here—I was terribly surprised. But my teacher did not think Route 66 counted as industry. So I had to call my report tourism—which is silly because when I think about tourists, I think about people with cameras and binoculars lookin' at birds and that's all they're doin'. Route 66 wasn't tourism like that—it was just the way you crossed the country and this is where you spent the night or had breakfast or bought a set of tires.

"Even today, I don't know about other roads. I live on 66. I work on 66. Both of my ranches are on 66. I can't think of another road we associate with as much history and romance. There may be roads from Chicago to Seattle, but I never hear about them. I wouldn't know their names.

"I don't associate 66 with wealth, either. I always associate it with people who are working hard. It's a hard life, but Middle America...happy. I think of Los Angeles and Chicago and I think of millionaires and people in lakefront apartments. But just Highway 66 I associate with people like us."

The bankers were gathering in the foyer. But Stanley had time for one more question—his own.

"Do you think there's a difference in people who lived right on 66, Tom—people who lived and grew up on the road *to* someplace? If you work at a gas station on the road to L.A., does that make you want to go there? I wonder if there's a difference in mental outlook between living on the road to somewhere as opposed to living at the destination. Does it make you more adventurous?"

I told Stanley I was finding out.

SEARCHING FOR 66

THIRTY-TWO

New Mexico had the longest maidenhood of any American state, going sixty-six years as a territory before adding the forty-seventh star to our flag in 1912. Still today, much of the rest of the country has trouble believing it's part us—tourists along I-40 compliment the natives on their fine English; New Mexican youth applying to out-of-state universities are referred to foreign admissions offices, letters come addressed to Santa Fe, New Mexico SOUTH AMERICA. A lady from Dallas once even called the Albuquerque Chamber of Commerce and asked, "If it's Friday in Texas, what day is it in New Mexico?"

Fact is, man has lived in New Mexico so long that the rest of the Union should have applied for admission to it. While glaciers still entombed the Midwest, Folsom Man was hunting bison on this state's vast plains. More recently, (about the time of the Nativity), Apaches and Comanches moved in to range and war over the land. More sedentary Indians arrived not too many centuries later and built pueblos. And there are still pockets today of the descendants of Spanish explorers—hardy wanderers who arrived a scant twenty years after Columbus made landfall in the Caribbean.

Given their seniority, it should be New Mexicans who look on the rest of this country as a strange, new land. But they have grown used to unneighborly treatment by their sister states and look on it now with a bemused tolerance. They've had Ann Landers do a couple of columns on the subject and *New Mexico Magazine* features an anecdotal column called "One of Our Fifty Is Missing." The rest of the country's ignorance doesn't bother them a bit. After all, *they're* the ones who live in the Land of Enchantment. Ninety percent of the people born in New Mexico end up dying there—a higher homebound rating than any other state can claim.

I had my visa stamped at the border, assured the guards I wasn't smuggling in any illegal Anglos, and bought some pesos at an exorbitant exchange rate in San Jon. I was ready for New Mexico. A sign just inside the border said "Los Angeles—1,007 Miles," but it would be Tucumcari tonight.

Like most other 66 towns from Oklahoma City to Los Angeles, Tucumcari owes its start to the railroad. Knowing that the Santa Fe would go through someday, early developers bought a north-south strip of sections in eastern New Mexico midway between Amarillo and Albuquerque. Once the rail line's latitude through their land was set, they built a settlement alongside it to service the locomotives. Robbers, rustlers, gamblers, prostitutes and drifters crowded into the new community, along with the decent folks. The site was first known as Six Shooter Siding, and in one violent night amid the roar of six guns, eleven men died.

TePee Trading Post, Tucumcari, New Mexico.

When the town incorporated in 1902, citizens thought "Tucumcari" would be a more respectable name. Their inspiration was the lone, flat-topped butte nearby. Rising in two stages a thousand feet above its arid surroundings, the solitary mountain is the tallest object within sight on Route 66. If travelers could drive to the mountain's top, they could see for a hundred miles. But they can't, because two ranchers co-own the mountain now and won't allow access to it.

Indian legend, embellished by white man, has it that a chief once ordered two braves to go to the mountain's top and fight to the death for the hand of his daughter, Kari. As the other brave's knife found the heart of her lover, Tocom, Kari rushed out from hiding with her own knife and stabbed the victor in the heart. She then took Tocom's knife and plunged it into her heart. When the chief arrived and saw the carnage, he removed Kari's knife from the "victor's" chest and buried it in his own.

"Six Shooter Siding" would have been equally memorable. But in opting for Tucumcari, the town's incorporating fathers also chose one of the most euphonic city names in America. Mention it and folks want to go there, even though they're not quite sure where it is.

The name's natural lure has been enhanced by smart business

practice. If Route 66 sired the Motel Age, then Tucumcari—with more motel rooms and neon per capita than any other city except Las Vegas—whelped it. "Tucumcari Tonight!" proclaim a series of billboards stretching westward from Oklahoma City. "2,000 Motel Rooms." Stretching westward from Oklahoma City and eastward from California, the signs have made Tucumcari not just a dot on the map, but also a point in time. Though I-40 sounded an apparent death knell for other New Mexico towns such as San Jon and Bard (whose only building is the post office), Tucumcari has remained a natural and prosperous stopping place. The president of Yellow Transit, the country's largest trucking firm, visited town incognito one day, liked the friendly treatment he got, and located a terminal there. Three other trucking companies followed suit. And the railroad, after a ten-year absence, came back. More families live in Tucumcari now than ever before.

Jene Klaverweiden owned an Indian jewelry store on 66 when I-40 shunted the Tucumcari stretch of 66 aside in 1980. He remembers the exact day.

"It was just like somebody closed the gate," he said. "There was nothing! And I said, 'I'm going to starve to death!' But so help me, that night we did more business than we did the same night the previous year. The bypass got rid of all those trucks and traffic that didn't want anything but were forced to come down here anyway. The ones that go through now want something. So it didn't hurt us a bit.

"It made me sick when the former mayor changed the name of Old 66 to Tucumcari Boulevard. I can remember when it was one lane. But now there's more traffic on it during the daytime than there was before."

Jene and I had met the night before at the grand opening of the Caprock Amphitheater near San Jon. This morning we were having an early breakfast before I headed west again for Santa Rosa. Jene had run his jewelry store, the TeePee Trading Post, for eleven years. For a quarter century before that, he'd run a Texaco station on the west end of town. He calls himself retired now, but only if you count serving a second term as mayor as being retired.

His round face and clear accent could have placed Jene in any American town. But his words wedded him to the spot. "I moved to New Mexico in 1940," he said over a second cup of coffee. "And I'll tell you, Tom, there's just something about it. It's magical. People leave here. They're gone five or six years. But then they come back. I know I'd sure hate to leave. I'm gonna die here."

"I've dealt with the public all my life," His Honor said. "We used to trade cattle years ago—buy, sell and swap. Quit that. Then I was with Texaco for twenty-five years. And I studied the traffic, I studied the tourists. I'd see a bunch of cars coming from a long way off and I'd get in my car and drive off about two blocks. I'd sit until they got within a block and a half of me. Then I'd pull out in front of 'em, come down here, turn my blinker on, and pull in. So I'd get one or two of those and three or four others would follow them in.

"Same thing with the jewelry store. I'd study the tourists. I'd see a woman in a car looking in the store, wanting to come in. But there was a truck in back of her and so much congestion that she had to keep on going. Sometimes she would turn around and come back. Sometimes she wouldn't.

"So whenever I could, I'd park two or three cars out in front because people are more likely to stop when they see other people are already there."

When Jene bought the TeePee, it had just been converted from a laundromat. In an inspired example of architectural kitsch, a brightly painted concrete teepee graces the store's entrance and customers have to walk through it to get inside.

Looking back to his shopkeeping days, Jene said, "I miss that old store. It was a fascinating business. And when I started out, I didn't know turquoise from your cup there. But after almost killing myself working twenty-four hours a day at the station, I really enjoyed the TeePee. I could wear nice clothes. And the heaviest thing we had in the store weighed five pounds.

"I like to visit with people. When a customer walked through that door, I spoke to him—asked him if he was having fun, having a good trip, where he was from.

"I don't know. Maybe folks felt like they were obligated, but they'd buy. I wasn't doin' it just to get a dollar off of 'em, though—I just enjoy visiting. And I knew tourists appreciated somebody talking to them because they'd come back the next year. That was a warm feeling to see 'em walk in—even if I didn't recognize 'em. That was what 66 was like."

SEARCHING FOR 66

THIRTY-THREE

Jene Klaverweiden retired from everyday work in 1981 to travel and be mayor. It isn't much of a job, he alleged, and he spends more money on donuts for meetings than he draws in salary. But he has managed to get a utility rate increase passed without rancor. And he was also a leader in promoting local support and state dollars for the area's brand new entertainment attraction, the Caprock Amphitheater.

"You talked with Betty Philley at the grand opening last night," he said at our breakfast. "So you know if it weren't for her, we wouldn't have it. But the rest of us worked hard, too. I remember the first time we were scheduled for a hearing at the state capitol for some funds. They came in and said there'd been a riot at the state pen. Everything just stopped. When we finally got our hearing, they cut us back from 2.5 million dollars to 1.6. They told us no money for production—don't even bother to come back. We had to raise that ourselves.

"So we did. Got the motel owners to support a new room tax. We would like to have had a drama about Billy the Kid because this is his old stomping grounds. But we couldn't afford the production costs and we settled on the play you saw. But we got the place built. Now it's up to the cast and the play. We could fill the place with just the people who stay in Tucumcari every night."

The play sported the metaphorical title *Dream on a Blue Horse*. Arty TV spots advertised it as far away as Amarillo and Albuquerque. Tucumcari's newspaper, The Quay County *Sun*, ran front page stories about it. Lou Rigdon, a former shopkeeper, featured it on her morning radio show. And flyers and talk were everywhere.

The *Sun's* article described *Dream* as "a collage of images conveying the spirit of the Land of Enchantment with the theme centered around the myth of an American hero, the cowboy." Rebekah Gossett, a native New Mexican wrote the play and was directing it. High schoolers and college drama students made up a cowgirl chorus called the Blue Ponies; five "authentic New Mexican cowboys" comprised a mounted group called the Skyriders. Tucumcari's Hyram Posey, a fiddle champion and a Southern

Pacific engineer, wrote and performed the music. The only imported talent was Kim Loughran of Hollywood, who played the Cowboy. His credits, recounted by the *Sun*, included roles on TV's *Trapper John* and *Night Court* and spots in commercials for Carlsberg Beer, Long John Silver's, Toyota Trucks, and Friskies Cat Food.

All these dreams and plans had had the humblest of San Jon beginnings—Betty Philley couldn't get to sleep.

"I had an illness in 1975 that didn't let me sleep well," she told me one afternoon at her cafe. "And I've always been a dreamer anyway. So whenever I was awake at night, I'd think of things to do. I remembered that in 1952 and '53 the people from San Jon and Grady had an Easter pageant out here. They didn't have a theater—just an open area—and the people would come out here early with their chairs to get a good place to see. And I thought, 'Wouldn't it be nice to have an outdoor drama here about New Mexico?'"

Betty started talking with her friends about the idea. That summer, she organized a trip to over by Amarillo to see *Texas*, that state's highly successful outdoor drama. In the bicentennial year, she gathered endorsements from area Chambers of Commerce. Then in January of 1977, she read about the University of North Carolina's Institute of Outdoor Drama in *Grit*. Sitting at her kitchen table with two friends present for moral support, she called Martin Sumner, the Institute's director.

"We had nothing, but he came here," Betty said. "He toured the area with us and said we had a real feasible location here for an outdoor drama because we're so remote. And we said, 'Oh, we know.'"

Sumner's visit gave Betty's group enough credibility to win a grant from the New Mexico Heritage Conservation Commission for a feasibility study and easements to a proposed site. On the strength of that, they raised enough donations to have an architect draw up plans for the amphitheater. Originally, they wanted to carve it out of solid stone on another section of the caprock. But the state arranged a deal for land which had once belonged to the Boy Scouts

Next came the competition with other projects for state funds, then more fund raising for the play itself. By the time Betty and her friends were done, they counted practically the entire population of eastern New Mexico USA as patrons.

A tall, curly-haired woman, Betty proudly claimed status as a "real 66 person" because the highway has cut through her land four times. Her speech was plain and came in calm country tones; if she weren't getting caught up in her dreams all the time, she might even be considered shy. But dreams won't leave her alone. Resting up from another illness, she sat on her porch one day four years ago, gathering wool and counting the cars coming into the gas station across the street. When I-40 had left San Jon in its wake, all the cafes and all the other gas stations had closed. But Betty thought she counted enough traffic that day to support a cafe, so she took some from her cattle business and started one. By the time I met

Betty, the cafe was not only a success—it was the informal center of town.

"Caprock's been a lot of long, hard work," she said. "Between the cafe and the ranch and the amphitheater, I've worked twenty-two straight days. After the opening, I don't know whether to take the next day off or mend fence. But I never thought of giving up. We had a few problems, but we kept on."

Dorothy Kvols was another ardent backer of the Caprock project. Until her husband died in a car wreck on 66, she'd run a Western Auto Store with him. For the past fifteen years, she'd been the Tucumcari Chamber of Commerce.

"We're realizing a dream tomorrow night," she said when we met. "You really ought to come." Then she reached across the desk in her award-strewn office and called ahead to reserve me a ticket.

At 5:30 the next afternoon, I drove back toward San Jon, turned south just west of town, and drove through fields of blooming bush cactus toward a dream. The road wound slowly up the Caprock escarpment, depositing me at the edge in a dusty, wind-swirled parking lot. Below me now, the ground stretched away like an ocean—almost too vast to look at. Chalk one up for the dreamers, I thought; the site was spectacular.

Barbecue was being served from a covered wagon on the amphitheater's picnic grounds. Dorothy, Jene, Lou Rigdon, and practically everyone else I'd met the past two days were there, holding their plates against the wind with one hand and eating with the other. A contingent of seventy-one Baptists had even come up from Clovis and were holding a group sing in the corner.

Dusk came, jackets were pulled on, and the expectant crowd—some 400 people in all—filed into the amphitheater. Eleven years' of community effort were about to culminate in _Dream on a Blue Horse_. But before the evening was over, not a few folks would compare the experience more to a nightmare.

I liked the Blue Ponies. They danced, played drunken cowboys in bar scenes, and served as the play's Greek chorus. "Tell us the story...the story...the story," they echoed to the Cowboy. "Dream on, New Mexico!...Dream on...dream o-o-on." Folks may not have gone home uplifted or wiser from a Blue Ponies performance, but they wouldn't go home offended, either. Nor did the Woman in Scarlet bother people much. But when the Cowboy swaggered onto the stage and started using words like "damn" and "shit," things went all to hell.

I was more offended by such Cowboy lines as "The orange of the sunset warmed the veins of my heart like the glow of a red, red wine (CHORUS: "Wine...wine...wine")." But his "hells" and "damns" were what bothered the Baptists. They left during intermission.

Dorothy and Lou left, too. They weren't offended or upset—they'd just had enough. _Dream_ played its second act to about half its original audience. The Cowboy changed from mythic figure to fading rodeo star. The Woman in Scarlet became Ruby, the Greek chorus a car full of whining children who snuck out at night with long-haired cowboys. By drama's end, there was very little dream left.

Caprock board members who hadn't left during intermission stuck around when the full performance was over. When the greetings and congratulations and other formalities were over, they met for an hour and a half—not to discuss the play's artistic merits, but to figure out what to do about its offending language.

On the way home two months later, I stopped in San Jon on the afternoon of *Dream's* final performance. Betty urged me several times to go see it with her. But I had to be in Amarillo by morning and settled for a reprise.

After a few more "hells" and "damns" from an unruly and exuberant cast, Betty reported they'd finally rid the play of its problematic language and gone on to have a pretty good year.

"How many people did you draw?" I asked.

"We got eighty," she said.

"Eighty *thousand* people for the season?" I multiplied the amphitheater's thousand-seat capacity by sixty nights and got Standing Room Only.

"Eighty people a night, Tom."

"Oh." On opening night, Caprock directors feared a Baptist boycott. As things turned out, it was hard to tell who wasn't coming because nobody did. And here I was bringing up the subject to the play's chief dreamer. But Betty took no offense. She was still dreaming.

SEARCHING FOR 66

THIRTY-FOUR

On a Sunday morning in Santa Rosa, after two months on the road, I finally decided to take a day off and just wander around. My first stop was the Blue Hole in Santa Rosa. A natural artesian spring, ninety feet deep and sixty feet wide, it flows at 3,000 gallons a minute. The water comes up clean and clear through a bell-shaped granite cleft in the earth. But because of the water's great depth, dissolved alkali in it color it aquamarine. Then it pours out of a natural spout on the north side of the Hole and flows on to fill six other smaller lakes.

I sat in the shade of the manzanita trees which border the Blue Hole and watched scuba divers sample its depths. Down deep where it was so blue that I could see only vague forms, air perked in thousands of bubbles through the divers' gear. They joined together, then together again and again. Unhindered by currents other than the gentle upward push of the air inside them, the now-huge bubbles floated like stately, glassine spheres to

Abandoned adobe home in Puerto de Luna, New Mexico.

the surface. Once there, instead of popping or bursting, they just quietly returned to the atmosphere in gentle ripples. And then, as a diver exhaled, another chain of ephemeral jewels began its journey upward.

South of town an hour and a half later, I saw a bare, simple road sign that said "Puerto de Luna."

"Gateway to the moon," I translated. Thinking it might give some poetic balance to my earlier visit to the Blue Hole, I turned in the sign's direction. The road wound through a series of flatlands and low mesas. Several times I crossed a clear, sandy-bottomed river. Next day, I learned this gentle stream was that rowdy river of legend, the Pecos. But today I would never have guessed. It looked so cool and inviting that I parked my car and walked down.

At the bank, I stripped off my shoes and socks, rolled up my pants legs and waded in. Perfect. So perfect that I waded around a bend away from the road, laid aside the rest of my clothes and let the current carry me for the next hour.

Back on dry land and the road, I found Puerto de Luna was a dusty, 400-year-old footprint—an ancient adobe village founded by settled-out troops of Coronado. Thanks to their native soil, the adobes had a distinctive red caste. Many were abandoned because of age or economic exodus. All were small and, though the horizon was distant, few rose far against it. An air of vague sadness pervaded; the only moving object besides myself was a small herd of cows coming home for supper. I wandered around the centuries awhile, then got back on the road.

On the way home to Santa Rosa, near the bend where I'd gone drifting, I stopped to take a picture of an abandoned adobe farm home. It was an oddly-shaped house, with a narrow hallway connecting two one-room wings. Climbing back into my car, I glanced once more at the adobe and by chance noticed, on the tip of a distant butte, a huge white cross. Small roadside crosses commemorating highway deaths were once common sights along the length of 66. But this one in its distance was a very personal monument, I imagined, one which marked what must have been an immense tragedy.

Refreshed, relaxed and sandy, I tuned my car radio to the Santa Rosa station. After a conventional newsbrief at 5, it featured a most unusual show by a most unusual man: "The Old Route 66 Hour" with host Ron Chavez. I reached town in just a few minutes but, entranced, kept driving back and forth along the main drag until the whole hour had passed.

Ron Chavez, I learned, owned the Club Cafe on 66 in Santa Rosa. I'd bypassed it for breakfast that morning, though the large, circular painting of a smiling fat man above the door had seemed attractively tacky. I'd thought about going there for supper; soon there was no question.

The show's announcer served as disc jockey and interviewer. He played "Kawliga," then invited Ron to talk about his cafe.

"The Club Cafe is for real," Ron said sincerely and with the lightest trace of a Spanish accent. "Fifty-one years in the same location. But we've been bypassed. A huge freeway zooms right past us. Radio's the only way we can tell you about our sourdough biscuits. We know their starter is at least twenty years old—it may be fifty—and they are a real treat. Fresh, hot sourdough biscuits with honey is a true experience. [Did he pause ever so briefly to let listeners smack their lips?] It's the goldrush days again. It's the daring mountain man. It's you at the Club Cafe munching sourdough biscuits."

The DJ played "Wabash Cannonball." Ron talked about his gravy: "A French chef has complimented it. We've never had somebody tell us it was not good." Helen Reddy sang a tune; Ron bragged about his salsa. After "Streets of El Paso," the announcer posed a question.

Ron Chavez at the Club Cafe, Santa Rosa, New Mexico.

"Tell us, Ron—what makes Club Cafe chili so right, so delicious, so doggone special?"

"Customers have told me horror stories about how it's cooked elsewhere," came the soft tones. "But when we set out to make chili, we started analyzing it. My grandma can make you a bowl of chili that is just something heavenly. A lot of people can say that, though. But what are you going to do when you make it in hundreds of gallons? This is where the test comes in. Yeah. You have to make it *different*. There's a *different* chemistry involved in the cooking. So we worked on it and evolved it and created it."

Another brief pause for lipsmacking.

"When we set out to feed people, Mike, we set our standards high. Well, the only standard you can set when you're feeding people is to satisfy their appetites. What you get at the Club Cafe represents chili cooked with a lot of love, a lot of care. And we want to make sure when you eat the chili that it satisfies your appetite for chili."

"One bowl of red chili," I said to the waitress right after the show. Ron wasn't at the cafe that night, but by the cash register I found a business card with his home phone number on it. Back at my motel, I called him. From those first moments on the phone and throughout the nine hours of conversation Ron and I would eventually have, the talk flowed full, fast and smooth—like there would never be enough time for it all.

"What did you do in Sahnta Rossa today?" Ron asked early in our first conversation.

"I spent an hour at the Blue Hole."

"That's on old, old 66."

"In the afternoon, I went to Puerto de Luna."

"No kidding? That's my hometown!"

"And then I took a 'dip' in the river."

A distinctly American chuckle came over the wire. "That's the Peckos. I spent many, many hours as a boy in that river. I know why you went."

Next morning I came down to the cafe early for breakfast. The Club has no plastic mansards, no backlit menus, no trim that was stamped out on a press, or peeled out of a mould. The cafe's sign used to be neon, but is now white block letters. Flush above the windows which run the building's length and breadth, a Navajo-style rendering of a road runner is repeated several times. Interrupting this design above the entrance, on a seven-foot wooden circle, is a head-and-shoulders painting of the Fat Man—a double-chinned, no-neck fellow with a receding hairline, almond eyes, well-padded cheeks, and an enigmatic wedge of a smile. He may or may not have just eaten—I couldn't tell. But he was thinking about it and he was happy. After biscuits with chile-flecked gravy, so was I.

With their sharp, angular features, ninety percent of the Club's help—like ninety percent of this town—looked like they could have been a Chavez. Later I would learn that a great many were. But I sensed this morning that none of them were Ron and I left the cafe unannounced for an hour of gazing at the Blue Hole.

I came back promptly at 10, walked up to a stocky, salty-haired man standing by the cash register and said, "Ron?"

"Tom! Come on back to my business booth and sit down!"

A waitress poured coffee and I sketched out my trip to date.

"You're doing very deep research," Ron said, more in appreciation than compliment. "Everything has meaning to you, whether it's interesting or uninteresting."

Like Reba Collins, I sensed Ron would need no warming to his subject, so I got right down to some of that deep research.

"*Who* is the Fat Man?" I asked

"The Fat Man is more famous than the rest of us put together," Ron said, extending a palm grandly toward the sign. "He used to be on twenty-six billboards! But he's strictly a figment of the original owner's imagination. Phil Craig wanted to create an image. He wanted to have this man with a white napkin spread across with his arms sticking up, getting ready to dig into a big, big steak."

Ron tucked in an imaginary napkin and held up invisible utensils, a constant choreographer of his speech. Craig never did get the look he was after, Ron said, but he did create a look which no one's since been able to duplicate: a smile at least as mysterious as the Mona Lisa's—and seen by millions more in person. The Fat Man isn't Ron, as some people think, but he could well be a Chavez.

"I never had an inkling what impact the Fat Man had on people, though, until Lady Bird Johnson introduced highway beautification," Ron said. "I got letters from all over the country—You can't imagine!—for me to send that face at any cost *collect*. That's when I realized how important he was."

From that realization grew a movement which, said Ron, saved not only the Fat Man, but all billboards along all American highways.

"It was part of Lady Bird Johnson's Highway Beautification Campaign," Ron said with unusual calm. "I went out there and they were chopping on my boards. They were actually chopping on them. And I thought, 'Here's an old, old tradition about to disappear.' So being a fighter and having nothing to lose, I protested—I filed an injunction to stop it. At the time, I had no-o ide-a how I would stop it permanently. But Route 66 would have lost a lot of its flavor without the Fat Man."

That simple, lone act of protest soon put Ron in the national forefront of people protesting highway "beautification." He wrote letters, called congressmen, and traveled to hearings as far away as Washington, D.C. Fellow Santa Rosa merchants even sponsored his trip to the final, decisive hearing in Dallas. One of the few private citizens there amidst batteries of government officials and sign company lawyers, Ron gave the testimony which turned the tide.

Back at the cafe, my host jabbed his index fingers down and brought them together for emphasis. "And all I did was tell the story of Route 66...of people," he said. "Everybody was allowed fifteen minutes, but all I spoke was five. I concentrated. I said, 'Look, we're just folks out here in little bitty towns. Insignificant to the big picture. But we're folks. And it's a way of life.'

"I said, 'Let me give you the history of my people. We were farmers in the little village of Puerto de Luna. Along came the trucks that would haul produce and goods across the country, so it was no longer profitable for us to raise crops on those little farms.

"'In the meantime, Route 66 was established and a tourist business developed and we got into it. We moved to Santa Rosa and became dishwashers and cooks. We weren't even owners yet—we came in through the bottom.

"'Then the interstate came—and another major upheaval. Done by somebody else making the decision. No consideration as to what it was going to do to the economic system of the people, to the traditions. You take 66 away and bypass us and the only way we have to tell people about us is the billboards. Now you want to remove them, too!'"

The triumph flashed brand new across Ron's face. "That brought the house down," he said. "I told them, 'Look what you're doing to us! You're going to dry up the little towns which add flavor to anybody's travels. Do you want us all to move to the cities and live like rats? Or are we going to sustain a rural people?'

"And I never once used the restaurant. Never once did I mention it. I touched on us as a people, as a way of life, as a tradition. And would you believe that they still haven't taken action on the billboards? It's still in suspense!"

Ron leaned back, arms propped on the booth's cushions, and relaxed in victory remembered.

"I started getting calls from all over the country to go speak on this because no one had thought of that approach," he said. "But I didn't take them up. I didn't want to be away from my business that long. I told them to just pick up the same theme. I told them if they can't tell their own story, then I certainly am not."

A hard judgment, seemingly, but the only owners who've survived along 66, Ron said, are the workers and the fighters.

"I started out here as a shoeshine boy out front," he said. "Came in as a dishwasher, a bus boy, and learned how to cook. Then I left the scene. I was in California eighteen years. When I came back, I came back with new eyes and a fresh mind. I had to promote. Before, when 66 went by, you didn't have to do that. You would just open the doors and—bingo!—you were full.

"That's when I came up with the radio show idea. Route 66 really was a cross section. And when you count who crossed it, then you have the whole country. So I talked about the highway on my show. And by golly, it worked. It started to work. People started coming and finding us again. Most of them were old customers—they'd just got disoriented."

As a hedge against the interstate's onslaught, Ron has built a new restaurant, the Red Rooster, just off the superhighway's eastern exit ramp to Santa Rosa. Operating on the "Summer makes it and winter takes it" principle, he's in the black. But Ron thinks the Club's future will always be perilous and even the Red Rooster may not survive. As the noon crowd came in, he explained why he has such doubt. It's a problem which he calls the "Blanding of America."

"They tell me if this restaurant were anywhere else, you couldn't get into the place," he said. "A man told me if I moved this restaurant to New Orleans, I would be a wealthy man. But I'm *not* there and I don't want to *be* there. I came back here and I have a very good life here.

"But I think this one-of-a-kind restaurant is disappearing fast. It's too labor intensive. The average cook in my organization has been here over eight years. I have to give my people good direction. I have to find ways to get them to take pride in their position. They have to love pleasing people with food. They have to take pride in those plates."

He sighed. "They built a Pizza Hut in Santa Rosa not long ago.

That's a sign. They all have absentee owners. They're faceless. They have no personality. You just see some little gal there with a cute hat and a name tag. That's it. And that's what you're gonna see across country."

I speculated there might be an innate need for places like the Club.

"I certainly hope you're right, Tom," Ron said. "But you can't just survive—you have to thrive. I'm riding on the seat of my pants now. It gets thinner and thinner and I can't tell you how much longer we'll be able to exist.

"See, we're not educated people here. We don't have a business tradition. We don't have a large inheritance. This *is* our life. You see the la-a-ast of it, the last....of needing to have it. When that vanishes, so will Route 66. The minute they put a McDonald's in this town, that's gonna be the punch. You can kiss my ass good-by."

I'd never seen a man face a gloomy prospect like that and yet be so enthusiastic.

"I'm in my own envelope here," Ron explained. "In the old days, if you didn't have a desire to go to California, you weren't a good New Mexican. So I went and managed a meat department in a grocery store in Monterey for eighteen years."

"But I wanted to come ho-ome," he said, bringing the word safely in with a wave of his fist. "I realized that when I started to write. I was trying to write about people and places back here and it wasn't working. So I came home.

"I like the semi-desert. I know there's more beautiful wooded lands and things like that. But I like the semi-desert. I like to go out on the llana—the plains. I like to give people tours of it and show them things they wouldn't notice on their own. It's one of the driest and flattest areas in the country, but the contrasts make it beautiful. Knowing that your family's been here for four or five centuries helps, too."

I mentioned that on my own tour the day before, I had seen a large cross on a distant mesa. Ron was amazed.

"That's part of the mystique of my tours!" he said. "When I was a little kid, I walked up the hill to that cross. It's huge and it's white and I have never found anybody who knows why it's there. So on my tours, I've manufactured stories."

I said I'd love to go on one those tours and hear a few of those stories. Ron had a full afternoon of appointments, but asked me to come back at 6 for dinner—he'd do the ordering—and then we'd go on a Chavez Special Tour of the New Mexican back country.

Dinner, for which I arrived punctually, featured salsa and green chile for appetizers, a chile relleno, a tamale, an enchilada with shredded—not ground—meat and carne adovada, which is pork marinated in pure red chile. For dessert, there were sopapillas and apple pie ala mode sprinkled with cinnamon. I lost ten pounds during my search for 66, but certainly none of them at the Club Cafe.

On our way to Puerto de Luna after dinner, the late sun darkened one side of the road while giving the other side its most brilliant colors of the day. Land of contrasts, Ron said, land of enchantment. He pointed out rock streams—flows of boulders down mesa sides which might take a thousand years to reach the bottom. Yet Ron can tell when they move. He pointed out a broad spread of mesquite being strangled by the sand which its foliage caught from the wind and piled up. "That'll be a desert someday unless they take the mesquite out," Ron said. Driving on, he explained how junipers survive on otherwise barren slopes by trapping rainfall in natural rock cisterns.

We poked the car through the same herd of cows as the day before and got into Puerto de Luna just as the sun was setting. Standing at a corner of a 200-year-old adobe, Ron showed me how the bricks had fused together over the generations.

"Someday, I plan to retire from the Club Cafe and write a novel about this area," he said, propping an arm on the old adobe. "I'll start it with a young Comanche boy when his nation was still strong, then take him to when it was a remnant. The Comanches were so savage.....because their way of living was strictly hunting and raiding. Nobody liked them, but that was their way and this is what I want to bring out. They were very, very little in religion—they ran by the seat of their pants, by their wits. And because of that, they survived for a hundred and fifty years.

"Then I'm gonna have a young Spaniard, which is my character, come along when the Comanche's an old man and tell his story through my eyes."

Ron drifted off a century or two. "You know something?" he finally said. "They call America a melting pot. But I see it more as a mosaic. We fit together some, like a puzzle. But we're still separate peoples with our own edges. That's what makes this country beautiful. That's what makes us strong."

Route 66 in its earliest form was also a mosaic—a motley, ill-fitting gathering of contiguous bits of road, trail, path and avenue. But just as concrete bound it together, 66 became the glue which bound the larger mosaic called America. Now that glue is cracking. The interstates bind us today and the mosaic we had is melting away. Owner-operated businesses like the Club are giving way to franchise management just as surely as Puerto de Luna gave way to Route 66. In Ron's book, one seat-of-the pants survivor tells the story of another. But who will come along when Ron's an old man and tell *his* story? Who will survive the Blanding of America?

SEARCHING FOR *66*

THIRTY-FIVE

"Be sure you have your auto jack. A short piece of wide, flat board on which to rest the jack in sandy soil is a sweat-preventer. Include a steel tow rope, tire tools, tire pump, tire patches, and tire chains. It is assumed that you have adequate brakes, lights, license plates, and a good windshield wiper.

"Carry a spare gallon of gas and spare water in the desert areas. Throw a can or two of motor oil in the rear compartment, too. One of those war surplus foxhole shovels takes little space and comes in very handy. Put new batteries and a new bulb in your flashlight. For chilly nights and early mornings, you'll find a camp blanket or auto robe useful—and it comes in handy if you find inadequate bedding in a tourist cabin. Don't forget sunglasses for each member of the party. An altimeter and auto compass may also come in handy.

"You probably won't use all of this stuff, but an hour spent in assembling it before you leave will give you peace of mind, and may save you half a day of discomfort if something does happen....Hardly a month goes by that some motorist does not die who would have lived if he had had such equipment."

Jack Rittenhouse, former Hoosier and aspiring writer, published these pearls of caution and advice in his 1946 volume *A Guide Book to Highway 66*—the first book length treatment the highway ever received. Fellow Illinoisan Sandy Schackel, who'd read my letter in the Albuquerque *Tribune*, told me Jack lived in Albuquerque now. So when I got there, I found a decent motel, then called him. Before I could ask, he invited me over.

"On the road, it's wise to sleep a little longer than you would at home since you are in a "strange bed" and are more tired physically. Try going to bed early, getting up before dawn, so you can take the road with the first faint light.

"In night driving—if you must drive at night—drive until you feel sleepy, then stop and sleep a while in the car, sitting up. The cramped posi-

tion will not allow you to sleep long, but the nap will "take the edge off" your sleepiness, and allow you to drive another good stretch before you again feel sleepy.

Jack had studied history and English at Indiana Teachers College in Terre Haute for three years. But when the Depression dropped the bottom out of the job market, he dropped out of college and went to New York. By 1934, he was a clerk in a magazine store in the Bowery "for a salary of $5 a week and the privilege of sleeping on a cot in the back room."

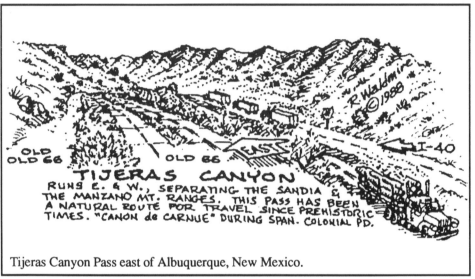

Tijeras Canyon Pass east of Albuquerque, New Mexico.

"But I'd always wanted to be a writer," he said. "So I rented a typewriter. It cost me $2 a month. And I'd get up every morning about 6, cook breakfast, and write. I'd do two or three pages about some character or person that I'd seen on the street the day before. I kept it for awhile, but eventually threw it all away. I wasn't writing for publication—just for practice."

World War II came, bringing Jack marriage, a job writing technical manuals for the Air Force in Los Angeles, and a constant battle with his draft board.

"I had a whole scrapbook full of draft cards," he said, holding up an imaginary string of them and letting them fall down. "I went all the way from 3-A (married) to 1-A. I even went all the way up to 'You are to be inducted. Report for your physical.' Then they decided I was too old—32—and put me back to 2-A."

Jack finally put his draft board to rest by volunteering for stateside active duty in the National Guard.

"They made me a mess sergeant—and I didn't even have any kitchen equipment. I must have done pretty well, though, because they made me a second lieutenant after six months. Then I resigned my commission and went back to civilian life.

"And I never got shot at—as far as I know."

"On the road, don't drink too much liquid, because your kidneys will soon proclaim the strain, which is bad enough after several hours' driving anyway. Do not eat heavy meals in the morning or at noon, and avoid starches.

"And DON'T WORRY! There are no impossible grades and you'll never be more than a score of miles from gas, even in the most desolate areas."

Jack's longtime desire had been to someday write a book. Tech manuals notwithstanding, he was approaching middle age and still hadn't reached that goal. But he was always looking for the right idea, the right chance. It finally came for him in 1945 as the war was winding down.

"I had a hunch that when the war was over, a lot of people would be heading west on 66," he said over the whine of a window fan and the clink of ice in our tea glasses. "I also knew to anyone—there was no TV then—the only landscape they'd ever seen was in *National Geographic* and *Life Magazine*. There was always this wonder about what was out beyond. So many people had never been over 66—they wouldn't know where the desert begins, how to get over the mountains, or anything. Friends thought I was kind of nutty, but I thought easterners could use this book. So I did it."

Jack started out by reading the WPA's writers' guides to each state along the way. He corresponded with Chambers of Commerce on the route and his wife wrote down the elevation of each town from an altitude dictionary. To bring it all together, he made a month-long sweep from LA to Chicago and back.

"I drove all by myself in a '39 Bantam, the successor to the American Austin," Jack said. "It was a tiny little car and had about twenty-two horsepower, but the wartime speed limit of 35 miles an hour helped me.

"I kept a clipboard on the seat beside me and just wrote things down as I went. I couldn't see because I was driving—I'd just write. At night, I would type my notes up, then mail them back to my wife the next day. That way, if something happened to me along the route or if the car caught fire, the typed notes would survive."

Back home in L.A., Jack set the type, drew the pictures, and self-published three thousand copies of his book for $900. He sold it by mail order to businesses along the route, charging them 60 percent of the book's $1 cover price. At about the time he should have been considering a reprint, a map company back east came out with a 66 book which *retailed* for only 60 cents.

"It didn't have half the information," Jack said. "But it had enough. That was the end of my travel book career."

A lifetime of book learning has given Jack's speech an articulate, precise tone. He spoke readily, even with excitement, yet knew the purpose of every word he used.

"Getting that Library of Congress number on your card was like seeing your epitaph on bronze in Westminster Abbey," he said. "This is going to be forever. I am immortal. It was my first book and I've got to admit—it was a pleasure, a kick. I never felt the same about anything else I wrote. I've had more satisfaction out of other books since, but...."

Jack moved to New Mexico in 1962, where he eventually retired as editor of western books for the University of New Mexico Press. He continued to self-publish fine books as a sideline, issuing such tomes as a book on Wendish, a German-Czech-Polish dialect spoken in 19th century Texas by immigrants. In retirement, he runs a mail order business in rare books. Only in the past few years has he become the subject of research himself.

"I'm somewhat embarrassed to be considered knowledgeable or an expert on Route 66," Jack said. "I wasn't an expert. I was one guy who made the trip and took notes. That's about the best I can say."

In methodical fashion, one guy's *Guide Book to Highway 66* lists each town on the route, its altitude, population, and distance from the next town in each direction—plus all the major tourist attractions, hotels, motels, gas stations, cafes and garages. The narrative is a mixture of travel advice, local lore, and occasional sociologic observation:

"*SAYRE, Oklahoma*—Joseph Benton, who took the stage name Giuseppe Bentonelli when he became a Metropolitan Opera star in 1935, came here as a child and still has relatives here. Jess Willard, a famous prize fighter, once drove a wagon freight line from here and also ran a lodging house.

"*Near the CALIFORNIA-ARIZONA Border*—Water faucet at the roadside here for cars that need water on the climb driving east.

"*BETHANY, Oklahoma*—This town was founded in 1906 by the Church of the Nazarene and they laid down certain community regulations which still stand. No cigarettes, tobacco or alcoholic drinks are sold in town, and there are no theaters.

"*HOUCK, Arizona*—Navajos are nearly always lounging around the trading post, drinking the soda pop they enjoy. The Navajos are a quiet tribe, whose deft ability in silverwork made them useful in many war plants requiring fine assembly work during the war. They are not allowed to vote, but were subject to the draft during the war.

"*Near EL RENO, Oklahoma*—the U.S. Southwestern Reformatory was built here, costing over a million dollars. No admittance to visitors.

"*WINSLOW, Arizona*—In the Lorenzo Hubbell Motor Company showroom is the world's largest Navajo rug: 21 feet by 37 feet. It required two years to weave and weighs 240 pounds.

"*ELK CITY, Oklahoma*—An unusual experiment in group medical care is being conducted in this community: each family pays $25 a year, for which they receive all medical attention. The Farmers Union has supported the project, which was launched by a local physician.

"*GOLDROAD, Arizona*—For eastbound cars which cannot make the Gold Hill grade, a filling station here offers a tow truck which will haul your car to the summit. At last inquiry, their charge was $3.50, but may be higher.

"*DESERT TRAINING CENTER, California*—Where U.S. troops trained for the North African campaign during World War II. Hunters and prospectors still find abandoned jeeps and other equipment, and recently found the body of an officer who died of thirst when he became lost."

Food was a common object of Jack's attention:

"*In BRAIDWOOD, Illinois,* is the famous Peter Rossi Macaroni plant.
"*CHANDLER, Oklahoma*—The town ships considerable honey and pecans.
"*EDGEWOOD, New Mexico*—The principal business here is the shipment of pinto beans—a western dish you have probably sampled by the time you have reached this far.
"*GRANTS, New Mexico*—is perhaps most noted for its vegetable crops, of which carrots are the most prominent.
"*VICTORVILLE, California*—Once there were many orchards here, but now it is devoted to turkey ranches and potato farms."

He discovered Route 66 had a lot of cemeteries:

"*MOUNT OLIVE, Illinois*—Here there is a monument over the grave of "Mother Jones," a famous woman leader of the miners who died in 1930 at the age of 100.
"*West of LUTHER, Oklahoma*—At 89 miles, you pass an old cemetery with a few old graves with old fashioned markers.
"*CANUTE, Oklahoma*—The town contains several cotton gins in sheet metal structures and a Catholic cemetery with some unusual bronze statuary.
"*OLD CEMETERY in New Mexico*—Originally a boothill in the roaring days of nearby Montoya, but now a burial ground for the Mexican people of the vicinity [actually Spanish New Mexicans] who decorate the graves with bits of colored china, glass, broken toys and other bric-a-brac."

Jack's thumbnails of the route's smaller towns were often poignant in their brevity:

"*HOFFLINS, Missouri*—Truly a small town; one store and a home. But it has a post office.
"*FANNING, Missouri*—The new 66 almost cut off the one store and meeting hall which comprise this community.
"*BAXTER SPRINGS, Kansas*—A green and quiet town with an ancient, bloody history.
"*BUSHLAND, Texas*—A few railroad buildings, three grain elevators and a church complete this small village on the flat Texas plains.
"*ENDEE, New Mexico*—Only three establishments in this hamlet, including its school. "

And though it would be sixteen years before Jack made New Mexico his home, he was already experiencing its pull. He devoted twenty-three of his book's 128 pages to the Land of Enchantment—more than any other state got:

"After a few more twists and dips, you suddenly come out of the Tijeras Canyon. Opening before you is the wide valley of the Rio Grande, in which Albuquerque is located. If it is at night when you approach the city, its myriad lights will resemble an upside-down heaven spread before you.

"...West of Albuquerque, the highway enters upon an area of richly colored desert and mesa, upon which herds of sheep and occasionally cattle graze. The vistas stretch interminably into the distance, and the inverted turquoise bowl of the sky becomes a mingling of indescribably beautiful colors at sunset.

"...You truly now are in a fabulous land."

But the poetry, the affecting descriptions of towns hanging on to the edge of existence, the often trenchant sociological observations were all incidental add-ons. And Jack's book's eventual place in the pantheon of 66 history wasn't even dreamed of.

"It was only a little 128-page thing to help people through their trip," Jack said. "And they were small pages at that. I meant it to be strictly utilitarian. When people were on this road, they didn't need romance. They needed information.

"And I didn't think of the mystique of Route 66 when I did the book, either. That highway was like the steam locomotive. Nobody glamorized the steam locomotive until it was gone. We were living with magic and didn't even know it."

When I left, Jack sold me an original copy of *A Guide Book to Highway 66*. It was a small book, just like he said—about the size of a dime western—and featured a stagecoach and cactus on its cover. I got it for the going rate of $25. Three years later, demand for the book had grown so much that the University of New Mexico Press republished it. It's now available up and down the route for only $7.

SEARCHING FOR 66

THIRTY-SIX

New Mexico's strong spiritual pull on its people—be they native or immigrant—has found artistic expression as diverse and striking as the land itself. Georgia O'Keeffe, an Amarillo emigree, juxtaposed mountains, cattle skulls and wildflowers—elements from her reality—to create images of haunting, unforgiving beauty—unmistakably New Mexican. Novelists Willa Cather and Conrad Richter lovingly and skillfully recreated the New Mexico landscape in some of their best work. Santa Fe's annual chamber music festival, set in the shadow of the Sangre de Cristo Mountains, is as dramatic as the O'Keeffe posters which advertise it. And Indian artists in cities, pueblos and hogans have taken formerly frozen forms of weaving, pottery, carving, sculpting, painting, and jewelry-making into individualistic new dimensions.

In the world of New Mexico arts, Albuquerque for decades lay in the shadow of Taos and Santa Fe, its more glamorous neighbors to the north. Since World War II, though—inconspicuously at first and then with increasing boldness—the Duke City has laid claim to the considerable title of Cultural Capital of New Mexico. A self-proclaimed "cultural corridor" in the city stretches from the state fairgrounds eight miles west to Old Town. It includes seven museums, a dozen public art galleries, fifty private art galleries, twenty theaters and other sites for live performances—plus dozens bookstores, cafes and studios.

The acknowledged spine of this burgeoning corridor is an old friend in an unfamiliar role: Route 66. A blue collar, commercial backbone for most other cities it traverses, the Father of Highways in Albuquerque has become an invocation of the arts.

As part of the city's second annual arts festival, I saw along 66, called Central Avenue here, a series of displays called *Art Windows on 66*—art exhibits in storefront windows which ranged from traditional paintings to mannequins in feather dresses to elaborate Dungeons and Dragons sets.

Even the neon which decorates the hundreds of motels, cafes and other businesses along the corridor has been elevated to the level of folk art. A committee of arts backers, ring led by expatriate Brooklynite Alice Kaufman, spent hundreds of hours cruising the strip early in 1986, debating the merits of each neon. They then compiled the best of the signs into "The Central Avenue Drive-It-Yourself Neon Tour." The tour's brochure features a map, plus commentary on twenty-two "must-see" neons along a 15-mile stretch.

The Westward Ho Motel, the guide says, "looks like a set from a Sam Shepard play." The lasso-throwing cowboy at the El Don Motel "embodies the spirit of Route 66." Johnson's Rib Hut has a "good neon Pig." The Route 66 Boutique sign is praised as "an energetic example of New Wave neon with Russian Constructionist roots." Neon trim on the portal of the Yen Ching Chinese Restaurant "gives it the look of a Sunset Boulevard car wash." And at the Zia Motor Lodge, art aficionados are advised to "forget the sign—the zias (Indian sun symbols) on the windows and the zig zag trim on the eaves are the stars of this show."

Albuquerque's Old Town is the oldest part of the oldest city on Route 66. It was originally a colonial farming village and military outpost on the Camino Real. Today it is a densely-packed half square mile of shops, galleries, restaurants, museums and open air markets—the western anchor of the Arts Corridor—and a great place for wandering.

In a room off the courtyard of an adobe-style mini-mall, though, I thought I'd wandered too far. The sign outside had been safe-sounding enough, but as soon as I walked into the Native American Art Gallery, a sense of foreboding hung on me. From every wall and rafter, angular, exaggerated faces of Indian men peered out. Silently but boldly, they gave this paleface intruder the once-over. They numbered at least a hundred, and before I knew it, I was entirely surrounded.

Dressed in blankets and ceremonial robes, the braves presented a traditional veneer. But outsized, elongated feathers, jutting chins, stretched-out bodies and brilliant colors on light backgrounds gave the figures a clearly modern, even surreal look. Several men also wore sunglasses which had been glued to the canvas. One held an ice cream cone. Titles like "That Guy" and "Modern Guy #2" predominated. Soon the threatening look faded to merely impenetrable; I relaxed and enjoyed their company.

"See anybody you recognize?" Sam English, the gallery's owner and artist-in-residence, had been leaning back in his chair, feet propped up on the easel, talking into a Mickey Mouse phone when I walked in. The phone rang often during the half day I wound up spending with Sam. Since each caller got the courtesy of an unhurried conversation, leaning back was a common position for him.

"I think I see you once or twice," I said. "But who are these other folks?"

"They could be reservation Indians, urban Indians, Indian people that I met at powwows—which is where I got the idea for sunglasses." He pointed to his work in progress. Four men stood in ceremonial dress, the bright colors of their robes running down into the ground like fading roots. "This guy here could be a lawyer during the week. This one may be a doctor or a ditch digger or a tribal councilman. They could be anybody."

Which is Sam's point about Indians in general.

Sam English, Albuquerque, New Mexico.

"Artists must feel close to their people and feel very concerned about them," he said. "And I just couldn't do that painting pictures of a brave on a pony with a spear. I think Native American covers everything that's happened to us, and that includes modern times. Indian people live *today*—and that's a lot different than yesterday."

We wandered in and out of other subjects for a while. One of us told a joke. Sam laughed easily and heartily. A phone call came. After an indeterminate length of time, we started talking seriously about Sam's art.

"I admit I've never seen Indians like this before," I said, gesturing to the assembled tribe. "But how can you call them modern when they're all wearing blankets and robes?"

Sam smiled, perhaps patiently. In repose, his features were rounded. But in mirth, they showed the strongly angular lines I'd seen in his paintings.

"It's the way they feel," he said, "the way they look. I don't think many Indians have made the transition from traditional to contemporary. Most of them leave the reservation and they drink and die....or they stay home and drink and die. Others leave and forget where they came from. But the people in these pictures have made it. These guys here could be doctors and lawyers during the week, but they're also Indians. They may be urban like me, but they also have their culture and traditions. I want to show both.

"And I want to show their sense of humor, too, because if we didn't have that we wouldn't have survived. That's why I have things like sunglasses and ice cream cones."

Sam has drawn and painted all his life. But it wasn't until he reached 33 that he got away from the brave on a pony with a spear.

"I'd been married and divorced and I'd had my own war with alcohol," he said, feet propped back up on the easel. "I was thirty hours short of a degree in business administration and I was in a training program with the Bureau of Indian Affairs to become a tribal operations specialist. And then I thought, 'Where are you going? Are you going to spend the rest of your life this way?'

"You have to make decisions. You can get into the easy life and be there all your life. Or you can get creative. I decided to be creative and devote all my time to painting. So I got a $35,000 loan from the SBA. Now I'm working damn near every day, but I have a studio and a gallery and a place to live. And I can change and find what I want to do."

Sam leaned forward in his chair, picked up a brush, and added a lavender stripe to a lawyer-brave's robe. Though one-quarter Anglo (his grandmother was a kidnapped English woman, hence his last name), nothing but his dominant Chippewa blood showed in his intense expression.

"Why do all the men have two feathers?" I asked.

"One represents birth and the other represents coming of age," Sam said. "I haven't gone beyond that yet—I don't know about the guy who's going to have three feathers."

Might that third feather represent immortality—the immortality which Sam might gain through his paintings?

The artist's chunky face rounded into another smile at the thought. "I don't know," he said. "I don't want my pictures to become worth a lot of money after I die. I don't want people to look at one of my paintings a hundred years from now and say, 'Poor guy.' I want the money now."

Starting his own gallery instead of working through other galleries and middle men was a correct first step in the money direction. Sam spoke self-assuredly of the strategy.

"Art is a very tough, competitive business," he said. "A lot of very talented people don't make it. A man creates a watchband that should market for $500, but he's lucky to get $300 for it. That's because the buyer and the gallery have to make money, too. Plus, the artist has to be sure to make a watchband that the middle man and the gallery like—he's at their disposal.

"That's what you have to contend with, being an Indian artist. For decades and decades, tourists from back east would come through here on your Route 66 and want to buy a rug or a pot just like what their neighbor bought last year. Buyers and galleries knew this and they played it safe. And that's how we got the brave-on-a-pony syndrome—they told us that was what people wanted, so that's what we did. Indian artists had no control over their situation. If they wanted to do something new, they were on their own."

Which is exactly the way Sam likes it. He's one of a small, but growing handful of Indian artists who run their own galleries. A recent issue of *Arizona Highways* had called modern Indian artists "The New Individualists." The term applies in the business world as well as artistic sense.

"If I didn't have this gallery, I would certainly be painting," Sam said. "But I would be at other people's disposal. So I'm not. If people buy my stuff now, they're gonna come here. They're not gonna go anywhere else. So they may bypass me. But that's the risk I have to run.

"It's been tough. There aren't that many people around to buy $500 paintings. But the last five shows I've been to, I didn't have to ask—I got invited. I just keep going and keep going—New York, Chicago, St. Louis, all over the West. I don't know if my work has risen to fine art yet, but it is getting a lot of national attention. And I like it—it makes me feel good."

Maybe someday it will make Sam rich, too. As he approached 40, he was an Indian artist in two senses of the word: he painted Indians and he was an Indian who painted. Might he one day shed one of those senses, I wondered, and become just an artist who happens to be an Indian?

"Oh yeah," Sam said readily, looking forward to the possibility. "In fact, I'm working on a painting like that now. But I have to do my own culture and tradition first. It gives me the opportunity, the visibility, the chance later on to try something else. I'm certainly not going to sit here and try to produce the likes of Picasso or El Greco—they represented their own life, their own experience. If I did anything else now, I couldn't survive.

"One thing I like about this work, though, is that I've met people from all over the world—New Zealand, South Africa, the Sudan, Brazil, Israel, Hawaii. And I get to travel a lot, too. I like driving 66, but someday I'd also like to go to Greece. I don't know why. The mythology, maybe. I'd also like to go see Turkey—you read about it and hear about it, but you don't know what goes on down there. And I'd like to go down to

Mexico and visit the pyramids and the Yucatan."

Already an artist and businessman, the New Individualist is also becoming a citizen of the world. The risk of this is that the Indian may someday not be red anymore, but just another shade of off-white. And the irony is that Sam himself is an agent of the process. He's mixing the cultures in his painting now. But someday he hopes his work will be....less Indian. He isn't selling out, though—like millions before him on 66, he's selling in.

SEARCHING FOR *66*

THIRTY-SEVEN

Auto court, motor lodge, motor inn, motor hotel, auto hotel, cottage court, auto motel, travelers' home, tourist court, tourist cottages, tourist inn, roadside cabins, roadside inn, motor court, hotel court. Roadside lodging along 66 has had many names. But whatever the label, if you could park outside your door, it was a motel. The first were mom and pop affairs. The latest are corporate franchises. The lot are an American institution.

Before paved highways, we had downtown hotels. They offered crosscountry and professional travelers leisure and community. But as 66 and other new highways let Americans travel farther and faster, convenience and speed became more important. Thus the motel. Early ones were often hasty affairs—simple clusters of cabins around a driveway. For furniture, they offered little more than beds—and those had flat springs and thin mattresses. Clothes were hung on hooks, toilet facilities were communal, and "air-cooled" meant you got a fan. But as the Depression waned, improvements began. First, the mattresses got better. Then toilets and showers were installed. Next came heat and furnishings—bed lamps, chests of drawers, closets and full length mirrors. Outside, the grounds were landscaped and pools were built. Some even added restaurants. Daily rent ranged from $4 to $8. At the industry's pre-interstate peak, there were 20,000 motels in America with an average of 22 rooms apiece.

During their first three decades, most motels were owner-operated—true mom and pops. And so long as cross country traffic flowed along their highways, they flourished. But in the interstate age, travel patterns changed dramatically—frequently overnight with the opening of new stretches of superhighway. Mom and Pop may have liked to move up to the new road, but they couldn't. All their capital was tied up in brick and mortar back on 66. So they left the interstates to chains and franchises and stayed on the old road until they either retired or died.

Most of this first generation of owners survived even in the interstate age because their expenses were low. But new owners, who carry all the old expenses *plus* a mortgage payment, are not faring as well. Many old motels rent a portion of their rooms to weekly tenants now. Some rent by the hour. Others have been converted to permanent apartments. At least a third are closed, but still standing. And not a few are owned by Asian Indians whose last names are almost always "Patel"—the Hindi word for innkeeper.

El Vado Motel, Albuquerque, New Mexico.

When I was on the road, owners of other small motels often criticized Indian innkeepers. "Their motels are rundown, they have no facilities, and the owners are unfriendly," these other owners said. Many advertised their motels as "American owned." But I liked the Indians' prices, usually about $15 a night, and ended up staying in quite a few of their motels. The odor of curry in their offices was pervasive, their chenille bedspreads were often worn thin, and their owners often were asocial. But I attributed that as much to my differences as theirs. We still did business.

My first routine on reaching a town where I'd spend the night was to cruise its main drag (Route 66) to check out the motels. In Albuquerque, where the highway is called Central Avenue, this search took more than an hour. The street's eighteen-mile length, plus a heavy rain reduced my usual smooth cruise to a slog. Most of the Duke City's motels, as elsewhere, were too expensive for my budget. Many had that faint air of decrepitude which I found too depressing to work in. On my second circuit, I finally settled on the El Vado—its neon sign of an Indian chief in full head dress being the deciding factor.

When I rang the office doorbell and a slight, dark-skinned man walked out from the living quarters in back, I knew I had come upon another Indian-owned motel. At first I was vaguely displeased and planned to stay only one night. But I ended up staying a week. In four months on the road, I'd unpack my car and set up my gear at many fancier motels, but never at a better one. The El Vado is an adobe jewel.

As the owner approached the office door, I could tell he was giving me a proprietary once-over. I repaid the favor by giving his motel the same treatment. It stood next to a golf course which in turn bordered the Rio Grande. Forty miles to the south, the sacred mountains of the Isleta Indian Reservation presented a dramatic backdrop. Built in the early days of connected units, its fresh white rooms—each with turquoise trim and a covered parking stall—fronted a well maintained courtyard. Four o'clocks bloomed in small plots beneath each window. Vigas, exposed logs which supported the ceilings, protruded through the outside walls of each unit. The place was clean, attractive; I thought I could stay. The owner must have thought so, too, for he unlocked the office door and let me in.

The man's family was watching television in a large open room to the right of the office. On a blanket on the floor, a dark brown nut of a baby played, then started to cry. When mother's hushings didn't quiet him, she picked him up and took him through a door to a further part of the family's living quarters. Able to be heard now, I smiled and said that a baby's cry in any language sounds the same.

The man smiled back. He offered me his best room, a free bucket of ice, and fifteen minutes worth of advice on what to see in Albuquerque.

The room was average size, but white stucco walls and recessed door and window frames gave it a bulky air. The bedspread was quilted (not chenille). An orange recliner sat by the window, a blonde desk and chair stood opposite the bed. From the bathroom window, I could yell "FORE!" at unsuspecting golfers next door. Crowning it all were the vigas, dark and varnished. My El Vado room didn't have the pseudo-luxury veneer of many modern motels. It didn't even have a phone. But during my week's stay there, I knew I was somewhere. Almost home.

I paid in advance that first night, stowed all my gear in the walk-in closet of my room, set out a few pictures and knick knacks which I carried along to call a place home, and went out for a coke.

The soda machine was just across the courtyard, but the owner was out watering the lawn. I soon learned that any trip which crossed his path meant at least a twenty-minute visit.

"Are you heading west?" Ali Hakam asked, directing his spray toward my four o'clocks.

As a matter of fact, I was.

"On 66?"

Hmmm. Not many Indian innkeepers knew about 66. I stayed and talked until the watering was done and full darkness came. Ali's speech had that high-pitched, irregular rhythm which makes Indians' English so hard to understand. But with practice I came to understand it. The next night, we met by chance again and talked until dark once more. From then on, we met on purpose. Usually we'd talk in the evening when I got back from my day's searching. Even if it was raining and there was no need to water the lawn, Ali would see my car pull in and have some reason to come over—a question, a comment, a curiosity about my day. And if he didn't come, I would have a reason to go see him.

As with most of my friends, I liked Ali because he resisted the stereotype. He had the dark skin, angular features and slight build of other Indian moteliers, but that was all. He was social and openly curious. His last name wasn't Patel. And while most of his countrymen in this business have come directly from India to their motels, he 'd taken a roundabout route—through eleven years in Sweden and three more as assistant manager of a Holiday Inn in Texas. He wasn't even Hindu like the Patels—he was a follower of the Aga Kahn ("Is that a picture of Jose Ferrer behind the counter?" "No, it's the Aga Kahn").

One night as Ali and I talked in the shelter of my carport, three carloads of tourists pulled in the front driveway in quick succession, glanced around the place in appraisal, saw Ali, and drove on. Did the bad reputation of other Indian-owned motels hurt his business as much as it appeared, I asked?

"You just see that," Ali said, pointing at the rear end of the third car as it scooted back onto 66. "Unfortunately, most of my countrymen's notion of motels and lodging is very bad." He scratched his head in the universal sign of puzzlement and added, "But it's not just the reputation."

"It's not?"

"No. It is also jealousy. You have this statue here. She says, 'Bring me your tired, your hungry, your weak.' But these people she talks about were poor. Today, you have East Indians come and they have money or they can get it. They do not start at bottom and you think..."

A tank-topped couple drove up in an old Impala. They were barely out their doors before Ali was waving at them.

"No vacancy!" he called. He'd just told me he had three empties. "We have no vacancy." The couple closed their doors and pulled back out.

"I have to screen people, only let the nice ones in," Ali justified. "The first owner told me to be choosy. I won't rent to hookers. I won't rent to junkies. Then we become a piece of junk, like other motels.

"When I first come here, I thought, 'Oh, this mud house.' I thought it was awful. Now I realize this is not just any motel. This is El Vado. This place is special."

When I finally left Albuquerque one afternoon, I stopped by the El Vado office to say good-by. Ali was gone to buy supplies. But his wife Salma, in her halting English, bid me a gracious farewell.

"You like cold cock?" she asked.

Uhhhh.....That was a tough one. Refuse the offer, and I might hurt intercultural relations. Accept it and I might be worse off. I took a chance.

"Uh, sure....That would be nice."

My hostess turned to her son. "Go get cold cock," she ordered. The intrigue deepened as the lad disappeared through the back door. Would this parting gift be served with curry, I wondered?

When the boy reappeared, he was carrying a can of Coca Cola. He handed it to his mother, who then gave it to me.

"Cold cock," she said and smiled.
"Very cold," I said. "Thank you."

Three years later, Ali left the El Vado. His partner, the motel's majority owner, wanted to cut maintenance costs and rent the entire motel out to weekly tenants. Ali couldn't live with that and he disappeared for a year. Rumors circulated among his friends that he had returned to Sweden. Then in the summer of 1990, a welcome letter came. "I am back at El Vado and Route 66," Ali wrote. "I am back where I belong." He'd bought out his partner, given the El Vado a new coat of paint, and rented its rooms back out to 66 travelers. In a twist on the tactic of American motel owners, he'd even hung a proud new banner outside the office: "Back under the management of Ali Hakam."

Note to 3rd Printing, 1992: In the summer of 1991, shortly after this book came out, Ali and the El Vado's owner reached a parting of the ways over how the motel should be managed. As a result, Ali and his family left the El Vado once again and returned to Sweden. Farewell, good friends.

SEARCHING FOR 66

THIRTY-EIGHT

West of Albuquerque and climbing, Route 66 passes by Laguna, the only pueblo along its path. Built after the Spanish era began, Laguna is the newest pueblo and—because of its mining claims—reputedly the richest. But you couldn't tell it by looking. Nor could you tell by the size of its welfare roll. In fact, Laguna doesn't even look like a pueblo. Chalk that up to the blandness of modern design—the community's first buildings went up in 1800.

I passed through Grants, self-proclaimed uranium capital of the world, at breakfast time. They have a little restaurant there called the Uranium Cafe. I wondered if I could have my eggs scrambled, over easy or irradiated.

Near Thoreau, the former backbone of America's highway system crosses the enduring backbone of America—the Continental Divide. At 7,263 feet, it is Route 66's highest point. A wooden sign and three souvenir stores mark the site.

The road plied on through red rock and high desert country as I approached the Arizona border. Driving into Gallup, I picked up Station KYVA on Sally's radio. A traditional kiva is a circular pit used by pueblo Indians for religious ceremonials. This KYVA, however, played contemporary country music. And mindful of his primary audience, the announcer spoke in Navajo—his speech a smooth, melodic stream, interrupted only by such occasional anglicisms as "Fourteenth Anniversary Sale," "wireless remote," and "American Express and Master Charge credit cards accepted."

Gallup was sustained first by the railroad, getting its name from a Santa Fe Railroad paymaster. Then mining became its chief industry. Then 66 and tourism came. But today the city's primary business is none of these. As the largest city of size close to the largest and most populous reservation—the Navajo—Gallup claims the title "Indian Capital of the World."

With 200,000 Navajos close by, most businesses in town either sell to the Indians or buy from them. Car dealers advertise "reservation-ready" trucks. Laundromats on the edge of town are must stops for most Indian families on their visits. Saloons are frequented by the younger men and women, while older folks patronize the liquor stores. And pawn shops, business heirs to the trading post era, loan as much as $4 million a year to their Indian customers.

"Most of it doesn't go dead, though," said one shop owner. "Pawn is just a specialized small loan business. We deal in the type of collateral Indian people have. The same concho belt may be pawned three or four times a year. If we let the collateral go dead, we lose a customer."

I tried many times in Gallup to start a conversation, but Navajos were a taciturn lot. The closest I came was in a bar one night. I had just lit a cigarette and the Navajo man next to me tapped me on the shoulder. He motioned toward the burning Kool. I offered him one from the pack, but he didn't accept. He pantomimed smoking a cigarette, then waved it off and solemnly cupped his hands over his lungs.

I moved down to the other end of the bar and finished my smoke. Throughout my stay in New Mexico, it had truly been a land of enchantment. In its Indian country, however, it was more a land of puzzlement.

SEARCHING FOR 66

THIRTY-NINE

The ground yellowed and vast banks of clouds commandeered the sky as I drove 66 into Arizona and through the southeastern corner of the Navajo Reservation. Many long stretches of the highway still survive here, running in sinuous counterpoint to the interstate. But they've not been tended for many years, the patches on the patches even look old, and occasional clumps of tumbleweed grow along the median stripe. In other areas, I-40 has claimed most of 66's roadbed and the old highway survives only as short exit roads to old trading posts like Jackrabbit, Yellow Horse and Twin Arrows.

At the Painted Desert, vegetation gave way completely, revealing the most beautiful badlands in America. Red, violet, green and gray layers of clay were laid down here by an ocean several epochs ago. Desert winds of succeeding eons sculpted canyons, buttes and mesas from the pliable material, leaving it in soft heaps like nature's chat piles.

The Nevin trading post near Houck, Arizona

On the search again next morning, I stepped around a couple of dozing gentlemen and climbed the steps of the Holbrook, Arizona, courthouse. Just inside on the left, a matronly lady sat beneath a beehive hairdo, playing the piano and singing "Ballad of the Green Berets." She would be a feature performer in a concert next evening at the courtyard gazebo.

On the other side of the hall, the old jail had been preserved as a museum. Nobody home. Up a few steps, I met several ladies at the local historical society museum. Terry White came downstairs from her Chamber of Commerce office and we all spent a pleasant half hour swapping 66 stories.

"Sixty-Six has been part of our lives," said chief historian Garnette Franklin. "And we resent having the name changed." The other members concurred. They told about a Route 66 display they were planning for later that summer and they suggested numerous cafe owners, waitresses, and gas station and motel operators as possible interview subjects in Holbrook. But it was an embarrassing moment Terry had suffered three years earlier, and not these suggestions, which led me along the right path today.

"We almost had a depression here when the I-40 bypass went through," Terry said. " Forty-five businesses closed down the first year. Now this lady Joy Nevin had done a little bit of everything along 66. At the time they pulled the plug on the road, she was director of our senior citizens center. And even though businesses were closing right and left, she decided they needed to build a $150,000 addition at the center. Everybody thought she was crazy for trying, but a year later we dedicated the place. So when a federal commission decided to give out woman-of-the-year awards, Joy was picked from Arizona.

"The awards were going to be presented in Washington, D.C. The athletic director at the high school, a friend of Joy's, borrowed a Cadillac convertible so we could drive her down to the Phoenix airport in style. I was going along as representative for the city."

"Now I'd lived in Holbrook all my life except for two and a half years at Arizona State," said Terry, who'd just turned 30. "But I'd never met Joy. So I was waiting down here by the courthouse with the athletic director when another man drove up in his pick-up and got out. He was wearing a cowboy hat, boots, jeans, and he had a pack of tobacco stuffed in his shirt pocket. I turned to the athletic director and said, 'That woman of the year better get down here soon or she's going to miss her plane!

"'This is the woman of the year, Terry,' my friend said. 'This is Joy Nevin. Mrs. Joy Nevin.'"

"Hi. I'm Tom Teague."

The woman extended a warm, calloused hand. "Joy Nevin, Tom. Sit down. Terry told me you were coming."

Early in our conversation, Joy pulled a tobacco pouch from her shirt pocket as she talked. "I haven't always dressed like a cowboy," she said. "I was actually raised in Providence, Rhode Island, in a historic old house on the Post Road. I even went to finishing school in the same class as Gloria Vanderbilt."

Joy creased a cigarette paper, poured just the right amount of tobacco in it, gave it a couple of finger taps to smooth it out, then rolled it up and licked it shut—all without looking. When the cigarette was dry, she struck a safety match to her belt buckle and fired up.

Joy Nevin, Holbrook, Arizona

"But I hated all that," she said on the exhale, flaring her nostrils to catch the secondary smoke. "Rhode Island was too small for me. So when I caught polio about that time, it was easy to move out west to recover. I lived with a chum in Wyoming for about a year. But I kept having spasms, so I headed down here. A friend of a friend had an outfit up on the rim of a canyon. Stopped by to say hello and ended up working there a year and a half. Haven't looked back since."

A new homemaker for the senior center came into Joy's office with a problem. She hadn't been filling out a timecard and she'd just discovered she needed one to get paid.

"No problem there," Director Nevin said. "Just ballpark it. I don't have to have it all in black and white."

Joy asked the homemaker about a client, then turned back to me. "I was rough as a cob in the early days," she said, leaving no doubt of the truth. "One day a partner and I worked all day, rounded us up a bunch of rodeo horses. We had them underneath the bridge here on 66 so we could ship them off. And I mean those horses were wild!

"We had 38-40 head and had them about all calmed down when I looked up and this tourist family was stopped right on the bridge. The father saw us and said, 'Oh, look!' and this kid started shooting his cap gun. He started whooping and hollering and down the river our horses went. It took us all the next day to round them back up. Of course they were more spooked than ever.

"I looked up at that kid when the horses bolted and said, 'You stupid sonofabitch! You just wasted a whole day's work!' And I meant every word."

Joy tilted her hat back to let the breeze cool her close-cropped, gray-speckled hair. "Afterwards, though, we couldn't stop laughing about it. You have to laugh about those things—you couldn't cry all your life. If it's not going to matter fifty years from now, it doesn't matter tonight.

"That's the way I look at things now, anyway. I didn't when I was younger. But the wisdom of the years has given me that."

Much of that wisdom, Joy proudly claimed, was gleaned from Route 66. She and the road made their imprints on each other early.

"The ranches were pretty isolated when I first came here," she said. "Some were fifty miles from the nearest town. So I came up with the idea of a store on wheels that could go to them. I bought a pick-up, stocked it with vet supplies, and started making the rounds on 66. It was mostly animal supplies, but then I had any kind of things like needles, thread, cigarette papers, tobacco. I even went up into the reservation and did some swappin'."

Occasionally, Joy's cargo also included exotic animals.

"I had an old boy who ran a gas station on 66," she said, stretched back in her chair in this rare moment of relaxation. "He said if I could catch a gila monster when I was down south, he would give me $35. So one day when I was down by Show Low, I roped one of 'em and put him in a gunny sack in the back of the truck. He scratched like a sonofabitch and I thought 'Oh Christ! He'll chew his way out of there!' Meanwhile, I had a load of bone oil back there and it stinks like hell...Damn lizard broke three bottles of it before I could get him out! So I lost the bone oil and the gila monster and I never did get my $35."

Joy also met her husband on Route 66. He had a gas station in a hollow east of Holbrook and she stopped by one day to swap Navajo rugs with him. They ended up swapping vows as well and soon she was running his gas station with him.

"It was the tail end of the Dust Bowl days," she recalled. "There were fruit pickers and migrant workers and they brought everything with them—including the goats and grandma and grandpa. Basically they were pretty good folks—they were true America. They couldn't help it because, hey, they went broke.

"Now there were bandits runnin' places along the highway—chargin' poor strangers $40 for a tire they wouldn't get $20 for from a friend. It's things like that have always irritated me—to see people held up like they were."

Joy's eyes narrowed even now, her jaw set, and her fist drew in on itself.

"You treat America like your next door neighbor!" she said. It was not a request. "It pays off psychologically and you earn a dollar. So what if folks are just transients? If you have a nice room in Holbrook, a nice stay, then you're gonna go home and be sittin' around a table with your friends havin' a beer and you're gonna say, 'Holbrook.'

"So if poor people needed a second hand tire or a water pump, I sold it to them. But I didn't try to rob 'em blind. My husband and I had many a fight over that. It's one reason we split up. So their money ran out! What're you gonna do—leave 'em there? You can't help your own plight 'til you help your fellow man."

Joy rolled another cigarette and leaned toward me so I could light it. Under her shirt, I noticed a patch of hard plastic and gauze over her heart. Wires lead from it to a monitor which rested in the shirt pocket she didn't keep her tobacco in.

"I talked to all the people, too," she said. "Told them about local conditions. And they were interesting. They had something to say to me, too—good and bad. Maybe it was a family fight. Sometimes you could even help with those. By the time they left, the wife was talkin' to the husband again."

If a traveler was sick, Joy would call the doctor in Holbrook and he'd send medicine out on the next bus. One time she and her husband and their hired man helped an out-of-gas plane land on the highway in front of their station. "Mixed him up some new gas and sent him on his way. It wasn't flight fuel—but hey, it got him to Winslow.

"Another time, I had somebody die in the privy. Grandma died in the privy! I was afraid they might think it was foul play or something, so I roped the place off so nobody else would go. Left Grandma just sittin' there—where else could I put her anyway?

"It took all day to rectify this and what are you going to do meanwhile? You're gonna feed her family, of course! Get them inside the house. This weather here can be rugged."

Landing planes on the highway. Roping Grandma off in the privy. Giving shelter to truckers when glare ice forced them off 66. It was the neighborly thing to do. Or, as Joy said, "Hey, it was great to have 'em! They'd come in and visit. I'd put 'em up.

"And among the few real neighbors we had, there was a great comradeship. I was down under the canyon rim one day. This fellow looked kind of suspicious, all dressed up. He said, 'You acquainted with any people down here?'

"I knew them all. 'Ehhhh. Not too many,' I said. 'Why?' He said, 'You know a guy named Jim Thompson?' I thought, 'Uh-oh!' I knew him real well—he had a still down here. So I said, 'Naw. That name isn't familiar.'

"This guy said, 'I'll tell you a story. During the war, I had a crash landing down there. It was the rainy season and I couldn't get out. I stayed two or three weeks with Jim and he made the best bootleg hootch! So now I got a case of scotch in the trunk that I'm trying to get to him.'

"I said, 'Hell, I know Jim. No problem.' And I gave the man directions. Before he left, we opened one of the bottles and had a couple of samples. I mean it was good stuff!"

Joy had retired from her more active pursuits about ten years ago when she got a finger shot off. It was just as well, she thinks, for an era was coming to a close.

"Nobody trusts anybody on the highway anymore," she lamented. "I bedded down many a night by the side of the road. Nobody'd stop. Nobody'd bug you. If they did, it was because they needed help. Now you're scared to talk to 'em.

"Tourists today are always on that racetrack. But they don't see the country. In order to know a state or anything else, you got to know the people. You got the job done on 66. But now, hell, people don't even know when they cross from one state to another! Nobody takes time to say hello to the next one. We don't care about people anymore. And it worries me.

"So much good comes of progress. But it's hard for me at the age of 62 now to relate to it because I much prefer the old way. I tried I-40 one time. You see a good bull out there, but you gotta go fifteen miles down the highway to get off and find the silo and go over and take a look at him! Ooh chihuahua!

"So this center job came along at just about the right time. Actually, I kind of fell into it. We had a little seniors' group here have a potluck every once in awhile and I'd volunteer to help. The nutrition and social service programs were just getting started then. I didn't know anything about them myself, but bein' younger, I thought I could do some P.R. Before too long, I was the director."

The occasional potluck grew to 33,000 meals served a year—plus other programs—in a town of less than 6,000 people. The century-old house that the center started in was quickly outgrown, leading to Joy's decision to build an addition across the driveway. So, though businesses were closing around them at the rate of three and four a month, she set about raising $150,000.

"I wrote to seven hundred foundations across the United States," she said matter-of-factly. "Some of them would give me a piddlin' amount. One of them gave me forty-five thou. And we had bake sales."

She treated her Woman of the Year award just as casually.

"My biggest decision before going was whether to buy a new pair of boots or not," Joy said. "And when I got there, I just wanted to make sure I saw Ford's Theater and the Vietnam Memorial."

Heart trouble the past three years had Joy planning retirement in a few months. She'd trained her secretary Carmen, who's worked at the center since graduating from high school six years ago, to take over soon. For herself, Joy planned to go back to volunteering. Other people faced with this prospect might take a relaxed, placid view of things. But Joy still starts her mornings out by pouring a little cream over a bowl of nails.

She pointed to a computer on the other side of her office where

Carmen was tapping away.

"I'm an old lady," she said. "I dress my own style. I do my own cigarettes. But these computers are taking our individuality away from us. Burp now and the government knows it. It's fast getting....ironic to me that I'm sitting here filling out papers on people, taking their own identity away from them. Paper says nothing about what a person's really like! It stereotypes people—their social security number, their name, their income bracket..."

A nail or two flew out. Joy dealt the air a lethal blow with her fist.

"I mean who the hell cares?"

Certainly not me, ma'am.

"I went to a meeting last Wednesday in Flagstaff about a new form. Fourteen pages! Fourteen pages of your ailments and all the goodies that go with it just so we can feed you or visit you!

"So I got there early and I talked to the headmaster of the state. I said, 'I presume that we should also shave all the seniors' heads and tattoo each of their arms.' She said it would make it easier to track them....I don't think she understood."

Another cigarette rolled. Another battle remembered.

"I told her about this one particular client. He lives in a pig sty. But he wants to live that way and he's been judged competent. He sits in his own excrement and the state says he's competent. They say he's competent to take his medicine, but not one pill is missing from the box. The state says he's competent, but you have to fight your way through his trailer to the kitchen sink. Mice, rats, roaches. Everytime I've been there, I've had to throw up when I got out."

"You do a lot of your own casework?" I asked.

Joy sneered—one of her kinder reprovals.

"I won't subject my staff to something like that," she said. "I'd be a hell of a boss if I did!

"So I filled out the fourteen pages the way they're supposed to be filled out—told them nothing! And I showed it to the headmaster. She said, 'Well, there's room for narrative.'"

Joy gave me an appraising glance—a monitored heart beat away from death, yet still challenging that machine on her chest to beep.

"You're proud of your country," she declared. "I can tell that. So what would you do? All the centers are scared they won't get funded if they don't do their paperwork. Which is true. They probably won't. We won't, either. But I'm not going to intimidate my people and ask them if they have hemorrhoids and how long. It's none of my business! So I take the forms home and do them myself on weekends.

"I just refuse to join their system. It's a pain in the ass. But you have to keep battlin' because you still care."

SEARCHING FOR 66

FORTY

"I have met the last of the Iroquois; they were begging."
Alexis de Tocqueville
Democracy in America
1833

In his landmark book, Tocqueville said the driving creative element behind American society was equality of conditions. We were, he said, the world's first true democracy.

But this was an observation, not a recipe to be automatically followed. While the French nobleman deeply admired the American experiment, he also warned of the dangers of a democracy left to its "wild" instincts.

"Men would seem still unaware of its existence," he said, "when suddenly it has seized power."

Things haven't changed much in a century and a half. American Indians may not know Tocqueville well. But they know what "equality of conditions" means. For them, it means they can't be different anymore. Witness the Navajo-Hopi Relocation dispute along Route 66 in Arizona.

The dispute has its origin in the Navajos' and Hopis' inability to accept the concept of arbitrary boundaries for land—and the government's insistence that they do. The boundaries in this case were for a million and a half acres of land in northeastern Arizona. Until recently, the Navajo and Hopi had both used the land, if not always harmoniously. But now a barbed wire fence split the disputed area. A federal judge had declared that one side now belonged to the Hopi and the other to the Navajo. To consummate the "solution," he ordered all Indians living on the other tribe's land to move.

"Relocate" is the government's word for this process. It has more syllables than "move" and the not so incidental advantage of being a word foreign to each tribe's native tongue. July 6 1986 was its deadline. Any Indians left on the other tribe's land then would be in violation of a federal court order. The Navajo-Hopi Relocation Commission described the consequences of such violation in a public notice: "If a relocatee refuses to move, the Commission can require the relocatee to appear before a hearing and show cause why he cannot relocate. If the relocatee still does not relocate, the Commission can apply to court of competent jurisdiction to order the relocatee to relocate."

Bonuses were offered to Indians of both tribes who relocated quickly—$5,000 if they moved during the offer's first year; only $2,000 if they waited until the fourth year. Allowances were also given for moving costs and for the value of existing housing and improvements. Many families even got government-built replacement housing. But the commission had determined such housing couldn't be built economically on the reservations and put up subdivisions in Flagstaff and Winslow instead.

Unschooled in the ways of a money economy, many relocated families mortgaged their new homes to buy trucks. Then, when they didn't make payments on the trucks, they lost both. The result was banks with lots of cheap houses to sell and as many dispossessed families back on the reservations. By 1986, over a billion dollars had been spent in the relocation effort and many of the Indians were living in the same huts and hogans they had left behind. Tension grew in both tribes, but mostly in the white community as the final relocation deadline of July 6 approached and 10,000 Indians were still on someone else's land. While the rest of America celebrated the rededication of the Statue of Liberty, activists and news media were gathering near Flagstaff, some of them predicting another Wounded Knee.

It struck me as ironic, then, when I learned the Hopis were going to celebrate the Fourth of July with a rodeo. So I drove out from the DuBeau Motel in Flagstaff to join them. I'd expected turmoil, bitterness and unrest. What I found, though, was three or four hundred folks sitting under makeshift sun shelters, quietly taking in some cowboy action. Ivan Sidney, the Hopi tribal chairman, was on hand, but didn't address the crowd. Only the announcer made any political statements, and he worked those into his patter between bull rides and calf ropings.

"The day we are having here is also the day they're having a big thing with the Statue of Liberty," he said. "We hoped when she first came here that the statue would make things good and friendly with the folks over there. But what did they do?...They invaded the Native American United States!" This brought light laughter and a smattering of applause, but then it was back to the steer wrestling.

After the rodeo, I passed on the country-western dance that the Mormons were having and headed south and west again toward Flagstaff.

"My grandfather taught me and my cousins how to ride bulls," said Emery Bontovi. "They weren't rodeo bulls, either, which are tough enough. They were range bulls. Territorial. This was their land, man. But my grandfather would stand close by when we rode. If we fell off before our time, he would use his bullwhip on us. We were more afraid of that whip than the bulls."

Hitchhiking in the rest of this country is a crap shoot. But on reservations, it is a form of mass transportation. The main danger is not to drivers who pick them up—Indian hitchhikers are peaceful and law abiding lot—but to the hitchers themselves. Many are hit at night as they walk or lie along the dark reservation roads. So when Emery had heard me cruising homeward after the rodeo and hung out a thumb without even looking around, I'd decided to pick him up.

"Don't run over that snake, man," he advised. "They hold spiritual power for my people."

Emery ("Just like Emery Express") had waist-length hair pulled back in a glossy cord. His round face and short, stocky build said he was Hopi. His breath said he had had a few.

"I have a Navajo buddy from high school down by Thumb Point," he said. "Let's go see if he wants to party."

We drove on down the mesa-studded road, picking up and letting off two Navajo hitchhikers along the way. One offered us $2, which Emery insisted I take. Forty-five minutes later, we pulled up to a cluster of government-built houses and a hogan.

"Just honk once, man," Emery advised as we stopped by the first house. Most Indians, he explained, don't honk at all—they consider it unnecessary and impolite.

Soon a Navajo woman came to the door. Emery got out of the car, stood respectfully by his door, and asked if his friend Robert was there.

"We don't know any Robert," the woman said. In her expressionless tone, she could have meant anything. We drove on.

"My sister in Winslow is throwing a party today," Emery said, undaunted. "Want to go there? If you like her, you can have her!"

On the way, Emery talked about the different paths his life may take him in.

"I'm supposed to start initiation into the tribe in about a month," he said, playing with his hard-won moustache. "I'm my father's only son, so I suppose I have to do it. But that takes almost a year and I'm broke. You know the difference between good and bad when you're done with initiation, but I don't know if I can wait that long. I need a job. The job training program taught me how to be a heavy equipment operator, so I may go back to Denver next month and work on a freeway."

He tossed out another alternative as the desert wind rushed through the car. "Or I might go join the Marines."

Wasn't that third choice essentially the white man's initiation, I wondered?

"Not really," Emery said. "I had an uncle get killed in Vietnam. Besides—I may be Hopi, but I'm part of this country, too.

"You sure you don't have any reefer?"

We took a couple of right turns in Winslow and pulled up in front of his sister's government-built apartment. Being in the white world now,

Emery walked up to the stoop and used the doorbell.

No one was home. Emery walked slowly back to the car where I sat waiting.

"I bet she's down at her favorite bar," he said.

No such luck. I drove Emery on into Flagstaff. When I dropped him off at a corner downtown, he was still looking for a party. I was more interested in getting back to my motel. The DuBeau, at 60, was probably Arizona's and Route 66's oldest surviving motel. Its new owner, transplanted New Jerseyan Doug Hughes, had converted it in the past two years to a bed and breakfast inn and youth hostel. It also continued to be a popular resting point for foreign travelers who started coming there because it's close to the railroad station—at my six breakfasts in Doug's living room, I would meet people from France, Holland, Brazil, Scotland and Germany.

The DuBeau steadfastly refused to carry the conventional amenities—phone, TV, pool, ice machine—but it did have an easy camaraderie among its varied lot of guests. And on the Fourth of July, Doug installed a keg in his kitchen and invited everyone by. He scrounged an old black and white portable TV from somewhere, we all got a little pie-eyed, and an international audience watched President Reagan's speech and the Statue of Liberty fireworks. It was good to be home.

The fireworks which many people expected on Relocation Day never came. Navajos and their Anglo supporters held a symbolic fence cutting on newly-partitioned land. Hopi Robby Honani, accompanied by tribal officials and the news media, brought six sandstone rocks down from his mesa-top home and marked off a three-acre homesite on former Navajo land. A reported stabbing incident was whittled by the truth down to a fingernail scratch. The Hopis said they wouldn't force any Navajos off their land and the government—whose idea Relocation was in the first place—said they couldn't until it had built adequate replacement housing. Ross Swimmer, Secretary of the Bureau of Indian Affairs and a Native American himself, said he wasn't sure of the reason for Relocation because he hadn't been with the bureau when Relocation was mandated in 1974.

Another federal deadline had come and gone. But the reprieve, even though more than four years old now, is only temporary. Tocqueville's equality of conditions is a ruthless, homogenizing force. As a society, we court it. As parts of society, we often resist it. It claimed the Iroquois in Tocqueville's day. Someday it will likely claim the Navajos and Hopis as well. Who then will be its next target? Who will survive the Blanding of America?

SEARCHING FOR 66

FORTY-ONE

Saturday, October 13, 1984, Williams, Arizona (Gateway to the Grand Canyon). A 300-foot extension cord snaked up to the new I-40 overpass and crawled across a flatbed trailer to a microphone. By the microphone stood a piano. Next to the piano were two rows of folding chairs filled with dignitaries. At the east end of the overpass, the Williams High School marching band tuned up. At the west end, the Bill Williams Mountain Men sat on their horses, absorbing the day's bright sunshine in their buckskin and fur. In between the two groups milled most of the rest of Williams' population, plus about two hundred miscellaneous curiosity seekers. Recording it all were media crews from as far away as London and Yugoslavia.

Faintly at first, then with growing attention, the whop-whop-whop of rotary wings could be heard approaching from the north. Officials started clearing the area in front of the makeshift stage. Soon a helicopter descended and let out a lone, silver-haired male passenger.

The crowd and the media crews pressed back into the open area as the man briskly climbed the makeshift stage. Joined by a bass player, the stranger stood by the microphone, waiting for quiet.

"My name's Bobby Troup," he said. "And this is my song." Then he sat down to the piano and the jazzy strains of the national anthem for a generation of dreamstruck travelers rode through the autumn air and onto the interstate:

> *"If you ever plan to motor west*
> *Travel my way*
> *Take the highway that's the best*
> *Get your kicks on Route 66."*

His musical advice concluded, Troup used oversized scissors to cut an official ribbon. A paper banner with "Route 66" emblazoned on it was stretched across one end of the overpass and a '52 Packard drove through it. At the other end, a brand new Dodge pick-up tore through a banner labeled "I-40." Fifty-eight years after it had been designated a national highway, U.S. Route 66 was passing into history. This overpass in Williams was the last completed link in the interstate system which replaced it.

Originally, federal officials planned to end 66's days as a national route in McLean, Texas. But Williams had fared better in gaining court delays. By October 1984, it claimed the only cross-country stop lights still in use between Chicago and L.A. But now it was time for them, too, to go. Williams, a town of 2,500 people, accepted three exit ramps and a tourist information center in exchange for dropping its court actions.

Eric Eikenberry was director of the Williams Chamber of Commerce when the end came. Though an Arizona native, the volume of media attention which began to focus on the upcoming closing surprised him.

"Quite frankly, I was not aware of the significance of Route 66," he said when I called on him at the information center. "I was really too young to appreciate it. To me, the closing meant my members might be losing 15,000 customers a day.

"But the media kept calling. Usually you have an event and you try to get the media's attention. This one was completely backwards. We had the media's attention, but we had to hurry up and make an event out of it.

"So we figured, 'Let's do something really flashy!'"

There was a back on Eric's chair, but he seldom used it. If he wasn't stroking his neatly trimmed beard or waving a phrase grandly home, he was leaning one way or the other, driving his chair like a car. It didn't surprise me later to learn Eric's degree was in speech communications.

"The media thrives on the negative," Eric said. Holding an imaginary microphone and downshifting to a mock dramatic tone, he went on. "'What's going to happen to this poor little town of yours?' they asked. We were already facing cuts in the forest service. Tourism was down. The past winter had not been good. And everybody was up here. Gloomseekers and doomseekers. It was just awful! People's faces were so-o-o long. Like a funeral.

"But Williams is a tough little town. One of the ways we thought we could counteract the negative atmosphere of this passing was by saying, 'By golly, we're going to meet this closure on a positive, upbeat note.' The closing of 66 was done so unsentimentally and unceremoniously everywhere else. But we decided to have a party!"

Eric had moved to northern Arizona in 1981 when his wife got a job teaching in nearby Ash Fork. He had substitute taught a year until the Chamber vacancy came up. Today, as Director Eikenberry, he spread cupped hands, brought them to his chest, and said, "I was the *obvious* candidate for the job! I organized the whole show in two weeks. And I'll tell you, I was a busy boy. But I had plenty of help. I mean this town pulled together like you can't believe! I'd ask to get something done and they'd do it just like that. It just grew and grew and grew."

Two weeks of hectic planning finally bore fruit on October 13. "Here we are sitting at 7,000 feet elevation and it was October already—but we had an absolutely gorgeous day," Eric said. It was a Chamber of Commerce day.

"Bobby Troup actually flew in to Flagstaff and I drove him over on Old 66. But we put him out at our local airport and flew him to the overpass in the helicopter. It was all just for flash." His beard parted in a grin. "Yeah. Flash. Bobby sang his song and where it says 'Flagstaff, Arizona. Don't forget Winona', he said 'Williams, Arizona.' Then he cut the ribbon and we had a parade: first the Mountain Men, then the old Packard, then the truck. Very symbolic, huh? Oh boy! Was that gushy or what?

"Afterwards, we had another parade downtown and a street dance. Gave away two thousand hot dogs. Everybody drank too much. It worked out great!

"And you know what was a neat moment, Tom? After the party, I took Bobby back to his motel. We got there just in time to turn on the TV and see Dan Rather. Both of us were sitting on the edge of Bobby's bed when Rather came on with his closing piece. He said, 'If you ever plan to motor west, travel my way, take the highway that's the best. Get your kicks on Route 66.' Those words were written more than 40 years ago by songwriter Bobby Troup. Tomorrow, that road will be closed forever. And CBS's Bob McNamara is there.'

"And there we were sitting on the edge of the bed, Tom. Bobby had written the words and I had alerted the networks...It was just really neat! I shared that with my wife, how neat that was.

"I'll tell you, Tom. Nothing will ever top that day. It was the high point of my career—the high point of this job, without a doubt."

I made some hopeful comment about the future, but Eric wasn't buying.

"No," he said at his usual horsepower. "Nothing could ever match it. Nothing."

"Your career peaked in a party?"

"Our party really had more meaning than capitalizing on an event," Eric said. "It went much deeper than that. It really did. Don't think that many of our people weren't very, very frightened. They grew up with 66. Their livelihoods were dependent on its traffic.

""The day after the party it was quiet. I'll tell you that. It was quiet. You see how my office is on this little peninsula between eastbound 66 and westbound 66? Before the interstate opened, you and I couldn't sit here and have this conversation with that window cracked open even half an inch! Eighteen-wheelers would come down off this hill with their jake brakes. Rru-du-du-du-du-du-du! And the traffic and the dust and the smell—it was horrible! It'd be like sitting out on the I-40 median trying to talk!

"But we were prepared for this. We weren't caught by surprise. And the business community really drew together. Today the chamber's membership is larger than it ever was before. Stores are being painted. Nobody expected it, but business now is at least where it was, if not slightly better. The exit signs and the information center helped, but we worked hard, too. And we survived."

Several months after the party, Eric had been out in the country hunting supplies for a cowchip throwing contest when he saw a stack of traffic signs in an old, unused barn.

"I thought, 'Gee, maybe there's a 66 sign in there," he said. "And there was one! I was just thrilled! I'm still thrilled. It's my most prized possession. I can't tell you how much that sign means to me. It's like I earned it."

My host came to a rolling, almost reflective stop.

"Before the party, I wasn't much on 66," he said. "And I had people coming up to me saying, 'What do *you* think the significance of Route 66 was?' They're asking *me* these questions. I'm just a young guy here. I don't know. So I started to find out more and more about it. And as I found out more about it, I got closer to it.

"Really, in my own way—whether anybody else knows it or not—in my own heart and mind, I know that I have a place in history with Route 66 because I organized the closing events of it. That was neat. I'm not trying to stroke my own ego. It's not for my glorification. It was *fun* to be able to be involved in something that I now have learned is truly significant."

During its fifty-eight official years, Route 66 touched the lives and careers of countless millions of Americans. Andy Payne was the first. Here in front of me sat perhaps the last. It didn't look like things had changed much in between.

SEARCHING FOR 66

FORTY-TWO

Before leaving Williams, I'd used one of the phone numbers Reba Collins had given me back in Claremore and called Will Rogers Jr. "I'd love to talk about Route 66!" he'd said. "Come on down." Down was Tubac, Arizona, a small town about three hundred miles south of Route 66 and thirty miles north of Latin America. Will Jr., who prefers to be called Bill, has lived there the past twenty years. The next day, I drove down to meet him.

"I've been up and down your Route 66 quite often," Bill said when we met. He had the same high-pitched voice of his father, but not the twang. "From Joplin west. In fact, a 66 Association meeting was one of the first things I attended after my dad died.

"What I liked about the national association was that they kept speaking about their group and how they had to stick together. 'Don't promote Gallup. Don't promote Needles. Promote the whole highway.' I thought they were pretty liberal and I stayed with them many years—and not because their highway was named after my father. We did do a promotional tour on 66 with them when the movie about Dad came out, but basically they were just a good group."

"Everybody I've talked to who knew your dad has deified him," I said about an hour into our conversation. "But they said you might not. I was wondering why."

Bill paused a moment. perhaps adding up years of his life that he'd already spent considering this same question.

"Dad was quite a person," he answered deliberately. "He was quite a guy. Everyone regarded him as a friend. You see his old movies and you can see why. He was not the movie star way up there tall. He was your friend across the silver screen.

"Actually, we had a fairly normal relationship. He would say, 'Come on, son. Get out of bed. Get your nose out of that book. Come on, ride those horses. Go do this, go do that.' I thought I was the most lazy teenager in the world. When I had *my* teenage son, I thought *he* was the most lazy one in the world."

Two similar photographs hung on a richly paneled wall near Bill.

One showed Will Sr. on a platform twirling his lasso around twenty-two smiling people. In the picture below, Bill recreated the trick in a scene from his father's film biography. But there were only four people in his loop.

"Dad was disappointed that I didn't take up horsemanship very much," he continued. "I look more like him, but Jim actually had to pose for one of the statues in Claremore. I just didn't like it. I was always the intellectual of the family and my brother was the cowboy. I was always a talker. Like when I was at Stanford, I took part in the first international, transoceanic radio debate with Oxford.

"And Dad was intolerant of some of my ideas of the time, too. We had lots of arguments. Terrible arguments. But actually, I found him very perceptive. He'd been around. He was very well informed, very well read. The Okie exterior was purely a way of speaking. His writing was by no means hayseed writing."

"Did that mean that there was a difference between the public Rogers and the private person?" I asked.

"W.C. Fields had the best comment about that," Bill said and switched effortlessly to Fields' voice. "My little chickadee! Will Rogers? Why, that man is a fraud! He talks like that all the time!"

Bill chuckled at the line and his performance of it. It was a rich, rolling chuckle, lower-pitched than his voice. "Good old LaRouche!" he said later when talk turned to my home state's politics. His chuckle rolled out again, fed on itself, and he couldn't stop.

"No, there was almost no difference between the public and private Will Rogers," he said at last. "He was very much the same all along. And that's very rare. It gave Dad an easygoing way. I think that's why people liked him."

"Was it really just like Kennedy, then, when your father died?"

After some thought, Bill said, "Yes, but you have to remember this: Dad's accident was the first major accident that occurred after the world became a global village. International radio had come in. We had been interconnected for only a year or so. So when Dad died, BANG! Everybody knew it in Los Angeles. Everybody knew it in New York. Everybody knew it in Oklahoma. And it happened in Alaska!

"But the reaction did surprise me at the time. I really had no reason to judge my father or pay much attention to him as a public figure until after he died. You don't pay attention to those things, hardly, when you're young. Doesn't everybody have a polo field? Doesn't everybody live the way you do?

"You have to go outside your environment to realize how specific that environment is. And that can take a long time."

We walked down the hall to Bill's library so he could look up a favorite piece of writing about his father. While he rummaged through the two shelves of Rogers books, I noted such homemade categories as "Books by Friends," "Watergate and Beyond," "Communism" and "Communism, Disillusionment with."

"You were interested in Communism once?" I asked.

"Oh yes," Bill answered readily, still looking for his book. "A lot of people were when I was young. I never called myself a Communist, but it was a very major factor in California when I was out there.

"And it was all open and up front. One of the nuttiest ideas for ending the Depression was '$30 Every Thursday.' That was the Townsend Plan. You can't get more radical, more communist than that. But it was indigenous American Screwball. It wasn't Russian.

"After the war, though, being tied into the Left became a very harmful thing. When Nixon ran for the Senate, he lambasted a very good friend of mine, Helen Gehagan Douglas. There was no doubt she was pretty far left, but he smeared her really pretty unfairly. I served a term in Congress before the war. But if I had run for reelection after the war, even I would have suffered."

"The son of Will Rogers—Will Jr. himself—would have been branded a Commie?"

Bill just laughed.

"Yeah," he said. "I bet Dad could have made a good joke about that."

Bill dropped out of Communism about the same time, he says, that he dropped in on Route 66.

"A few months after my father died, I, uh, purchased the Beverly Hills *Citizen*," he said. "After I got wounded in the war, that's what I went back to. It was right by 66 and that's basically what I was for eighteen years—a newspaper publisher.

"And then I made probably the only smart business decision I ever made. I saw very quickly that the Los Angeles *Times* was absorbing the area and I sold out. The *Citizen* was once the biggest weekly paper in the West. But a few years later it did go out."

Later, Bill treated me to Steak Diane at the Tubac Country Club. Talk continued about his career.

"After the paper, I made a movie of my father's life for Warner Brothers," Bill said. "Then I did two more movies after that. Quickie westerns."

"It was....odd," he said, twisting that last word into about five high-pitched syllables. "Looking back, I'm surprised how cavalierly I treated the movies. I didn't pay much attention to them and I didn't really like them very much. But I walked in first class, so I never had to fight for things.

"Then I went east to CBS. CBS was floundering around, as they are right now at this moment, for a morning show. I was the emcee, like who's on now? Bryant Gumbel! I was their man for two years against Dave Garroway and I enjoyed it very much.

"Looking back, it was amazing how primitive TV news was then and how long it lasted as a primitive arrangement. I remember one time having an argument with the producers. We wanted to go down live for a remote to....."

Bill spread his hands in gee-whiz amazement, a 75-year-old boy.

"...Washington, D.C.! 'Oh, my goodness!' they said. 'Oh, that would just wreck our budget forever!'"

He had another nice long chuckle.

In yet another career after CBS, Bill's Indian heritage landed him a post with the Bureau of Indian Affairs.

"I was with them a year and a half," he said. "It was mostly publicity and promotion. If they wanted to crown an Indian princess or something, I was there. I was also to make reports on education. I remember visiting some reservations and seeing some awfully horrible situations."

Bill's hard blue eyes narrowed. He continued in a quieter voice. "I didn't make any recommendations, though. We are eradicating the Indian traditions. There's no doubt about it. We're doing very little except words to give Indians the strength to hold onto their traditions.

"And I don't know what you're going to do about those people, even today. Education starts a hundred years before you're born. With no books in the home, no magazines, parents who can't read and who are drunk half the time, it negates the whole process."

After the BIA, Bill and his wife, Collier, bought a 400-acre ranch near Tubac and settled into semi-retirement. When Collier died of emphysema ten years ago, Bill built an adobe duplex in town and moved into it with his son, Carlos, and Carlos' family. He spends his days now visiting his grandchildren in Tubac and Tucson, working on various literary projects with his computer, and co-managing the Rogers estate with his brother and sister.

"Are there still Will Rogers-type of people around today?" I wondered. "If your dad was alive today, would he be doing the same thing with the same success?"

"Everything has changed so much," Bill said, doubtful. "Each person has to take advantage of the culture and the techniques that are available at the time. And Dad was a master of that. A great deal of his columns were actually news. I remember one time at a Chamber of Commerce affair in Los Angeles here was Will Rogers bringing a report *fresh from Washington!* He had been there only three days before!

"The techniques of the two times are quite distinct. Dad today would be a political commentator. But a political commentator today is an adversarial person. That's the way it's done—you bounce off the opposition. Dad could have done that all right, but he was much better when he was just pontificating.

"And I don't know if Dad would have made it on television or not. He was much faster than Twain, who would really milk a gag a long time. But he was still much slower than today's fast action television. And since he and Twain both wrote all their own material, they'd both have real trouble keeping up."

How about an occasional guest host shot on the Johnny Carson Show?

His father a latter day Jay Leno? The concept amused Bill. He had a short, pleasant laugh about it.

"Yes, Dad would have done that well. But if he lives, it will be because of his writings. And he lived in the right age for that.

"Dad's column perfectly fit his times. It was like being on all three networks every morning. People would read the headline and what Will Rogers said about the headline.

"I didn't realize it until after he died, but Dad was a powerful man in Washington. He could make people or break people. And he was probably the last col-yumnist who sat on both sides of the aisle. The only time he was really critical was of the Hoover Administration in the Depression. He sided with the Okies and the Arkies, of course. But even so, he had a humorous way of doing it."

"Now quit blaming the Democrats and quit blaming the Republicans," Bill said in an absolute copy of his father's voice. "They're not smart enough to have thought of all this themselves!"

Back in his own voice, Bill continued, "Dad was perceptive. And he was powerful. He could make or unmake, even hurt or advance people very much. But I think his political analyses lacked a certain depth. He didn't have time is why. He was writing everyday. Maybe if he had lived longer....

"But humor is ephemeral and doesn't last forever. Dad was the best read and best quoted person in the country and he handled that well. He was a friend of both Republicans and Democrats. He came up from the Ziegfeld Follies and he was unquestionably the greatest roper of his time. But that doesn't put him in a class with Mark Twain, who was a much better and more lasting analyst of this country.

"It just makes me blush with shame when people go on about Dad. Especially those Oklahomans. But now I'm 75 years old and I'm looking back from a long perspective of history. Dad was a major, outstanding figure of his time. But that's about all you can say."

A pause. A brief long-away look.

"But that's quite a little, too.

"And isn't that the same thing you could say about your Route 66?"

SEARCHING FOR *66*

FORTY-THREE

The longest, straightest surviving stretch of U.S. 66 lies between Seligman and Kingman in western Arizona. Its roadbed arcs gently northwest from Seligman, following the Santa Fe's tracks through Yampai, Nelson, and Peach Springs, capital of the Walapai Indian Reservation. Arcing back south from Peach Springs, it follows the railroad again through Truxton, Hyde Park, Valentine, Hackberry, Crozier and on to Kingman, the last town of size before California. Along this 81-mile length, the yellow land dips and rolls and crosses scores of washes. But there are still straightaways of ten, eleven and twelve miles, plus numerous shorter ones where even the weakest of cars can reach top end and cruise.

When 66 was still a national thoroughfare, a band of life stretched across this high, treeless land. Many Walapai families made their livings running the stations, cafes and motels along the way. But when I-40 replaced 66 in the early '80s, it discarded the Yampai-Peach Springs-Hackberry arc and headed straight west from Seligman to Kingman. Peach Springs, at thirty-six miles, gained the unsought distinction of being the town most thoroughly bypassed by the interstate system. And travelers flowed as if by gravitational force along the new highway.

At 700 members, the Walapai Indians are one of the smallest distinct ethnic groups in the world. For uncounted centuries, they lived in Grand Canyon country as nomadic hunters and seed gatherers. The land surrendered its sparse treasures reluctantly, leaving the Walapai little time to develop the elaborate culture, ceremonies and arts of other tribes. They didn't even see their first white man, Father Francisco Garces, until the year that Thomas Jefferson wrote the Declaration of Independence.

On a material level, the Walapai never did prosper. But it took that first white man (and the millions more who followed) to make them realize how poor they were. Before Father Garces, everybody worked. Now sixty-five percent of the tribe is unemployed. A reservation's boundaries squeezed them together first. Later, Route 66 and centralized government housing concentrated them even more. A subsistence economy became a money economy became a welfare economy. Before Father Garces, the Walapai claimed their supper with an arrow or trap. Now many of them claim it with food stamps.

Marty Whatsoniame (what-so-knee-ami) is Assistant Development Officer for the Walapai People. When my letter was published in the Kingman newspaper, he sent me a formal reply.

"It would be advantageous for you to include a scheduled stop at the Walapai Indian Reservation," he'd said. "Route 66 runs directly through the reservation and we have many people who have 'lived, loved, driven and died along its way.'

Marty Whatsoniame, Peach Springs, Arizona.

"Please feel free to contact me on your journey thru."

So I did. I found a dark, heavy, round-faced man of about 30. He had long hair and glasses, which are not uncommon among Indians. But he also had a beard—the first one I'd seen on an Indian—and spots of a moustache above the corners of his mouth.

"Before I got this job last October, I hadn't even heard of development," Marty said in his paper-strewn office at tribal headquarters. "Now I'm a development officer.

"The problem is whether to have development and the changes it will bring or maintain what we have now. We have uranium in the mountains, but it's not being mined. Here in town, two-thirds of the people are unemployed and they're going into Kingman all the time for food stamps and surplus food."

Officer Whatsoniame spread his dark, lined hands to show the choice's extremes. If it tapped its ore reserves, his tiny tribe would be among the nation's wealthiest per capita.

"But some people like things the way they are," he said. "Some Walapai believe that digging into the earth is like digging into their heart, or their liver, or their lungs. They would protest."

Like most of the younger Walapai, Marty had spent half his life off the reservation. The U.S. government required that all Walapai children attend school, but it closed the one on the reservation long ago. Marty, like Indian children from a dozen other tribes, was sent to a boarding school in Phoenix for five years. When he reached his teens, his mother moved the family to Long Beach. After six years, she'd had enough, returned to the reservation, and married a Navajo. An older brother enrolled in an Indian urbanization program and moved to Chicago—where he was fatally rolled outside a bar when he flashed his first paycheck. Marty stayed behind in California awhile, trying a series of odd jobs and colleges. Following 66, he gravitated slowly homeward—first to San Bernardino, then to Barstow, Needles and King-man. In 1985, he finally came back to the "Res."

Marty appreciates traditional views on mining, but thinks *some* development would be healthy. A more benign form, the one he seeks, is tourism. He thinks that 66, so rich in history and sentiment along its route, is a natural draw. In his Datsun pick-up, he drove out to show me why. An expert guide, he showed me the trading posts, the old motels, the crumbling gas stations, the abandoned school.

"Some of these could be fixed up if we could get 66 tourists coming through," he said. "It would be real historical."

At a graveled pull-off west of town, Marty pointed out the Grand Canyon in the dust-fogged distance.

"The Tribe has raft trips down the Colorado," he said. "It's the most scenic way to see the Canyon."

Out in the middle of scenic nowhere, Marty pulled up to a gate. I held it open while he pulled through and we drove down an ancient cinder road, dodging truck-high weeds in our path.

"This is the original 66, man," my guide said. "The Main Street of America. Who would have thought it?"

After the tour, we stopped by to visit with Marty's mother.
Beth Wauneka, her husband Louis, and Marty's sister Pinky live in a stucco, ranch-style home in a Peach Springs housing development. Except for the bare yards, the neighborhood could be a modern subdivision most anywhere in the west. I even noticed a water meter at the side of the house as we walked up to the door.

"Yeah," Marty said. "The government put them in a few years ago so we would all have to pay individually for our water. But they've never hooked them up."

Beth, Louis and Pinky are all artists—a rare occupation on the Walapai Reservation. A loom, an easel, supplies for beadwork, a quilt in progress, and various arts and crafts paraphernalia fill their living room, leaving not even space for a couch. The family gathering place is the dining room table, where we all sat with glasses of fresh tap water. Marty stayed until a conversation was well underway, then went back to his office to finish off some paperwork.

Marty said his mother knew all about 66. Before I could find out much, though, I had to tell her all about myself. Where was I from? What did I do for a living? What was this book I was writing? Did I have any pictures? Was I married?

When Beth's curiosity was finally satisfied, I got to ask her how life had changed on the reservation since I-40 had bypassed it.

"Fewer dead Indians along the road," she answered quickly. and her well-rounded frame shook in appreciation of her humor. But she was also serious. When 66 was a national highway, she said, as many as one Walapai a week would lose his life when a truck or car would stray off the concrete and onto the shoulder where he was walking or lying. I-40, while taking away a major source of the Walapais' livelihood, had also taken away one of their leading causes of death.

Louis nodded in agreement. Sporting a long and wondrously stringy beard, he carved a piece of wood as we talked. For his benefit as well as my own, we all spoke in the only language he and Beth share—English. He'd been a policeman and then an alcoholism counselor on the Navajo Reservation. In newspaper reports on roadside deaths, he said you could always tell when the driver was also an Indian because his name would not be mentioned.

I'd heard that an Indian's liver and other vital organs were different than the white man's, less tolerant of alcohol, and thus more susceptible to the drug's abuses.

"That's not true," Beth said readily. "There's no difference between my organs and a white person's."

She paused as we considered the remark. Her frame. though racked by arthritis, began to shake again.

"Except my organs may be larger."

Beth's journey to California during Marty's teen years had been her second. As a girl, she remembers traveling 66 to Los Angeles where her mother and an aunt worked at a Chinese laundry.

"They'd work all day long beating laundry for this Chinaman," she said. "When they asked him for pay, he walked around a lot and finally said, 'You want sex?'

"And another time they worked all day for another Chinaman and asked him for their pay. This one was right on 66. He hemmed and hawed around, went in his office like he was going to get the money, then finally came out again. 'You want sookie?' he said. 'You want sookie?'" She laughed again, but not so easily.

"But that's all over for me now," she said. "I'm home. I suppose the Chinamen have Mexicans working for them now."

When I left to go see Marty again, Beth walked me slowly to the door and watched me away. As I started my car's engine, I heard her call to her husband in the kitchen.

"Louie, did you get that steak out of the freezer yet?"

SEARCHING **66**
FOR

FORTY-FOUR

Five o'clock in Walapai land, like everywhere else in America, is quitting time. Marty invited me to supper, I accepted, and we locked the doors to the tribal headquarters and drove down to Goldenstein's Cash and Carry on Old 66.

Bob Goldenstein's dad moved to Peach Springs 50 years ago to run a trading post. When Bob grew up, he married a Walapai woman and kept the post going, evolving it today into a modern grocery store complete with a game room and videotape center. While I talked with Bob, the only white man I'd meet that day, Marty gathered up a box of spaghetti, a jar of Ragu and some lettuce.

Marty's home is the former living quarters of a century-old trading post. Unusually for an Indian, he lives alone—except this week his brother Chris was staying there.

"His wife kicked him out, too," Marty said. Chris just smiled and took the groceries. While he fixed supper, Marty and I went to run a "few" errands.

First we crossed the Santa Fe tracks to a small house where Marty's ex-wife, Jean Fielding, and their children live. He talked with her briefly while the children lay stretched out on the living room floor, chins propped up in their hands, watching a big screen TV. On the way out, he waved at three kids playing in the camper top of a pick-up.

"Cousins," he explained.

By scenic back roads, we wound our way across Peach Springs to Beth's house. He took a can of corn in and came out carrying a check.

"Now don't put *your* name on it!" Beth called after him.

By yet another route, we took the check over to Jean's and gave it to her, then drove to Goldenstein's for something Marty had forgotten. In the parking lot, we met a cousin who needed a ride. She stuck her groceries and her kid in the back of the truck, pulled the tailgate down and sat passively on it as the truck bumped and rattled its way up a dirt road to yet another cousin's house.

Back home, I helped Chris clear off a tiny dinette table in the living room and set it for supper. While we worked, Marty propped a 5-inch TV on a nearby stool and carefully tuned it into the news "because I like to see how somebody's fucking up while I eat." I brought in a six-pack from the car. The three of us sat at the table in the last strong rays of sunlight and watched a clever news segment about a cinnamon roll shop in a Phoenix mall.

Between Truxton and Valentine, Arizona.

Meeting with Bill Rogers had meant making a loop around the entire state of Arizona. When I got back to Peach Springs, I stopped to see Marty again. He recognized me through his screen door and hailed me on in. Jean had brought over her big screen TV and she, Marty, and two other Indian men were watching video movies on it. The man nearest the door looked at me in challenge and interest as I opened the door and walked in.

"Hey! A white man!" he said in unaccented English. "My name's Russell Means!"

"Hi, Russ," I said. "I'm Dennis Banks."

Marty waved at my inquisitor. "It's all right, man. This is my friend. He's writing a book about Route 66."

And then to me: "Come on and have a beer."

The first man was not the activist Means, but Ned Beecher, a cousin of Marty. The other man was "Moon," a lanky, Walapai-Pima crossbreed and also a cousin. They'd been drinking beer and watching videos with Marty since six o'clock that morning. An office-size refrigerator, freshly restocked, stood in one corner.

Ned stood up and commanded me to take his seat on the couch. For the next two hours, only Moon paid much attention to the movies as I quickly learned Beth Wauneka is not the only skilled interrogator among the Walapai.

Jean had had a softball game at noon and had been with the men only an hour. A beautiful, trim woman whose white blood gave her a finely chiseled nose and a sunburn. she took the first turn. Her questions were friendly and almost easy: What's it look like in Illinois? Why do you want to do a book about Route 66? Are you married? Where are your children?

Ned was stocky and wore closely-cropped hair and a football jersey. He was also friendly enough, but his questions gave me more of a chance to screw up: Why do you want to write about us? What can a white man say about the Walapai? What's the sense of a book, anyway? And, underlying all the other questions: How did the white man manage to muck things up so much?

My sincerity fogged the air and eventually Ned eased off. Earlier he'd admonished me for saying I was part Cherokee ("Don't say that. You can't be *part* anything."). Later he boasted that he was one quarter Irish himself and had even spent two years at San Jose State before coming back to the Res. For a white man, he guessed I was a nice enough guy. At one point, he even sang a song for me in Walapai. Marty, who understands the language but doesn't speak it, followed the words with hand motions.

In between movies, Moon walked over to me and laid a hand on my knee. "Don't write about us, Tom," he said earnestly. "Leave us alone. Don't write about us." His hand pressure tightened.

Marty broke in. "Hey bro, this is my house, right?"

Moon turned. "Right," he said solemnly.

"You're my cousin, right?"

"Right."

"We're number one, right? You know I love you, right?"

Moon nodded.

"Then lighten up."

So he did. He took his hand off my knee, listened to the rest of us awhile, then ambled out on the porch and out of view.

"I know what he was trying to say," Ned said. "Sometimes I wish the white man would just go away and leave us alone." Marty brought him a fresh Bud.

When the children in Beth Wauneka's crafts class at nursery school get unruly, Beth sings to them in Walapai. They don't understand what she's saying, but the novelty of the sound calms the kids down. It's a language they'll probably never speak themselves. Jean and Marty's seven-year-old daughter has been to San Francisco with an Indian dancing troupe; but she'd also spent a good part of the afternoon boogieing to music from the TV set. The Walapai talk of the independent life, but live the dependent one. Which isn't so different from the rest of us. And that's what rankles them.

"To-om!" Moon's disembodied voice, hoarse and toothless, floated through the screen door. "To-om!"

His appeal took an insistent tone. "To-o-om!"

"Should I go out and see him?"

Marty said nothing. Ned and Jean exchanged short glances. "I don't think so," Jean said. "Stay in here."

The refrigerator emptied out. Marty, who would lose his job a year later when money for it ran out, crashed. Moon ambled back in. The conversation continued another hour or so, a series of swapped tales about 66 and the Indian life. Ned, who a month later would be decapitated in a car crash east of town, wanted me to drive us all to a cave near the Grand Canyon to camp out. But I remembered how deep the ruts in reservation back roads can be and I declined. It was time to go on to Kingman.

Ned held up a palm. "Not so fast, white man!" He had one more question. "We've just spent all this time telling you what it was like to be an Indian. Now you tell us what it's like to be a white man."

"Yeah!" Jean encouraged. "Tell us what it's like. Where do you belong?"

I was stunned. It hadn't occurred to me before to define myself like that. My family's been in this country 350 years. We've diffused. I was just the mainstream now, what's left over when all distinct cultures and ethnic groups have been filtered out. I was everybody else. But I didn't know how to say it.

"I like to move," I said, thinking of my past three months on the road. "I like to see what's next, to have goals. That's what it's like to be a white man, I guess—I always have to be going somewhere."

"Then you don't belong anywhere," Jean said.

Yes I did belong somewhere, I said. In fact, I belonged everywhere. The Walapai are a land-bound, deeply rooted people. But so was I, I told Ned and Jean. The only difference was where they had just a million acres to fill, I had the whole country. That's why I needed Route 66.

Ned sat declaiming on the couch as I finally got up to leave Peach Springs. Jean walked me to the door. I leaned forward slightly, Jean did the same—and our lips met in a kiss. Then the road took me somewhere else.

SEARCHING FOR 66

FORTY-FIVE

"You have never lived until you have taken part in a high-speed chase over Oatman Hill."

Clyde McCune
A Man Who Ought to Know

Oatman Hill is Route 66's precarious gateway to California. Twelve miles of hairpin turns and shoulderless switchbacks west of Kingman, it is the most treacherous all-weather road in America—get to its top safely and you can almost coast to the Golden State. Many a driver has given his soul to God in return for a safe trip over this piece of the Main Street. And many of them have made that promise with Clyde McCune hot on their criminal tail.

"I retired three years ago after twenty years on the bench in the justice court," he wrote after seeing my letter in the Mohave *Daily Miner*. "Before that time, I had six years part-time and six years full time on the Mohave County Sheriff's Office. I also spent many years in the municipal court and as the Walapai Tribal judge.

"Since retirement, I've gotten quite independent. I hear a few cases in the municipal court as well as the justice court, but can generally arrange my schedule to fit my desires. When you come through Kingman, if you'd like to talk to me, I'm probably available."

Clyde was right about the word "probably." On my first loop through Kingman, he wasn't available. He was the second time, though, and we agreed to meet for lunch in the restaurant at the Quality Inn—whose owner, 66 enthusiast Jerry Richard, was putting me up for a few days.

"I'll be sitting at the counter," Clyde said over the phone. "All my hair's on my chin. Don't look for any on my head."

His Future Honor McCune had a '33 Chevy, a $20 bill and an invalid wife when he came to 66 country forty years ago. And that was all. Not a home, not a friend, not a job—not even an idea for one.

"I was an engineer's test pilot in Indiana during the war," he said when we got settled in one of the restaurant's booths. "A Chuck Yeager type. But my wife got Marie Strumpel's Disease, a vicious kind of arthritis that freezes up the whole spine. She couldn't move her head. She couldn't move her back, hips, shoulders, arms, hands and knees. She carried a lot of *pain* with her.

Clyde McCune, Kingman, Arizona.

"The Air Force offered to promote me to major if I stayed. But I had to make the decision—stay in and let strangers take care of my wife or get out and take care of her myself. The doctor said Arizona climate would be good for her, so I resigned my commission and here we come."

Clyde studied his cigarette ash, then flipped it expertly into a tray.

"She'd have done the same for me," he said.

The day's talk was fast, nearly non-stop, and came equally from both sides.

"I was raised in Nebraska in the middle of the Dust Bowl," Clyde said in his barbershop tenor. "First time I got into an airplane was when I got in with an Air Force instructor. You had to have two years college to get in. Well, I didn't. But I'd always wanted to fly and from the time I got out of high school, I studied everything I could in the way of advanced mathematics, physics. If you could take their entrance exam and pass it, you could get in. I was just egotist enough to think I could do that. And I did. Guys in the squadron used to call me 'Pappy.' I was 25 years old. But out of a hundred and sixty fellows, I had the second highest grade when we graduated.

"I had the best racket in the Air Force. There was nobody shooting at my tailfeathers. I wish I could have stayed. But..."

"I was feeling pretty lonesome when I got here," Clyde went on. "Then I heard Bob Goldenstein Sr. needed some help in Valentine—on the reservation. Went out there. I find out he used to run a grocery store in my home town in Nebraska."

Clyde went immediately to work as a dishwasher. Bob Sr. had a motel, a service station, a cafe, a grocery store and a post office in Valentine. Eventually, the former test pilot worked in them all.

"When I came here, I was looking for a job," Clyde said of his early work. "Then I started looking for a position."

That first position came one night at Bob's cafe when the superintendent of the Walapai Indian Agency stormed in.

"The reservation had its own power plant then," Clyde said, stroking the goatee he's cultivated as his hair's migrated south. "And the superintendent was all bent out of shape because the plant operator had got drunk. They'd fired him and bounced him off the reservation. Found out later he's the only guy who knows how to run the place and the voltage was going down.

"So I told the superintendent 'I'll be off work in about twenty minutes. I'll come down and see if I can straighten things out.' I've never figured out how I did it. But I knew electricity pretty good from my engineering test. I knew what the plant was supposed to be doin'. All I had to figure out was *how* to do it. And I did.

"So the superintendent says to me, 'Hey! You want to come work for us?' Hell, I was an independent. I said, 'How much do you pay?' It was about four times as much as I was making, so I went to work at the power plant."

Clyde worked at the plant until the Rural Electrification Administration sent its wires to Walapai Land. The plant closed down, but the Walapai wanted him to stay and offered him a new job as tribal judge. Clyde responded with his usual lack of low self-regard.

"I'd never been a judge before," he said. "But I figured I could learn. So I began to study law. Started out with just one of these home courses from LaSalle Extension. At the time, you could actually pass the bar from that course. Then after I took the course, they changed the law and I couldn't be a lawyer here anymore."

It was the only setback in the man's law career. Eventually, the same people who denied him the right to be a practicing attorney asked him to sit on the Judicial Qualifications Commission—and to help rewrite Arizona's lower court and criminal codes.

"At one time, I had a corner on justice on the reservation," Clyde said. "I was the judge for tribal misdemeanors, the deputy sheriff for the whites, and the felony investigator for the Bureau of Indian Affairs. I was the law west of the Pecos."

A glint of a smile reflected from Clyde's steel blue eyes.

"I learned early on that I was too little to whip too many people, so I learned to talk," he admitted. "One day my dad was visiting and we were driving back from Kingman. Got up ahead by Truxton Canyon and all these cars were backed up both ways on 66. I looked down and saw the tribal paddywagon parked crossways blocking the road. I figured the tribal officer was having some problem, so I says, 'Let's go up and help him.'

"We drove down the ditch, drove back up there and here was the tribe's chief of police, drunker than $300. He's got an old couple from Indiana stopped and he's waving his service revolver around the old man's nose. I told Dad to go on into Peach Springs—I was going to handle the situation. He said, 'You're gonna get killed, too.' I said, 'No, I'm not...I don't think!'

"So I took the chief's gun away from him, took his badge away from him, threw him in his own paddywagon and brought him back to Peach Springs. Charged him with assault."

Another time, Clyde said he'd tried talking again—only to be cut short.

"One night my wife and I drove into Valentine to have dinner with the public health nurse," he said. "We're sittin' at her kitchen table and I hear this high-powered rifle fire. I look out and this Indian boy's up in the rocks with a 30-30. He's shooting down into the Indian camp. I've known him since he was a little kid, so I step out the door and say, 'Jerry! Put that gun down and come down here!'

"And he spun around and he shot and that bullet sounded like a bullwhip goin' by my ear! I learned pretty quick how to dig a ditch in the hard road with my nose. I had a little two-inch hide out gun, five shells—that was all I had. He shot at me twenty-seven times. After the twentieth time, I thought, 'That's it. That's your box of shells'. Then he shot the twenty-first and I thought, 'Sonofabitch! You got two boxes!"

I refilled Clyde's cup and lit his cigarette. "It must take a lot of coolness under that kind of pressure," I said.

"I don't know," Clyde said. "I was terrified! Scared to death! But somebody had to take care of the boy. Somebody had to do something with him. That's what they gave me that badge for.

"Anyway, the stand-off went on for about five hours. Eventually, the Indian policeman came. I had him shake the brush down in the wash to draw the fire while I tried to flank the kid.

"I got about as close to him as from me to you. He had no idea I was there. I started to shoot. Then I thought, 'I believe I can whip this kid.' So I bulldogged him, got my arm around his neck, put my knee in his back, and jerked the rifle out of his hand."

The waitress came by with a second pot of coffee.

"No thanks, dear," Clyde said. "If I have another drop, I'll percolate."

Jerry's spent only two months of his life since then on the right side of a jailhouse door. The episode with Clyde landed him at the federal juvenile reform center in Denver until his twenty-first birthday. A month after he came home, he got into an argument with his father at a Kingman bar and stabbed him. The wound wasn't fatal, so Jerry's sentence was light—six years at Arizona State Prison. A month after he got out from that, the still-young man raped and killed an Indian girl. His return to Arizona State was swift and permanent.

"It got pretty bad on the reservation," Clyde said. "Every night they'd have these big battles or big parties. People would come to the trading post where I lived, kick on the door, and demand I do something about it. Eventually, I'd get up, go fill the jail with drunk Indians. Next morning, I'd go down, get 'em out of jail, line 'em up in front of the bench, see what I could do with 'em.

"Once I called the federal solicitor in Phoenix. I said, 'You got to do something!' He said, 'Is the tribe doing anything about it?' I said, 'No. They seem to be satisfied with it.' He said, 'Well, I'll get you a policeman up there one of these days."

Between Kingman and Oatman, Arizona.

After three years in Valentine, Clyde was persuaded to become the sheriff's dispatcher in Kingman. But after only three weeks behind a mike in Kingman, the sheriff put him behind the wheel of a patrol car.

"Hell, I don't know how to be a deputy sheriff," Clyde told the sheriff. "I think you do," the sheriff told him. A new deputy was off and rolling.

"The county covered 15,000 square miles, includin' a hundred and nine of Route 66," the jack-of-all-law said. "We had three highway patrolmen, three deputy sheriffs, and eight city policemen. We were all on the same frequency and everybody did basically what came next. You might find the highway patrolman in the city workin' a burglary and the city police officer out in the country settlin' the peace and the deputy sheriff on the highway.

"I had three robbers cornered once and only one pair of handcuffs. When I called for help, the city police, an FBI agent and a livestock inspector showed up. They still work together well out here."

The check came. Clyde won a gentlemanly dispute over who got the honor of paying for it by offering to arm wrestle me. I set a tip on the table.

"So it was during your Kingman time, then, that you had all those thrilling chases up Oatman Hill?" I asked.

"Actually, those high speed chases weren't so great," Clyde answered. "It's an all mountain road. Barely two lanes wide and no shoulder to slide off on. Some of the curves were so tight that the trucks and buses had to pull around partway, back up, and go on back through. We knew exactly how fast we could take every one of them. And the poor guy we were chasin' eventually would just give up."

Clyde glanced at his watch. Time to get back down to the courthouse and continue some research he was doing for a Phoenix law firm. I would have to take that life-defining ride up Oatman Hill on my own. Before we said good-by, though, he drove me down to the courthouse steps so I could get a picture of him. Our route was Andy Devine Avenue, nee 66.

"Just because that's all I talked about, don't get the idea that Route 66 was just cops and robbers and drunken Indians," my new friend warned. "There was also a lot of romance and history along that highway, Maybe Americans *are* restless. Maybe we *are* always lookin' for that pot of gold at the end of the rainbow. Sixty-six let us do that and be that, sure. But it also let us show a lot of good things about our character."

"For example?"

"For example, we always tried to help people along the road. We got the whole spectrum of humanity through here—from the crumb bum who's thumbin' his way across the country to the guy, maybe he was out on the coast, who suffered reverses that were no fault of his own. And he's tryin' to get somewhere else where maybe he's got nothin' but a dream in his eyes. And he's goin' someplace on 66 and he gets here and gets broke down. But he always got there—somebody around here was helpin' him.

"If people had a flat tire, we'd stop. A lot of us lawmen always carried extra water, extra gas. If I saw an old bum walkin' down the road between here and Topock, I'd pick him up and give him a ride. They may not have liked me for it in Topock, but that's the way it was.

"That helping spirit is still alive, too. I-40 may have replaced 66, but you got the same people."

"Like you, for instance?"

"Oh, I don't know," Clyde said. "I always felt you really don't know a hell of a lot...but you *do* exist. I've never been too damned impressed with my own importance. But I'm an independent. I enjoy life. I enjoy people. And I've had a lot of fun in life."

Other wonders and attractions along Route 66 had often failed to live up to expectations. But Oatman Hill did not disappoint. In allowing the Father of Highways through this barren moonscape of land getting ready to be a desert, Nature made the barest of compromises. Except for occasional piles of mine tailings, the highway is often the only trace of civilization—or even this world as we know it—and not a very reassuring one at that. It just kept going up and back and forth and up and back and up, up, up. If God didn't have my soul by the time I reached the halfway point, it was because He didn't want it. I saw now why there had been no fatalities on this stretch during its last ten years as a national highway—everyone was too scared to drive fast.

Oatman, Arizona.

At the top of the hill, at last, stood Oatman, a turn-of-the-century gold-mining center. Brochures called it a ghost town, but that was mostly for tourist appeal. Semi-tame burros wandered the streets, mooching hand-outs. Handpainted "66" signs dotted the main drag. And at the Oatman Hotel, the room which Gable and Lombard honeymooned in had been turned into a museum.

I took a pleasant walk around Oatman, then took a deep breath and plunged down the other side of the hill and toward Topock, the last 66 town in Arizona. As I crossed some reedy lowlands near the Colorado River—the land where the Joads' retarded son Noah had left his family—I said farewell, after two and a half weeks, to Arizona.

SEARCHING FOR 66

FORTY-SIX

Spire-like rock formations east of town gave Needles its name; July and August gave Route 66's first California town its longtime title: Hottest City in America. Days during those months when the mercury fails to break 100 are rare; days when it reaches 110 are only average. Before air conditioning, railroad men sent their families to nearby mountains every summer to escape the heat. It is so hot in Needles, says Johnny Carson, that even the thermometers get heatstroke.

Folks in Needles are an easygoing lot, but they could do without the notoriety, so a few years ago they moved the city's official thermometer from downtown to the airport. The elevation gain was only three hundred feet, but it succeeded in shifting the hottest town duel to a daily slugout between the nearby Colorado River boomtowns of Bullhead City and Lake Havasu City, Arizona. The move didn't cool Needles even a fraction—it's still as hot as ever there. But the town relinquished its title gracefully.

Grandma Joad was buried in Needles. Calamity Jane once ran a whorehouse on the edge of town. The Hotel California on 66 welcomed guests to a "unique air conditioning system guaranteed to keep your room temperature between 74 and 75 degrees." And during the route's heyday, shops and stations in Needles thrived on sales of thermostats, blocks of ice, flaxen water bags, swamp coolers you could hang from your car window, and other hot weather aids.

Until the Corps of Engineers tamed the lower Colorado by turning it into a series of lakes, the chance for travelers to buy survival gear was Needles' major draw on passing tourists. Its population topped off at 7,000 shortly after World War II, then fell to 4,000 when the interstate went through. Cars were better, roads were faster; who needed Needles? The Hotel California, once such a lovely place, has been boarded up. The county seat is two hundred miles away. There weren't even any bookstores when I passed through. Only in the past few years has there been a modest upturn—"Snowbirds," retirees from colder parts of the country, have found Needles a comfortable, affordable place to build a winter home. There's also been some spillover from Laughlin, a new gambling resort a few miles upriver in Nevada.

Even with this development, the desert can be a sparse and lonely place. But Maggie McShan, a local historian and community pillar, has lived in Needles for two-thirds of her seventy-five years—and she has no intention of leaving.

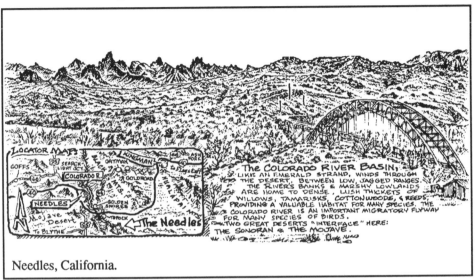

Needles, California.

"We know there aren't any trees here," she told me. "But that's compensated for by the ground being easier to see. The desert is a tremendous place for studying geology and rock hounding and hunting pretty stones. And we have a fabulous flower show in the spring."

Maggie, though, can see beauty anywhere. But a seven-year-old boy who's just moved to town might see things quite a bit differently. Not knowing how to compensate like Maggie does, he might think it's pretty lonely out here on the edge of nowhere. And if he should move away again in just a year, his memories of Needles' heat and isolation might be heightened with the passage of time. Then if he should grow up to be a world famous cartoonist and choose to write about his desert days, you would have Charles Schulz and his Mojave alterego, Spike.

Schulz lived a half block off 66 in Needles during second grade. Later in Minneapolis, his family got a little black-and-white mixed-breed dog they named Spike.

"He was the smartest and most uncontrollable dog that I have ever seen," Schulz says. "You could say to him, 'Spike, do you want a potato? Why don't you go downstairs and get a potato?' and he would immediately go downstairs and stick his head in the potato sack and bring up a potato."

When Schulz created the comic strip "Peanuts" in the mid '50s, Spike was the inspiration for the beagle Snoopy. And in the early '70s when Schulz started recounting his Needles days, he did it by giving Snoopy a desert-dwelling brother named Spike.

Like the original Spike and his better known sibling, the new Spike is a black-and-white, beagle-type dog. Unlike Snoopy, though, who is bareheaded and clean shaven, Spike sports a battered fedora and a droopy moustache. And where Snoopy views the world through slits or spots, Spike has full-fledged eyes. They also droop, making him look tireder and more world weary than his brother.

You never see any adults in "Peanuts"—only children and animals. In his Mojave scenes, Schulz carries this isolation motif one step further: Spike is always entirely alone. There are no kids, no other dogs—you don't even see the coyotes which occasionally attack. Snoopy hitchhiked 66 once to visit his brother, but did not appear in the same panel with him when he got there. Like his creator fifty years ago, Spike is on the desert and he is alone, his only companions the saguaro cactus.

"Life here on the desert is hard and wonderful," Spike wrote to his brother one Sunday. "Sometimes it is very hot. And the nights can be very cold. Sometimes it rains and sometimes we have flash floods. Sometimes it even snows."

He tossed his fedora onto the arm of a waiting saguaro.

"But there are always beautiful places to walk and when I return home, I always have a place to hang my hat."

Spike carries on a continuous monologue with his cactus friends—dressing them like waiters so he can dine out, stringing lights on them at Christmastime, practicing field goal kicking through their upraised arms. Sometimes he'll go dancing with one of them, but only if it promises not to dance too close. And when seized by the civic spirit, he calls a meeting of the Cactus Club.

For a night out, Spike will hitch into Needles and play some video games. If traffic is sparse, he settles for a ride on a skateboard. For a living, he once tried a roadside art stand. When that didn't get many walk-ins, he set up a real estate office and advertised oceanfront condominiums for coyotes—which is why they attacked him.

I wondered if the folks in Needles liked the kind of attention that Spike brought them.

"My gracious, yes!" said Margaret Bemish, retired director of the Chamber of Commerce. "In the beginning, we had no idea why Mr. Schulz was writing about us. It was odd that he would make that kind of gesture and not explain why or visit here. I even had a call from—of all places—Tokyo and this young man was talking to me about Spike and Needles.

"But then one day Mr. Schulz was just driving through and he stopped to look up his old home. It was before the Bicentennial. He was very charming, but he didn't want any publicity. Just browsing. He said there'd be a surprise for us the next Father's Day. We looked and there was Spike writing a letter to his father from Needles."

Larry DeAtley owns a cold storage firm which caters to the Laughlin casinos. He's also president of the Needles Chamber of Commerce. Spike didn't bother him, either.

"My dad always used to say, 'I don't mind if you mention my name as long as you get it right,'" he told me. And that was as official as he got.

Down at the Hungry Bear Cafe on Old 66, a coffee klatsch from the Needles Police Department was said to gather every mid-morning. Crime would be strictly forbidden during this period as the lawmen discussed the day's events and checked the pulse of the town.

"I see we're in the funny papers again," a patrolman was reported to have said one morning.

"Yeah," said another, "It's because we're funny, that's why. We are funny. Anybody who would come here or stay here at this time of year..."

"Now just a minute," the chief intervened. "Things aren't as bad as all that. Think of the publicity. It's better than a big billboard."

In 1981, Mayor Dave Daniel declared July 4th Spike Day in Needles. Schulz has been invited several times to be grand marshall in the day's parade. He's always graciously declined. Far from being offended by their syndicated caricature, Needles' people have embraced it.

Jim Lambert, a local realtor, has done a particularly good job of embracing Spike—though he's reluctant to talk about it. His firm is called Spike Realty. His office is decorated with *Peanuts* paraphernalia, he keeps a scrapbook of all of Spike's strips for clients and other visitors to browse through, and he had a man-sized Spike costume made to wear in the annual parade.

"But the costume's retired now," Jim said, gesturing to where it hung in an office corner. "All I did was wear it in parades, but the Schulz people wrote and told me not to use it."

Yet Jim's kept the Spike Realty name. And he's planning a Spike Subdivision with street names like Snoopy Boulevard and Woodstock Avenue. Which is why he had little to say. But there was pride in his silence, even a hint of defiance. Route 66 is gone. The railroad is all but gone. And the interstate hardly stays in town long enough to say it's been there. But Needles hangs on. Who knows, the San Andreas fault may change our coastline one day and Spike might actually sell some of those oceanfront condos.

SEARCHING FOR *66*

FORTY-SEVEN

I headed west from Needles and into the Mojave Desert. Interstate travelers can cross the Mojave in less than two hours and without a single shift of gears. But early travelers on 66 counted themselves lucky to get across in two days. The route's first roadbed here was mostly graded sand. Bridges weren't built across some of the wider washes until the 1930's. And part of the road near Needles was even "paved" with redwood planks dragged into place by mules. Legend has it that a tourist saw a hat on the sandy road one day and stopped to pick it up. To his surprise, there was a man's head underneath. "I'll get a shovel and clear you out," the tourist said. "You better go back and get a tractor," the head replied. "I'm in my Oldsmobile."

Early Indian trails through this rugged terrain connected a series of watering holes, springs and intermittent rivers—each about a day's walk from the other. When the Santa Fe came, it built water towers and equipment sheds by these spots and, for administrative purposes, named them in alphabetical order: Amboy, Bristol, Cadiz, Danby, Essex, Fenner, Goffs, Home, Ibex, Java and Klinefelter. When 66 came, service businesses began opening in the alphabet communities and they became real towns. But when I-40 came through in the 70's, it bypassed every one of them. With their lifeline gone dry, several of the towns simply disappeared back into the desert. Others survive out of stubbornness or inertia.

Essex, among the bare survivors, enjoyed a day in the national sun in 1977. Its thirty-five residents sent a collective letter that year to the editor of the Los Angeles *Times* lamenting that theirs was the only town in America without television. Johnny Carson read the letter and invited the entire town of Essex to L.A. for dinner and an appearance on his show. A Pennsylvania manufacturer saw the show and donated a $15,000 TV translator to the town. Outside, it was just as hot and isolated as ever in Essex. But inside the people's homes, it could now be anywhere else in America.

I stopped in Essex at June Wellington's gas station-cafe-grocery store. A wooden sign outside commemorated the town's brief celebrity.

But Jim "Bronc" Howard, who was sitting at the formica-top counter having a Sunday afternoon Coors, was quick to correct the myth.

"It was all a bunch of hype," he said. "We'd actually had TV here since 1968 if you had a big enough antenna. Besides, the translator they gave us broke down three years ago and they haven't fixed it. It doesn't make much difference anymore anyway because most people have satellites and VCRs."

Business is generally slow at June's, except when the occasional busload of Marines stops by on its way from Twentynine Palms to Las Vegas. But the troops were off on a war games exercise farther west in the desert today and wouldn't be in. In their absence, June used a thumb nail to pry a Tums off its roll. Later, she took a Tylenol. She and her husband had moved to Essex four years earlier and bought this place. They thought it might save their marriage. Now they were slugging out a divorce. The "winner" would get the business.

Bronc ambled over to the cooler and served himself another Coors. He got his nickname, he says, because he's so hard to break—on a trip back east when he was three years old, he survived a wreck near Tucumcari which killed his mother. And where June had been in Essex only four years, that's all the time Bronc had been away. He even worked at the state maintenance yard in Essex, so weeks at a time could go by without his leaving town.

"I tried Arizona State for two years," he said, his tones like a country boy's from anywhere. "Then I bummed around for a coupla of years playin' pool. But I *like* Essex. It's home. So I came back. Flat, you say? Featureless? Not to me. I know this country. I know where everything is. There's plenty to do here, too. You just have to get a little more basic. I spend a lot of time working on my car, for instance. I fix things for June here. And I help people out. I'm not bored."

I wasn't bored, either, but the sky became overcast and I thought that would be a good time to start my journey again. So I left Bronc and June and Johnny Carsonville and headed west again across the desert.

Though not as colorful as Arizona's Painted Desert, the Mojave was not a monochrome. Most vegetation, except for an occasional cottonwood in a wash, was brown or gray. The soil, if rocks and pebbles can be called that, was tan or dun. Dull red stones lay everywhere, ancient black lava flows stretched toward the horizon, and the road was a silver mirage.

Running parallel to 66 in most places was a rocky gray embankment or berm built to divert the water of the desert's occasional cloudburst. Gathering colored rocks from the desert, people have spelled out their names or laid down designs on the berm, making it our country's longest string of graffiti. As long as something obscene isn't said, Maggie McShan says state maintenance crews let this graffiti stay. So I pulled off on the barest of shoulders, gathered up a few dozen black stones, and fashioned my own message on the rocky desert canvas: "66." I hoped the highway folks wouldn't consider that unauthorized signing and take it away.

SEARCHING FOR 66

FORTY-EIGHT

In Amboy, Buster Burris has been trying to sell his home for ten years. Also three other houses in town which he owns. Also his garage, his cafe, his 30-unit motel, his service station, and even the building which houses the post office. Amboy, California: 44 acres and all improvements, even a 3700-foot gravel runway. It's all Buster's and it's all for sale. You have reliable tenants. The road is well maintained. And it's yours for only $350,000.

Or make an offer. It's been ten years.

Buster didn't set out to own a whole town. In fact, he moved to Amboy in the first place for his health. But the takeover happened gradually over forty-odd years, a building and an opportunity at a time. Before Buster knew it, he had it all.

Jack Rittenhouse called the little kingdom "a popular tourist stop" in his guide to 66. In the town's heyday during the 60's, Buster says his motel-cafe-service station complex would bring in as much as $6,000 a day.

"But as soon as the interstate opened up in 1973—*that day*—that's when she went down," says the 77-year-old, deeply tanned monarch. I-40 passed sixteen miles north of town and more quickly even than overnight, business dropped 90 percent. Buster hung on for four years, then he put the entire town up for sale—lock, stock and airplane hangar. And then, because everything moves slowly in the desert except traffic on I-40, he waited.

Hee Haw, the country music show, investigated the town as a possible production headquarters. A Vietnamese group checked it out as a potential colony site. Dozens of other inquiries have also come in over the years. But only Buster has stayed. Even the school closed down when it could no longer enroll the minimum of twelve students.

Amboy's owner, general manager and majority voter still has hopes of selling the town. He's not planning any rapid departures, though—death will likely be his only exit. And when that finally comes to Buster, there will probably be nothing left in Amboy but a shell and a road once called the Main Street of America. Someday the desert will reclaim them, too.

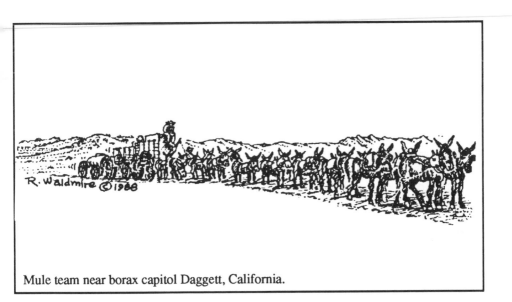

Mule team near borax capitol Daggett, California.

SEARCHING FOR 66

FORTY-NINE

North of Amboy in the Bristol Mountains, interstate highway builders planned to remove several peaks so that portion of their new road could hew straight, flat and uniform. Sixty-eight million cubic yards of earth would have to be moved, creating a gash through the mountains eighty feet wide and a hundred to 350 feet deep. To perform this prodigious feat, engineers proposed a novel means: nuclear bombs. They suggested detonating twenty-two atomic warheads along a two-mile stretch of the Bristols—the equivalent of more TNT than it is useful to imagine. Windows would be broken as far away as Amboy, the ground shock might damage some buildings there, and the radiation might take five years to dissipate to a safe level. But it would save $6 million and might even demonstrate a technique which could be used in building a sea level canal across Panama.

The Atomic Energy Commission had encouraged such uses of nuclear power through its Operation Plowshare program. Faced with an actual opportunity, though, the Commission began backfilling. It required more tests—seismological, meteorological, hydrological, geological. Everything but sociological. Finally the contractor for that stretch could wait no more and removed the earth in the conventional manner. Which is just as good. We should stick with Progress only so far.

The overcast held. The temperature reached scarcely more than 105. I crossed the Mojave with little incident. Back home in the midwest, the humid summer heat hangs on you, drips from you. But desert heat just beats you straight down. And when it takes you, it doesn't even leave a grease spot. Take all the adjectives used to describe desert country—hot, dry, treacherous, beautiful, isolated, lonely, barren, merciless, hot—then consider these modifiers apart from the word "desert." It induces few pleasant images. I was relieved to get across.

The road began climbing again 120 miles out of Needles. By the time I reached Barstow, the elevation was 2,000 feet and the temperature only 85. I found a motel with a big pool and swam the sand out of my pores. Later I went to a movie and felt naked and light in the coolness.

Gas station in Mojave Desert, California.

SEARCHING FOR 66

FIFTY

Several years ago, Stanley Marsh 3 discovered an apartment complex was about to be built near his home outside Amarillo. The wily Texan countered by erecting a sign on land adjacent to the proposed development: "Future Home of the World's Largest Snake Farm." Years later, the sign still stands. But the apartments never got beyond the design stage. Stanley had taken most proper advantage of America's longstanding love-hate relationship with roadside attractions—and who can blame him?

It's nearly impossible to name an animal that wasn't once caged and exhibited along Route 66. It's also hard to imagine a trinket that wasn't sold at one of the highway's roadside stands. Or a miracle of man or nature that couldn't be seen—for a reasonable fee. And when Tocqueville worried that American writing might get so far into the clouds someday that it would be describing a fictitious country, he may have presaged roadside advertising. With signs beckoning as far as 250 miles away from their sites, roadside attractions were irresistible—if not always genuine.

Schlock emporia, snake pits, wax museums, nature's oddities. We've loved them all. We knew we might get taken, but that was part of the thrill. And if the rubber blade fell off Billy's $3 tomahawk the first time he whacked brother Tommy with it, he only got what he deserved. As an institution, roadside attractions could never be considered highbrow or entirely respectable. But neither is the country which spawned them—and they have reflected that with flair and accuracy.

The interstate system has sanitized and franchised commerce along our highways, though, and roadside attractions have not fared well in the new environment. You can find gas and food at most interchanges today. You can even find a $3 tomahawk and pay $6 for it. But a two-headed cow or a mummified outlaw? How can you franchise that? "No surprises" is our travel motto now. That not only threatens roadside attractions—it threatens the whole idea of an open road. We don't want to *be* somewhere anymore when we're traveling—we just want to get there in encapsulated comfort.

Which was the mood I was in one afternoon while driving out of Victorville, California. It had been what I'd come to call a "texture" day. Nothing had sparkled. Nothing had glared. Nothing had stuck out a provocative foot of opportunity to trip me. My most exciting discovery had been something I couldn't even see: the Mojave River. Perhaps our country's wisest river, the Mojave crosses its namesake barrens as an underground stream.

By five o'clock and Victorville, I was thinking not of the road, but of getting through the Cajon pass and on to San Bernardino before nightfall. Not surprisingly, I lost 66 when I came to an interchange south of Victorville. Soon I could see the old route again from the interstate. I could have gotten to it if I had wanted to, but chose to keep moving fast instead. Consequently, I went zooming right past the last genuine roadside attraction on Route 66.

Fortunately, the female form—whether in person or in art—is an attractive one and my instincts caught sight of one for me in the corner of my right eye. She was a bit tall for my tastes—about nine feet—but she was beautiful. A flower graced her dark and flowing hair. A lei rested on her ample, though two-dimensional bosom. A knee was bent slightly, seductively parting her faded grass skirt. Her hands and hips swayed in a frozen hula. A toe had a spot of rust.

I found an exit and doubled back to see this raven-haired beauty. A sign near her said "Hula Ville State Landmark #939." But it was clear from first glance that this was no government institution. It was more like a shrine. Except where most shrines venerate the holy, this shrine paid homage to the discarded—discarded people, discarded things and a discarded way of life.

The hula girl stood on a stage at shrine center. Her floodlights were a series of empty wine bottles collected from alongside the road and lodged upside down on nails around the edge of the stage. Joshua trees, creosote bushes, and a dozen varieties of cactus surrounded her. A dead apple tree stood stage right, empty Coors and Olympia cans dangling on strings from its branches. And randomly throughout the shrine's half acre, hundreds more wine bottles perched bulbously on nails driven into the sides of weathered stakes. Even the state landmark sign had nails driven into it and bottles hanging on. And the late afternoon sun shone through everything.

A few steps to the hula girl's left a small mound had been built up. A hand-painted sign, adorned with an old work shoe suspended by its laces, dubbed the mound Boot Hill. Smaller signs dotted the memorial-within-a-memorial, each remembering a person symbolically buried below: Dirty Neck George, Soapy Smith, Hard Rock Bess, Rubber Tramp Ralph, Chuckawalla Slim, Bugger Red, Steam Train Wagner, Freeway Annie, Shoot 'Em Up Charlie, Stiff Orchid...

"I painted those signs myself," came a high-pitched voice from behind me. "They were all friends I met travelin'. Don't know if some of 'em appreciated 'em, but those were their names."

Miles Mahan, Hulaville, California.

It was the shrine's architect, owner, caretaker and curator—a white-haired, bushy-browed man with red suspenders, tomato seeds in his beard, a permanent gleam in his eye, and a name as worthy as any other on the hill: "Fry Pan" Miles Mahan.

"I used to ride the freights with this fella heah," he said pointing. "Faro Dealer George. We'd get in the accordion space on coal cars and ride. That was in the '20's. Then they went to juice [diesel fuel] in the early '30's and we had to find another spot."

Every nation or people has had its wanderers. But the rails and roads of twentieth century America opened a far larger area to wander in than any gypsies had ever enjoyed before. Though reared in a respectable home in southern California, Miles Mahan fell early prey to the open road's call. In answering it, he and the friends he memorialized were among the first true citizens of the whole country.

Young Mahan wasn't lazy, he made sure to say—his grandmother had cured him of any hope of that while rearing him. He just wasn't happy unless the wind was blowing in his face and today's scenery was different than yesterday's. He not only wanted to see what was over the next hill—he wanted to see what was over *every* hill. So for 35 years he traveled. His nickname came from the cast iron skillet he carried with him. Home was where he used it.

In Los Angeles once, Fry Pan got temporary work driving a pie truck for a restaurant chain.

"You didn't need no license *then*," he said, bringing each sentence to emphatic conclusion. "I come out of this alley and make a *turn*. Turned too quick, the truck flipped over and pies flew *everywhere!*

"And that's the only regular job I ever *had*."

The rest of Fry Pan's youth flowed by in low-budget adventures and the camaraderie of fellow travelers. Once he made a wager with an Indian and another man named Nig Wagner to see who could get from California to Chicago first—without paying for the trip. After three days and six different rides, Fry Pan jumped off a freight in nearby Hammond, Indiana, dropped a slug in the change box of a streetcar, and collected the bet at the speakeasy to which the three of them had mailed it.

"Spent a good part of it there, too," Fry Pan remembered. "Those were the Capone days. You could get away with anything then. All you had to do was have money."

He laughed, then remembered tougher times.

"But they had a sandhouse theah—that's the county jail. Ohh-h-h, that's the worst place in the world. They don't let you smoke or anything."

One day the open road took the young traveler to the beach in San Francisco and the start of a three-decade career in the carnival trade.

"I was lookin' for a job and I come by this scale," Fry Pan said. "And the guy said, 'Well, if you wanna, you can hand out prizes.' After awhile, I started helpin' him flash the joint—draw people in. Then I watched him guess the weights. Began to get on to it. So he had another place on the boardwalk in Santa Cruz and he says, 'Wanna go down there and run my operation, my weighing machine?'

"I stayed there all summer. After Labor Day, I went out on the fair circuit. That lasted until late November. Next year I bought my own scales and went into business for myself. And that was it."

In a poem he wrote later about the Kindell and Graham Show, Fry Pan said, "As nature comes forth without any strife, the carneys all crave the crossroads life." He had found his calling. And for thirty years he practiced it on crowded, dusty midways in the west and midwest.

"You gotta be a showman and make people laugh," the old pro told me. "You gotta make friends with 'em, crack a few jokes, maybe guess a few wrong ones. I'd have a little guy on the seat and I'd say, 'You weigh 200 *pounds*?!?' Even he would laugh. And that's what you gotta do."

Miles and the Hula Girl.

While he was in the trade, Fry Pan collected membership cards in showmen's associations in twenty states. "Toward year's end your mind seems hazy, but who don't like carnival life is crazy," he once wrote. Working the crowds, shooting craps on lazy midway afternoons, hustling pool for food money when everyone was broke, driving the same '41 Plymouth for twenty-nine years—he remembered it all and he loved it still. But when Dirty Neck George, a bar owner in Victorville, told him about this twenty-acre plot south of town, the first faint hair of a root took hold.

He bought the land in 1955. For the first several years, he worked seasons as a booking agent and spent only the winter on the parcel. Highway officials bought an eighty-foot depth of his road frontage in 1956 to widen Route 66. Then when the interstate system was declared in 1957, they came back and bought another eighty feet. Less than two acres of his land was left by then, but it was still enough to retire on, and now Fry Pan had enough money to do just that. After 1960, he left the carney life. In his career, he'd traveled past the entire country. Since his retirement, the entire country has traveled past him.

Hula Ville, recognized as an official state landmark in 1984, started as an answer to the new landowner's persistent litter problem. One day in '57, Fry Pan policed his frontage strip, but had nowhere to dispose of the debris. Rather than just let it pile up, he pounded a few nails into an available fence post and hung wine bottles on them. More discards brought another cactus, then another, then—in time—an entire garden. A friend brought the dead apple tree, giving the beer cans a permanent home. Another friend told Fry Pan about seeing the hula girl in an area junk yard.

"I'd always admired her," her rescuer said. "She used to be in front of a restaurant near here. When they tore the restaurant down in '58, we thought she was gone. But a friend come one day and told me he'd seen her in a scrapyard. I went down there and the only thing you could see was her toes stickin' up. I paid the man a dollar for her, brought her back here, set her up."

After a few moments of gazing at the girl, Fry Pan offered me the grand tour of the grounds. "It's free!" he said. Also priceless. We started by walking through a doorway made from scrap two-by-fours. There was no door, though. And no wall. Just a doorway. A hand-lettered sign above it said "Museum." On a reclaimed pediment above that was a line of beer bottles—preserved just as they'd been found in nature.

"That little bellboy theah with the coconut head—he used to hold a sign at the Claredge Hotel in San Francisco," my guide informed. "The thunderbird sign is an old one from the hotel in Las Vegas. And that bench is from an old gas station on 66."

As we talked, a ground squirrel darted tentatively out from behind one of the many poem-signs on grounds.

"That's Roberta," Fry Pan said. "She's kinda skittish these days. Her mate got killed tryin' to cross the road the other day and I think she's holdin' me responsible for it."

"You know your animals pretty well?"

"Oh sure," Fry Pan said, like he was acknowledging the existence of air. "This is what you might call an animal ho-tel."

Later, a raven left its perch a hundred yards away in a joshua tree and winged its way toward us. Then he saw me and wheeled back. "That was Keith," Fry Pan said. He had rescued the bird several years ago when it got its leg caught in a fence wire. Though the bird regained his health in a couple of weeks, he refused to leave. Soon his mate joined him at Hula Ville. Then a third bird came.

Like a desert Doolittle, Fry Pan has also had a roadrunner that would jump in his lap, a spiny lizard that would eat from his hand, as well as assorted dogs, cats and rabbits. As with all the other outcasts which have made their way there, each has found a home at Hula Ville.

After the tour, Fry Pan took a golf club from its resting place against a post and we played a round on his mini-course—nine cross sections of drain pipe buried in the hard sand at strategic locations. At a quarter a hole, he took me for six bits. Afterwards, we adjourned to Fry Pan's office for a rest. The room had a couch, chairs, a large braided rug, a refrigerator. But then like the rest of this most original place, it started deviating. There was no running water, no electricity. and no walls—just a framework of scrap studs with an old iron fence leaning against it. There was also no ceiling and no floor—just packed sand and sky. And in the center of the room, a joshua tree crowned the scene. Joshuas are a cross between a palm tree and a contortionist. Carefully tended by Fry Pan for 30 years, this one was a prime specimen. Its top arms curved out and then up thirty-five feet in a goalpost pattern. Other arms snaked out at all angles, dipping and curving as the fancy took them. Here and there they swung so low that Miles had propped them up with fence posts. And at odd intervals along them all sprouted bunches of yucca-like leaves.

In the joshua's richly-shadowed shade, in his days of reflection, Fry Pan turned to poetry. He wrote about his carney days, his roadside friends, his animal guests, the women in his life, restaurants he liked, a zoning battle he fought to keep the Hula Girl in place, and even the pleasures of shaving with an electric razor.

Most poets record their work on paper. Fry Pan had preferred to paint his on pieces of board and stick them in the ground. Then two years ago, he had collected and published the poems in a hundred-page book called *Poems from the Valley and Others We Tallied*.

"I want people to know that there once were guys like Seldom Seen Slim and Hubcap Willie," the desert bard said. "To do that, they have to be written down. Kids don't think about things like that, so I do."

Copies of the book were still available for $5—$1.95 off the cover price. "And they're autographed, too," Fry Pan said, assuring their value. I bought one and sat back to read it while its author went to give the grand tour to a couple from Ohio.

The style was distinctive, if not at the laureate level. And the poet showed a certain maturity in his willingness to ignore conventions of meter, rhyme and syntax as his art required it. There was only one rule he never broke, unless by accident, and that was a self-imposed one: All lines in a poem had to be exactly the same length.

In the verse "Comments", Fry Pan explained why:
"Poetry is known for those ragged ends
But with even lines some fun it lends
Yeah, the main reason for all of this
A game to play as I pondered in bliss"
In praise of friends, Fry Pan was unabashed, as in his poem "Smit-

ty the Barber:"

"Though he sleeps, on a sunny hill
Many tell of their haircuts still"

The poet gave clue to his fondness for animals in a poem, "The Stray Doggie":

"He's just a doggie who loves to roam
You may see him passing by your home
Call him Brownie and toss him a bone
Even your Fido may lose his way home"

In his many poems about circus and carnival life, the writer was positively reverential:

"We should be so glad and get down on our knees
Grateful we have so many well-performing fleas"

At other times, he lamented progress:

"Lo, the great freaks have seen their day
On the ten-in-one they were the mainstay
These rare people are in a strange plight
Because to some reformers it wasn't right"

And what poet worth his iambic salt has never written about love? In "The Doll House," Fry Pan wooed an amour who lived in Camarillo, California:

"Love is better the second time round
With all those things that do abound
Like that Matterhorn I came aground
'N near the magic land a pixie found"

But love just wasn't to be. The Crusoe of Hula Ville gave clue why in the book's final poem:

"Let's hope, my dearest
I will see you, I pray
And have a celebration
Upon our wedding day
I'll have a nice villa
For my lonely Travilla
Here in the high desert
...But not in Camarillo"

Fry Pan came back from his tour early. The couple hadn't wanted to play golf. Showman that he was, though, he continued performing. Grabbing a baton from its resting place against the joshua tree, he hustled me out to the "dance pavilion"—a makeshift stage lined with Lowenbrau bottles. On it, he demonstrated the flash routine which had made hundreds of thousands of people over the years suddenly decide to have their weight checked. The old carney strutted and twirled and called out his line. At the end, he told me I weighed 160 pounds. The audience rose and applauded as one.

Heading down toward the Cajon Pass much later than I'd originally planned, I thought how easy it would be for someone to think this gentle old man was lonely or alone. Out there in the desert amid his bottles and signs and other refugees from oblivion, how could he be anything else? Fact is, he's everything but. There are occasional twinges of regret, especially about matters of love. And once in a while the roadrunner hides in the joshua's leaves and picks off a cactus wren. But here in Fry Pan's 66 oasis, each day brings with it the chance for a new poem. And when the poet drives up every morning for a day with the hula girl, the lizard runs up the joshua trunk and waits for the fresh bug he knows his friend will lay there for him.

SEARCHING FOR **66**

FIFTY-ONE

"Been held down, nailed down, beat down, shut down, set down, drove down, shoved down, chopped down, hoed down, plowed under. held under, ducked under, dusted under, tractored under, shot at and missed, spit at and hit. But we ain't down yet."

Woody Guthrie
An Okie

The road kept climbing and winding. Scattered pine trees started showing up. Remains of old service stations became suddenly plentiful. Route 66 was girding itself for one last mountain range. Half an hour out of Hula Ville, I reached 6300 feet and the Cajon Pass—gateway to Southern California. A hundred miles more and I'd see the ocean.

Stories are told of westward travelers who've crossed the Mojave, finally reached Barstow after two hundred miles in the state, and then quit. "If that's all there is to California, I'm going home!" they've said. But if they'd just endured the desert to Cajon Pass, they'd have been rewarded by the route's most dramatically beautiful scenery changes. Constantly switching back on itself as it descended through the San Bernardino National Forest, 66 opened on a new vista with each turn—verdant, pineclad slopes, one right after the other, fading to a blue haze in the distance.

And then the valley, the golden land. Land of orange groves, vineyards and salad farms. Land of milk and honey. Land of dreams. Forget that first three hundred miles. This was where California began.

Fifty years ahead of me, the Okies—tired, hungry, broke, but not down yet—had stood at Cajon Pass or Tehachapi Pass further north and taken in the same view. Leaving their overheated, overloaded, patchwork cars wheezing and puffing on the roadside, these dispossessed dreamers had walked to the very top of the passes and gazed hopefully down at their future. Then they'd fanned off 66 and out into the valleys to lay claim to it

"There ought to be some yodelin' in this song
There ought to be some yodelin' in this song
But I can't yodel
Cause of rattlin' in my lung."

"Dust Pneumonee Blues"
Woody Guthrie

It all started with a trickle during the days of record crops in the late '20s and early '30s—just the usual quota of people seeking the other side of the hill. As drought came and deepened, though, the trickle became a steady flow. And when dust storms filled the skies in 1935, it became a flood. The Okie Exodus, the largest involuntary migration in American history, was upon us.

"The dust blew up like a rainstorm," historian Merle Woods had told me in El Reno, Oklahoma. "It covered the fields. Then it would come again and blow the fields down to the bare clay. From there it would go on and cover up other crops with the new sand."

"That dust would just blow in like a wall," Lucille Hamons had said in Hydro, Oklahoma. "It was terrible. One day I looked out and it was like piles of snow along the road. It had to come from Texas or New Mexico because we don't have white dust here."

A reporter coined the term "Dust Bowl" after witnessing the area's largest, most terrible storm on April 14, 1935. Though the region covered parts of ten states, a variety of factors conspired to make Oklahoma's cotton country the most dramatic victim. Because of this, though people from all ten Dust Bowl states left for California, the derisive label "Okie" was applied to them all.

Prolonged drought and high winds were the Dust Bowl's prime causes. But farmers themselves had contributed by taking greater pride in

Cajon Pass, California

plowing a straight furrow than in soil conservation. Banks and holding companies which owned the land had contributed by letting their tenants plant only cotton. Less than half a century after the state was settled, much of Oklahoma's soil was depleted and defenseless. Then came a double blow from mechanization and the Depression.

Franklin Roosevelt, who put so many other millions of people to work, hardly helped the Okies at all. His New Deal farm policies concentrated more on improving efficiency of the land rather than on helping the people who tilled it. Relief payments went to the landlords, not the farmers, and were used to buy more tractors, forcing more Okie tenants out. As one landowner put it, "The renters have been having it their way ever since the government come in. They have their choice now—California or WPA."

Faced with this Hobson's choice. people started leaving Oklahoma and other Dust Bowl states by the tens of thousands. Though its creators never envisioned this use, their path was made easy and logical by the recently-paved superhighway, U.S. Route 66.

> *"This land is your land, this land is my land*
> *From California to the New York island*
> *From the redwood forests to the gulfstream waters*
> *This land was made for you and me."*
> Woody Guthrie

John Steinbeck would later call Route 66 a road of flight. But Okies themselves didn't see it that way. To them, Route 66 was a road of dreams. They were simple dreams—a home to live in and land to work on—but they were sturdy. And as the Okies trickled onto 66 from its tributary roads, it never occurred to them to question their right to such things. When Woody Guthrie wrote "This Land Is Your Land," he implied no irony. He, like his countrymen on the road, truly believed that the whole country belonged to the whole people. Dispossessed in one part of it, they were simply moving to another part to take possession again.

The irony in Woody's words came when the Okies' California dreaming hit the bedrock of Depression reality. From New Mexico on, this wasn't their land at all. And they weren't our people. Instead of being welcomed as fellow citizens, Okies were treated as feared, despised strangers. The only good Okie was one that kept moving—or never showed up at all.

> *"The police in your town*
> *They shove me around*
> *I got them 66 Highway Blues."*
> "66 Highway Blues"
> Woody Guthrie

"When Okies came to the east end of Albuquerque, the police would make them wait—then escort the lot of them through town all at once," a businessman in that city told me. "I was just a kid then. I'd stand out there every morning and think I was watching a parade. It was years before I found out different."

Arizona didn't want the Okies, either. That state's cotton crop matured earlier than California's, and the migrants were welcomed during the harvest season. But when that was done, ranchers and lawmen actively prodded them on.

California was even less hospitable. For a month in 1934, police from L.A. were even stationed at the Arizona border to turn "undesirables" away. And in his 1934 campaign for governor of the state, socialist novelist Upton Sinclair was defeated handily after boasting, "If I am elected, half the unemployed in the country will climb aboard freight trains and head for California."

Soon afterward, California legislators passed the Indigent Exclusion Act to stem the flow permanently. They didn't need these people. The only work they could do was in the fields—and there were already plenty of Mexicans and Orientals to do that. Even worse, when the new migrants weren't working, they'd be burdening the relief rolls.

> *"They think they're goin' to the sugar bowl*
> *But here's what they find."*
>
> "Do Re Mi"
> Woody Guthrie

Maybe this wasn't their land. But Route 66 was their road as much as anyone else's and the Okies won their right to use it—if nothing more. The L.A. police went home. The Indigent Exclusion Act was ruled unconstitutional. Migrants kept pouring down from the Cajon and Tehachapi passes into the valleys below—battered from the journey, but dreams still intact.

Even if the growers had welcomed them, the Okies' problem was that they had no intention of becoming migratory workers. In fact, they resented even being called that. Steinbeck's Joads were an exception granted by literary license. When the crops had been worked, most real Okies resisted the system's tendency to push them onward and stayed right where they were. They built makeshift homes along ditch banks. They enrolled their kids in school. And though they didn't like the idea any better than Californians did, they went on relief—right in the counties which benefited most from keeping them moving.

Steinbeck may have dramatized it some, but his portrayal of the Okies' plight is essentially accurate. They lived in collections of tents and cardboard shacks called "Hoovervilles." Their children died of malnutrition or starvation. Annual outbreaks of dysentery took heavy tolls. Untreated injuries turned to gangrene. Vigilantes and sheriffs' posses torched Hoovervilles and sent the residents running.

Talk about the problem flowed abundantly. President Roosevelt considered resettling the migrants in the Columbia River Basin—his proudest public works project. A California state senator suggested Brazil as the migrants' new homeland.

Money flowed, too. But ninety percent of it went to growers and farmers. Okies got only grudging relief payments and not enough relief camps. And even these camps, well intentioned as they were, proved to be an unwitting subsidy for the growers by keeping wage pressure down. In another irony, liberal young camp managers prodded their residents—rejected by the state which surrounded them—to function as ideal citizens of an ideal republic.

Held down, nailed down, pushed down, shut down—the Okies' dream was turning sour on the vine.

With all America in depression, the country at large remained unaware of the Okies' plight for nearly a decade. This ignorance vanished overnight, however, when *The Grapes of Wrath* was published on March 14, 1939. Young John Steinbeck had already shown considerable power as a writer in *In Dubious Battle* and *Of Mice and Men*. In *Grapes of Wrath*, he would have his masterpiece.

Had *Grapes* been about Mexicans or Filipinos or any other of the many ethnic groups which worked California's fields, it may never have gained the prominence or notoriety that it did. But the Okies, after you gave them a bath and clean clothes, were Old Stock Americans. They were us. That's what made them so hard to take.

The nation was appalled; *Grapes'* first printing was an immediate sell-out. By the end of April, Viking Press was hard put to keep up with each day's 2,500 orders. By mid-May, *Grapes* was the country's best seller. By year's end, nearly half a million copies had been sold—one for every Okie—and the movie which followed would be second only to *Gone With the Wind* at the box office.

Praise and commercial success came quickly. But so did a dust bowl of criticism. The book's profanity and sexuality, though mild by modern standards, got it banned as far away as Kansas City. But the strongest reaction was political, not artistic, and much closer to home. Days after the Kansas City action in August, the board of supervisors in Kern County, California (Bakersfield), where the largest number of Okies had settled, banned the book, too. Only the supervisors charged it was not so much obscene as untrue. The novel falsely accused Kern County, they said—and, by association, the rest of rural California.

Much of the Okies' original negative image had been generated by growers' groups and government agencies. Now those very bodies accused Steinbeck of the same transgression. One of their reports said, "Steinbeck has offended our citizenry by falsely implying that many of our people are a low, ignorant, profane and blasphemous type living in a vicious, filthy manner." Counter-propaganda included a novel, *Of Human*

Kindness, and a film, *Plums of Plenty*.

The California legislature and the state's delegation to Congress had both been long divided on the migrant problem. Consequently, little had been done about it. Even when California had pled for help, other states had viewed it as a good-time Charlie finally getting what he deserved after years of self praise.

But when Congress convened in the fall of 1939, *Grapes* had introduced a new factor to the equation—popular pressure to do something about the Okie problem. After much wrangling, name-calling and a fist fight or two, lawmakers announced formation of the Select Committee to Investigate Interstate Migration of Destitute Citizens early in 1940. For two centuries, America had dealt with its poor by encouraging them to move somewhere else. At last there was recognition that this might not work forever.

California Congressman John Tolan headed the Select Committee. He and his colleagues traveled 20,000 miles, taking testimony from half a thousand witnesses. But in yet another irony, by the time they finally got to California in late 1940, they were too late to help the very people whose plight had inspired their work—the Okies.

Nor did unions contribute much to easing of the Okies' plight. Steinbeck, Woody Guthrie and others had advocated this approach. But it had two flaws. First, Okies didn't *want* to join unions, especially if it meant aligning themselves with Negroes and other minorities. Second, the strategy assumed that Okies would stay in agricultural work. The migrants themselves may have dreamed of such a fate, but history didn't allow it.

The solution to the Okie problem, when it did come, had nothing to do with either unions or government studies. What it had to do with was war. Hitler invaded Poland; the Japanese cast envious eyes over the entire Pacific. America's eventual conflict with these powers was a given. Anticipating it, President Roosevelt launched a preparedness program. Defense plants all over California suddenly needed thousands of new workers and the Okies flocked to them as quickly as they could scrape up gas money for the trip.

Only months after being recognized, the Okie problem was over. In fact, the Dust Bowl migration, as monumentally as it's been portrayed, paled beside the defense plant rush. Only half a million Okies came to California during the Depression; more than two and a half times that amount would come to work in the war plants. And when labor-poor growers imported thousands of new Okies in 1942 and 1943 to harvest their crops, the new arrivals were greeted not as pariahs, but as heroes.

Lela Bird and her family had been among the first Okies. They'd spent eleven years wandering the West as "fruit tramps," picking cotton in Arizona, peas in Idaho, and oranges, olives, figs, carrots, lettuce and asparagus in California. When Lela and her boyfriend Ed Angell decided to marry, they got a mail order catalogue and looked up the cost of the bare essentials needed to set up housekeeping. They compared that to the amount of money they had, decided that was enough, and the wedding took place. Four homes, one child and eighteen months later, Ed got a job in a defense plant. Their wandering was over.

In retirement, Lela wrote a book about her family's travels called *When the Birds Migrated*. It was self-published in Bakersfield, where she lives.

"All things considered, I suppose it is true that every dark cloud has a silver lining," she said of her people's Dust Bowl days. "In spite of all our trials and tribulations, all was never lost. I feel that we profited a great deal from our adversities. For had we not lived as we did then, we probably would not be living as we are now."

SEARCHING FOR *66*

FIFTY-TWO

San Bernardino. End of California's first county. Beginning of the megalopolis. Mountains gave way to rolling foothills as Route 66 changed terrains once again. Elevations ranged between 500 and 1,000 feet and there were ample western and southern slopes. With irrigation help from the Santa Ana River, these conditions had made citrus farming the county's leading industry for eighty years. In 66's heyday, groves and packing houses lined the route for thirty miles. Roadside juice stands—shaped like the fruit—aroused, then slaked the thirst of many a traveler. Okies worked the fields, children sorted the produce, and Orientals on treadmills kept the conveyors moving in packing houses.

A concrete teepee motel in Rialto, California.

Citrus is still a $14 million a year industry in San Bernardino County. But along Route 66 urban development has squeezed it out. In the 1920's, growers netted $150 from each acre of orange trees. Not bad then.

But that's all they can make today. However, they can get that much by selling three inches of frontage to a gas station or office building developer. Only a few small groves survive along the route today—and they're on the development market. Only one roadside juice stand survives on 66 in San Bernardino, but it's hard to find.

Route 66's pavement from San Bernardino to the eastern suburbs of L.A. survives as Foothill Boulevard. In Santa Anita it passed the race track, which was closed for the season. In Duarte it passed the 66 Bar and Grille, which was closed forever. In Rancho Cucamonga, which sounded so much nicer as simply "Cucamonga," the road passed an automatic bankteller—still open at 7:30 and with eight people standing in line. The Okies wouldn't have believed.

SEARCHING *FOR* 66

FIFTY-THREE

It was a sunny July day in 1983. The photographer, a few minutes early for his rendezvous, was passing time over coffee and small talk at the Maple Cafe in Joplin. The waitress already knew he was a stranger; she figured from his bags and tripods what he did for a living. So she asked him who he worked for.

"The Joplin *Globe*?" she wondered.

"*Life Magazine*," the man answered politely.

"Really? What would *Life* want a picture of in Joplin?"

"Bobby Troup."

"Bobby Troup?" returned the waitress. "Isn't he that mediocre guitarist who's married to Julie London?"

A silver-haired man in a sports shirt and linen slacks entered the cafe. Spotting the photographer by his baggage, he strode over like a golfer who'd just launched a 275-yard drive, reaching the booth as the waitress posed her last question.

"Excuse me, madam," he said in the tones of a seasoned diplomat. "I'm Bobby Troup. And I'm the mediocre *pianist* who's married to Julie London—not the mediocre guitarist.'"

Yes, he *was* Julie London's husband. But Bobby Troup was also a noted songwriter—"Daddy," written when he was a junior in college, was the number one hit of 1941; stars as diverse as Tommy Dorsey and Little Richard have made hits of some of his other songs. He's also been a TV star—playing Dr. Early on *Emergency*. And a film actor—speaking the last words in the movie *M*A*S*H* ("Goddamn Army!"). He was the father of five children—including three in one year with Julie. And today he was in Joplin for *Life's* recognition of his most memorable achievement—the writing of "(Get Your Kicks on) Route 66." Comments like the waitress's don't faze him at all. With great self-assurance, he welcomes them now as straight lines.

In February 1946, though, it was more a time of dreams and raw hope than of great self-assurance. Bobby and his first wife sat in a booth at a Howard Johnson's on the Pennsylvania Turnpike. A map of the United States lay spread out on the table before them. A '41 Buick convertible stood outside, its trunk riding low with the sum of their worldly goods.

Bobby Troup, Encino, California.

"I had just spent almost five years in the Marine Corps and I came out resolved to see if I had any talent as a songwriter," Bobby would later tell me. "My family had music stores in Lancaster and Harrisburg, but I told my mother, 'Mom, I don't know if I can be successful. I don't know if I have talent. I don't know if 'Daddy' was a happy coincidence. But this is what I really want to do. I'm going to give myself two years and see what happens.'

"There were only two places a professional songwriter could go—New York or California—so we packed the Buick and headed west. We picked up the turnpike in Harrisburg and the Howard Johnson's was our first stop.

"My first wife, Cynthia, was a society girl from Philadelphia. She was kind of wary about making suggestions to me about writing. But she said, 'Bobby, why don't you write a song about Route 40?' because that was the name of the highway we were on.

"I looked at the road map and said, 'That'd be kind of silly, Cynthia, because we're going to pick up Route 66 right outside of Chicago and take it all the way to Los Angeles.'

"She didn't make any more suggestions for awhile. Then somewhere in Illinois, she leaned over and whispered in my ear, 'Get your kicks on Route 66.'

"I said, 'That's a darling title! Goddamn! That's a great title!'"

That wifely tip and the song which followed have probably done more than anything else to inspire and build the mystique of Route 66—more than the Okies, more than Steinbeck, more than the TV series (which the song itself inspired). But in February of 1946, Robert William Troup just saw a cute title and an opportunity. Driving and singing, he wrote half the song while on the very road he was describing:

"If you ever plan to motor west
Travel my way, take the highway
That's the best—
Get your kicks on Route 66.
It winds from Chicago to L.A.
More than 2,000 miles all the way
Get your kicks on Route 66."

Eric Eikenberry—organizer of Williams, Arizona's farewell to Route 66—had given me Bobby's phone number. I'd worried that he'd probably been interviewed five hundred times already about that one song. But when I'd called, Bobby had graciously invited me over.

"Would you like a drink, Tom?" he said after ushering me into his Encino, California, home.

Not really. But I'd gotten lost on the way and had arrived late. Bobby was already standing by the counter and I didn't want to risk another discourtesy, so I said, "Sure."

My host gestured toward a well-stocked backbar.

"What would you like?"

My standard bottle of Bud didn't seem like the correct order here, so I said, "Scotch on the rocks, please."

"That's my favorite drink!" Bobby said. "You have good taste." He poured me a healthy shot of Dewar's in a tumbler and brought it over to the lowslung couch where I was sitting. Then he fixed a cup of coffee for himself and settled down on the couch across from me. For three hours, until a golf outing at 2, he talked readily and enthusiastically. A pair of Dobermans, a German Shepherd and an equally large mongrel wandered in and out, offering us occasional, enthusiastic company.

"I wrote 'Daddy' in Philadelphia for Wharton School's Mask and Wig Show—our rival to Harvard's Hasty Pudding Show," he said. "In it, a young doll tells her sugardaddy to buy her a brand new car, champagne, caviar because 'you want to get the best from me.' Sammy Kaye, who was like the Lawrence Welk of his day, thought that was too risque. So he changed the wording to 'you want to get the very best *for* me' and played the song on his radio show *nine* weeks in a row!

"And one of the greatest thrills of my life was when my family and I sat around the radio one Sunday evening and listened to the Ford Hour's symphony orchestra play it as the country's number one song. Honest to Christ, it sounded like Beethoven! They had sixty strings and woodwinds...God, it was exciting!

"I thought at the time that 'Daddy' would go on in perpetuity. As long as old, bald-headed men are looking for young girls—and that will be forever—I thought there would be a time for 'Daddy.' But I had no sense what a landmark this east-west highway was; I wrote '66' because it was a catchy title. Yet it's been far more popular and made far more money than any other song."

"Daddy's" success had led Bobby to a brief pre-war stint as a songwriter for Tommy Dorsey before he was called to active duty. When he and Cynthia reached California on their post-war journey, he used that Dorsey connection to meet Nat King Cole.

"Nat was my idol as a pianist and singer," Bobby said. "They'd named a room after him in the Trocadero on Sunset Boulevard and he played there whenever he was in town. So my friend, Bullets Durbin, arranged for me to play a couple of songs for Nat after the show. I did 'Baby, Baby All the Time.' And Nat says, 'Oh that 'Baby, Baby All the Time!' I love that!'

"I says to myself, 'I got an opportunity to play for Nat King Cole! What am I gonna play next? I got to find something he likes!' So I say, almost apologetically, 'Nat, I wrote a song in the car, but it's only half done.' And I played 'Route 66.'

"He said, 'I really like that!' and he sat down and played it. Then he told me to finish the song and he'd record both it and 'Baby, Baby All the Time' the next time he was in the studio—which would be in about five days."

Four decades later, Bobby clearly recalled the hectic rush to get "66's" second half written.

"I got a road map and Bullets got me a rehearsal hall at CBS Radio Studios on Sunset," he said. "Band members kept coming in for show rehearsals, so I had to keep going from room to room, dragging that map and looking for a piano. That's how I came up with the rest of the song."

> *"You go through St. Louie, Joplin, Missouri,*
> *And Oklahoma City looks mighty pretty.*
> *You'll see Amarillo, Gallup, New Mexico,*
> *Flagstaff, Arizona. Don't forget Winona*
> *Kingman, Barstow, San Bernardino.*

Won't you get hip to this timely tip
When you take that California trip?
Get your kicks on Route 66!"

"Did you go through Winona?" Bobby asked.

"Almost."

He smiled. "It's the only town I got out of geographical order. I don't remember going through it, either. But I needed something to rhyme with Arizona. It went out of order, but at least now people remember it.

"Anyway, Nat recorded the song about five days later. Capitol liked it so much that they released it right away. And that's the story of 'Route 66'—I had a hit song before I'd been here a month! "Since then, everybody's done it—Bing Crosby, Manhattan Transfer, the Andrews Sisters, Mel Torme, Perry Como, the Rolling Stones—just everybody! They're even using it for a Toyota commercial and to promote the state lottery in Washington. And Nat told me once of all the songs he ever recorded, he identified most with 'Route 66.'"

A Doberman came wagging by and knocked my drink on the floor. I was mortified, but it wasn't the first spilled drink Bobby had seen. Without missing a beat, he cleaned it up and insisted on fixing me another. Talk turned then to the TV series *Route 66*.

"That program brings back a lot of bad memories," Bobby said. But he didn't look disturbed—he looked more like he was about to enjoy a good story.

"Buddy Morris was the publisher of 'Route 66.' The head of his west coast branch was Sydney Goldstein. Sydney called me one morning about 11 o'clock and said, 'Bobby, ordinarily I would never tell a writer anything unless it's signed, sealed and delivered. But this is so almost certain that I'm gonna tell you because it's such good news.'

"I said, 'What?' He said, 'They're gonna have a television show about Route 66 and the papers are all drawn up and they're gonna use your song as the theme!'

"Anyway, Goldstein didn't call back in a week. He didn't call back in two weeks. He didn't call back in three weeks. Finally, I called him and said, 'Sydney, what the fuck happened?' He said, 'Bobby, I'm so embarrassed I couldn't call you. Everything was drawn up. It only needed Columbia's signature and at the last minute they said, 'Fuck Bobby's song! Let's get Nelson Riddle to write a 'Theme from Route 66' and we'll publish it and get the money instead of Bobby!'"

I mentioned that the jukebox at a bar I'd visited in Kingman, Arizona, had Riddle's song on it and not Bobby's.

"Oh shit! That's sacrilege!" Bobby said. I agreed.

"Nelson Riddle and I are very good friends," he went on. "I know it wasn't his fault. He wrote a good song—those piano interludes capture the rhythm of the road—but the producers were wrong. I know the royalties would have been marvelous for me, but they'd have gotten tremendous promotion from using my song.

"I mean if you're going to have a television program *Stardust*, you gotta use Hoagy Carmichael's song, don't you?"

On the strength of Nat Cole's promise to record '66'—plus first, second and third mortgages—the Troups bought a small home just off Ventura Boulevard. Other songs weren't so successful and Bobby, with a boost from Cynthia, drifted into piano bar work. For several years he paid his dues, but not much else. Finally his witty patter and smooth, sexy stylings attracted the entertainment set and overnight he became their piano darling. Among the many young female stars who flocked to see him was Julie London, his wife now of twenty-eight years.

"When I signed with Capitol, they said I might become the white Nat King Cole," Bobby said. "They kept me for two years and then they dropped me two weeks before Christmas!"

My eyes asked the question.

"I didn't sell any records!" Bobby answered. "Julie records 'Cry Me a River' and she's a major star in three months! It's amazing."

Which is a word Bobby also applies to his acting career.

"I never had any aspirations to be an actor," he said. "But I'm a ham; I love to perform. Cynthia said to me one day, 'Goddamn it, Bobby, you're such a good writer. You're so talented. Why do you spend six nights a week at these dumb clubs you play?' And I said, 'I guess it's because I love it.'

"She asked me who I'd rather be—Vic Damone or Cole Porter. I said, 'Vic Damone!' I mean, there's no comparison between the two men on their contribution to music, but I like the immediate gratification of having people applaud.

"Anyway, I'm playing the clubs and some very astute director decided he didn't like the way actors played musicians. He had a casting call for a pianist and a drummer and he said, 'Why don't we get real ones?' That's how I got into acting."

That bit role led to guest spots in *Perry Mason*. Later Bobby acted in *The Red Nichols Story* and *The Gene Krupa Story* (where he played his former boss, Tommy Dorsey). His co-stars included Charlton Heston and Jose Ferrer. And then Jack Webb, Julie's former husband, liked him and cast him in several *Dragnets*. Later Webb chose Bobby to play Dr. Early in *Emergency*.

"That was the greatest thing that ever happened to me—*Emergency*," Bobby remembered. "I love that because I lost the tag that he's Julie London's husband. Now people would say, 'That's Dr. Early on *Emergency*.'"

The energy of his conversation had worked Bobby to the edge of the couch cushion. Now he leaned back, folded his hands, and did some mental addition.

"I may have missed an opportunity or two," he said. "But all in all, I've been a very fortunate man."

Fortunate and, now that he's been a part of it for forty years, also appreciative of the 66 mystique he helped create.

"When I was in Williams for the closing of 66, I said, 'I can't really understand why you're celebrating this. I think it's terribly sad. You should be having a wake!' But there's tremendous enthusiasm for 66, I found. I don't think it'll die out. There's too strong a cult of people who will keep the memory of Route 66 alive forever.

"Of course, a song with a catchy title will help them."

I told Bobby that I'd made a tape of ten different versions of that very song. It had been my traveling music the past four months. And my license plate was KIX ON 66. He was pleased and allowed that although musicians were his favorite people, writers were all right, too. Then, though he's heard the song so many thousands of times, he walked over to his record library and sorted through it for his second favorite version of "Route 66"—Manhattan Transfer's Grammy winner from 1984. As it played, he complimented the piano player and the quartet's tight, jazzy harmonies.

Snapping his fingers in time, he said, "The song bridges everything." As had the highway. "Jazz, pop, country, rock 'n roll—they could all do it. The Rolling Stones' version was the biggest moneymaker, but this is *my* kind of music."

Along about Amarillo, the phone rang. It was Julie calling from upstairs. Bobby promised to bring her half a ham sandwich when he came back up.

We enjoyed the rest of the song. When it was over, my fellow traveler said, "Tom, I have to fix my wife a sandwich and get ready to go soon. I hope I'm not being rude."

How could he possibly be? Two and a half hours had just gone by as smoothly as one of Bobby's songs. I did plead, however, to take a picture of him before I left.

"Sure," he said. "Why don't we do it in the music room for it?"

"By the way, I love your saddle oxfords. They're very eastern."

Bobby seated himself at his Steinway as though he were becoming a part of it. "Emily" flowed from his fingertips in chordless simplicity. We talked; I took a couple of shots. Then Bobby spread both hands over the keys and brought them down in the opening notes of our mutual anthem. I went to heaven in the passing lane.

SEARCHING FOR 66

FIFTY-FOUR

Before I left, Bobby offered to arrange a visit between me and his ex-wife. Which is why, three days later, I braved the L.A. freeway system once again in search of Cynthia Troup's home in Ventura. I couldn't find it on the first try and had to call for new directions. Forty-five minutes late, I finally pulled in Cynthia's drive, walked up to the shaded porch, and knocked on the door of the house that 66 built.

Cynthia came presently to greet me. She was a petite woman, slowed by arthritis, but dressed to the nines—purple silk blouse, white linen pants, heavy silver necklace. And her voice, I quickly found, was hard as stone.

"Goddamn, Tom!" she said. "I didn't think you'd ever find this place!"

I was halfway into some lame explanation when she interrupted.

"Come on back and sit down."

We got settled on comfortable chairs in Cynthia's living room. Through a bay window, I admired her carefully tended back yard. I imagined my own back yard in Illinois, left to its own devices now for four months, was probably a jungle of brush trees and noxious weeds.

"Did Bobby tell you how we met?" Cynthia asked.

"Not much."

She hmmphed. "I guess I couldn't expect him to. We've been divorced, God, I don't know how long. But we met in 1940 at the Embassy Club in Philadelphia. I was a society girl, but I hung out there all the time. They had a thing in New York about then where debutantes started singing in night clubs. The Embassy Club's owners wanted to copy New York and they all knew me. So they asked me could I sing? And I said, 'No, but I can tap dance.' They hired me for $55 a week."

A spark of satisfaction flashed in Cynthia's voice.

"And the publicity! It was on the front page, all filled up. My mother's hair turned gray.

"So anyway, I'm there at the Embassy tapping away when Bobby came in. He was going to the U. of Penn—Wharton. And he came up to my table after my act and said, 'Would you like to dance?'

"I looked at him like I'm looking at you and said, 'You must be kidding!

"But people knew I always dated whoever was in the Mask and Wig Show, which was like Wharton's answer to Harvard's variety show. After Bobby left the table, somebody told me he was the star of it. So I went up to him and said, 'I *would* like to dance.'

"They played 'Honeysuckle Rose.'"

Cynthia enjoyed a moment of reverie. Then I asked, "So you knew Bobby when 'Daddy' became a hit?"

She nodded. "Yes, I did. In fact, I helped make it that way. The band at the Embassy liked the tune and made a little arrangement of it. Sammy Kaye came in one night, heard it, and had them play it nine times. I told him my boyfriend wrote that song. He said, 'Well, I'll be here again Thursday night.'

"So I called Troup and told him 'You better get down here Thursday.'"

With that initial boost, "Daddy" went on to earn Bobby enough to buy the '41 convertible that would later take him to fame on 66.

"I can remember that trip real well," Cynthia said. "There wasn't a decent motel or place to eat after St. Louis. But 66 had a sound to it. There was a mystique about it even then. And I can remember riding in the Buick, saying to myself, 'Six, nix, picks, kicks.' And then I said, 'Get your kicks!', which was very hep, hep, hep in those days. Then I put the two together and whispered to Bobby, 'Get your kicks on Route 66!'"

I nodded. "So you came out to Hollywood, got a hit song right away, and you were set—right?"

"Are you kidding?" she scalded. "We were on our ass! Bobby never made any money until after he left me."

In those dark days between the first round of royalty checks and the stardom he finally claimed, Cynthia explained, Bobby spent endless hours at his piano—playing, singing, writing, wondering if it really had been hip to make that California trip.

"That really bugged me," she said, anger yet in her voice. "Here we sat with three mortgages and no money, borrowing from his family—and all he does is play the piano! So I say, 'Why don't you go out and play the piano *for a living*, Bobby?'

"He just keeps playing. So I got in the car and went from one end of Ventura Boulevard to the other and stopped in every piano bar. I'd go in and order coffee. The manager would come up and I'd say, 'My husband's Bobby Troup. He wrote 'Route 66.' He doesn't need the work, but he might want to play a couple of songs for you.

"I got Bobby a job where he worked one week for nothing and they paid him the second week. Then I got him another job where they paid him scale and he kicked back money.

"He had very bad front teeth. So I got him a dentist and had his teeth capped. Got a barber to cut his hair. It was fun those days. We never could pay the phone bill or the milk bill, but it was fun. Then he got a job at the Encore in La Cienaga and overnight he was a hit. They'd even come over the hill from Hollywood to see him—which was unheard of.

"And then..."

Cynthia paused and folded her active hands. I waited a moment, then offered, "And then?"

"And then that's when our marriage went dow-w-wn hill."

"I told Bobby the other day I was sorry I was such a bitchy wife," Cynthia said after a bit. "Because, really, I was very bitchy. I was never bashful about promoting my husband's songs or promoting him, either. I'm still that way today, still telling everybody what the hell to do. After he left, I began telling my kids...and telling myself!"

She had a rich, deep laugh.

"Bobby and I are the best of friends now," she said. "He drops by nearly every afternoon for a visit. He even got our girls jobs in *The Girl Can't Help It*—then snuck back to Jayne Mansfield's dressing room with them to see if there were any tricks to her bra.

"But it really smashed my ego when he married Julie. At least I was the only mother of his children. Then they had a girl and twin sons all in one year. Boy!

"Julie's ten years younger than me. And she eats so badly. I mean, like spaghetti for breakfast. Never moves a muscle for exercise. Never goes outside. Drinks, smokes—the whole thing. It's amazing anybody can live that way and look so damned attractive. But she does. It's amazing. I keep waiting for her to look a little bit like she's going over the hill, but she never does."

"Sounds more like a compliment than a critique," I said.

"Well, listen, Tom, I can't complain. Bobby supports me like a queen. I mean this is the house that 66 built and I'm here. I did very well.

"I don't live in the past. I *think* of things in the past, but it's not like those were the good old days and I wish I was a kid and little again. But last night they had a tribute to Nat King Cole on TV. Natalie Cole and Johnny Mathis did a duet of 'Route 66.' I was watching that and I thought, 'Sonofabitch! Think of that! That was us, boy, forty years ago coming out here on 66, wide-eyed kids gonna take Hollywood by storm!

"Who ever would have dreamt it?"

SEARCHING *FOR* 66

FIFTY-FIVE

Like a grave marker, a bronze plaque stands low to the ground near the intersection of Ocean and Santa Monica Boulevards in Santa Monica. Put there in 1952 to promote Warner Brothers' film about Will Rogers, it marks the westernmost point on Route 66. After checking into a motel, I called Adrian Verburg, who had read my letter in the Santa Monica *Outlook*. We met by the pier and walked together to the plaque.

Seeing the marker, I thought, would end my journey. But as I stood before it with Adrian, I had no sense of having finished anything. The reason for this, I finally decided after several months, is that I **hadn't** finished anything. Route 66 was more than a few million yards of concrete, a path from Point A to Point B—it was a 2,400-mile long community. And in searching for that community the past four months, I had become part of it. For many people, Route 66's appeal is nostalgic. But nostalgia implies a sense of finality, a sense of something being over and done, and that's not

In Santa Monica at Santa Monica and Ocean Boulevards.

how I see 66. I enjoy it for what it is today. So there never will be any finishing for me—only continuing.

Other species fulfill their destiny by living like the past generation and bringing forth the next. But the human race has always felt compelled to better itself. We think, therefore we change. Then we call it Progress. And Route 66, the artery of so many lives, was both its agent and its victim. The highway paved our Manifest Destiny. At its peak, it inspired our dreams and then gave us the opportunities to realize those dreams—showing us not only who we were as a people, but who we could be. Then, in less than a human lifetime, we replaced it.

Chuck & Florence Binna of Bailey, Colorado, hitchhiked 66 on their honeymoon in 1930.

Unlike other relics, though, 66, has refused to slip quietly into history. But I think that's a matter more of resilience than defiance. And the community that 66 created, after some initial confusion about whether it still existed, is flourishing again. In 1987, Jerry Richard, a motel owner in Kingman, and Angel Delgadillo, a barber in Seligman, led formation of the Historic Route 66 Association of Arizona. Within a year, the group got a 160-mile stretch of Old 66 from Seligman to Oatman declared a state historic highway. Every year since, they've held a two-day "fun run" along the "new" road. In the past couple of years, associations in Missouri, Oklahoma, Texas and California have followed suit with similar events. Ron Chavez, my Santa Rosa friend, is vice-president of the New Mexico 66 association. Kansas also has a large, new group. And last year, I banded together with about 500 other folks to form the Route 66 Association of Illinois.

In the Prairie State, we thought a good way to help keep 66 alive was to establish a hall of fame. The folks at Dixie Truckers Home in McLean agreed and completely remodeled one of their hallways for us. On June 9, 1990, in conjunction with a motor tour from St. Louis to Chicago, we had the first induction ceremonies for the Route 66 Hall of Fame of Illinois. Our stage was a flatbed truck parked on a grassy field near the Dixie. American Legion members presented the colors; a bagpipe band from the Illinois State Police marched and played. Then we inducted the Hall's members. Francis Mowery, retired captain of a state police district which stretched from Pontiac to McLean, was the first. Then came Ernie Edwards, story-telling owner of the Pig Hip Restaurant in Broadwell. Next was Russell Soulsby, who's owned and operated a gas station in Mount Olive since 1926. John Geske, who founded the Dixie in 1932 with his father-in-law J.P. Walters, became the fourth member. Mr. Walters was inducted posthumously. In Litchfield the next day, we inducted Francis Marten, keeper of the Our Lady of the Highways Shrine near Raymond.

After getting his plaque, Ernie took the occasion to clear his conscience. "You know we've always used only the left pig hip at my restaurant," he said. "That's because when a hog has an itch, he has a tendency to

Hamel, Illinois.

raise that right leg to do his scratchin'. That makes the meat tough on that side, so we don't use it. Well, now that I have my plaque, I guess it's safe to tell you what we've been doin' with those right hips all these years—we've been sendin' 'em to John Geske!"

Route 66 Associations

Associations devoted to preserving, promoting and enjoying Route 66 have sprung up in each of the eight states along the route. Here's how to get in touch with them:

Arizona
Historic Route 66 Association of Arizona
P.O. Box 66
Kingman, AZ 86402

California
California Route 66 Association
2127 Foothill Blvd., Suite 66
LaVerne, CA 91750

Illinois
Route 66 Association of Illinois
2743 Veterans Parkway, Room 166
Springfield, IL 62704
Operates a Route 66 Hall of Fame at the Dixie Truckers Home in McLean.

Kansas
Kansas Route 66 Association
P.O. Box 169
Riverton, KS 66770

Missouri
Missouri Route 66 Association
P.O. Box 8117
St. Louis, MO 63156

New Mexico
New Mexico Route 66 Association
1405 San Carlos SW, #6
Albuquerque, NM 87104

Oklahoma
Oklahoma Route 66 Association
6434-D NW 39th Expressway
Bethany, OK 73008

Texas
Old Route 66 Association of Texas
P.O. Box 66
McLean, TX 79057
Operates a Route 66 Hall of Fame in restored gas station in McLean.

Two other organizations of interest to Route 66 fans are:

Route 66 Territory Visitors' Bureau
8916-C Foothill Blvd.
Rancho Cucamonga, CA 91730
Operates a small museum and promotes toruism.

Route 66—An American Adventure
c/o Dr. Tom Snyder
P.O. Drawer 5323
Oxnard, CA 93031

Society for Commercial Archeology
National Museum of American History
Room 5010
Washington, D.C. 20560

INDEX